CANADA'S SECRET COMMANDOS

The Unauthorized Story of Joint Task Force Two

**ESPRIT DE CORPS
BOOKS**

ABOUT THE AUTHOR

David Pugliese, a journalist with the Ottawa Citizen newspaper, has been writing about military affairs and the Canadian Armed Forces since 1982. His reporting on the Canadian Forces' 1996 mission to Zaire won him a Canadian Association of Journalists magazine writing award. Pugliese was also nominated for a National Newspaper Award for his articles on Canadian military operations in Bosnia. His freelance articles on military issues have appeared in more than a dozen publications. In 2003, David released another bestseller entitled *Shadow Wars: Special Forces in the New Battle Against Terrorism.*

Copyright © 2002 by David Pugliese

6TH PRINTING – MAY 2005

NATIONAL LIBRARY OF CANADA CATALOGUING IN PUBLICATION DATA
Pugliese, David, 1957 -
Canada's secret commandos: the unauthorized story of Joint Task Force Two
Includes bibliographical references and index.
ISBN 1-895896-18-5
1. Canada. Canadian Armed Forces. Joint Task Force 2.
2. Special forces (Military science)-Canada. I. Title.

U602.J62P84 2002   356'.167'0971   C2002-900250-8

Printed and bound in Canada
Esprit de Corps Books
1066 Somerset Street West, Suite 204
Ottawa, Ontario, K1Y 4T3
1-800-361-2791
www.espritdecorps.ca / espritdecorp@idirect.com

From outside Canada
Tel: (613) 725-5060 / Fax: (613) 725-1019

CANADA'S SECRET COMMANDOS

The Unauthorized Story of Joint Task Force Two

**ESPRIT DE CORPS
BOOKS**

OTTAWA, CANADA

ACKNOWLEDGEMENTS

This book represents the most information ever assembled in public on Joint Task Force Two, Canada's counter-terrorism and special operations unit. It was written because Canadians have the right to know something about the role this unit plays in their name on the domestic and international scene. As such, this book examines both the positive and negative elements of JTF2.

For reasons of security, I have not included the names of present serving members of JTF2 that I obtained through my research, nor some specific details on tactics the unit may employ in operations. The names that are presented in this book have either been previously put in the public domain or released in some form by the Government of Canada or the Department of National Defence.

Over the last 10 years, a number of Canadian Forces personnel have provided pieces of the JTF2 story or have helped me understand the development of counter-terrorism and special operations in the Canadian context. Others have helped during my trips to Bosnia, Croatia and Haiti to visit Canadian operations in those countries in 1995, 1996 and 1998.

Material released under the Access to Information law by the Solicitor General's office, the Privy Council Office, the Department of National Defence, and Foreign Affairs, has also proved invaluable. Those at JTF2 who handled my Access requests should also be recognized.

Material collected by retired Colonel Michel Drapeau, Brian Nolan and Scott Taylor helped form the basis for much of Chapter 4. I would also like to thank Warren Ferguson and Gary Dimmock for information they have provided. At the Ottawa Citizen, Editor Scott Anderson and assignment editor Bruce Garvey have always been supportive of my defence writing endeavors.

I am particularly indebted to Dr. Bill Twatio who lent his skills to researching and writing the chapters dealing with special forces units and terrorist groups from around the world. Thanks, of course, are due to Scott and Katherine Taylor, Cathy Hingley and Julie Simoneau of *Esprit de Corps* who designed and laid out the contents of this book.

ONE: A MEMBER OF THE CLUB

IN THE HIGHLY censored history of Joint Task Force Two, the afternoon of October 8, 2001, will be remembered as a turning point. While most Canadians were enjoying the Thanksgiving holiday, preparing turkey and cranberry sauce for the evening ahead, those with any connection to the country's top-secret counter-terrorism force were glued to their TV sets, waiting to hear from the country's Defence Minister.

Just before noon, Art Eggleton walked into a spacious conference room at National Defence Headquarters in Ottawa to meet with journalists. Most government offices were closed for the holiday, but Defence department planners had been hard at work, reviewing last-minute details of what was to become, in numbers at least, one of Canada's largest overseas missions. Looking grim, Defence Minister Eggleton stepped up to the podium. The Chief of the Defence Staff, General Raymond Henault, the country's top military officer, was at his side. Both men knew that the details they would unveil in the next few moments would be closely followed by American officials in Washington.

Less than a month earlier, the world had radically changed. By this time, television images of the September 11 terrorist attacks on the U.S. and their aftermath were still a regular part of most American and Canadian news lineups: video footage of two hijacked planes plowing into New York's World Trade Center; firefighters removing body parts from the rubble; construction crews pulling out pieces of aircraft and debris from the section of the Pentagon that had been hit by another plane; interviews with family members of passengers who had tried to prevent a fourth aircraft from wreaking similar damage. Across the United States and Europe, investigators were searching for clues to help them understand how a band of terrorists could seize four passenger jets and use them as kamikazes to strike at the heart of America's financial, political and military centres.

Not long after the strikes, intelligence agencies had identified the most likely culprit behind the attacks as Osama bin Laden. The Saudi Arabian millionaire was the guiding force behind al-Qaeda, a Muslim terrorist network that had vowed to punish the U.S. for its long-standing support of Israel. Bin Laden and his group had been behind the 1993 bombing of the World Trade Center and attacks on American embassies in Africa five years later. His men were also reported to have fought in Somalia, taking a key role in the 1993 ambush in Mogadishu which killed 18 American soldiers, most of them special forces troops.

Bin Laden was operating from Afghanistan with the full support of the Taliban regime which ran the country under strict Islamic law. The Saudi millionaire's training camps were churning out dozens of fanatics who, like those behind the controls of the passenger planes used in the September 11 attacks, didn't question dying for their cause.

Now the United States was on a war footing, with President George W. Bush vowing to bring in bin Laden, dead or alive. The American military was busy trying to make good on the president's promise and, just a day before Eggleton's press conference in Ottawa, the Pentagon had unleashed waves of cruise missiles and bombers to strike targets in Afghanistan.

At Fort Bragg, North Carolina, and other bases across the U.S., special forces units were preparing to move out. American and allied commandos were slated to play a lead role in this war. Though relatively small in number, members of the U.S. Army's elite Delta Force and the British Special Air Service were already rumored to be operating in Afghanistan, gathering crucial intelligence and scouting out potential targets.

In the world's Western capitals, and particularly in Ottawa, leaders were faced with less-than-subtle pressure to contribute to the war effort. President Bush had made it quite clear that his government would take note of those nations that did not rally behind the American-led campaign against terrorism.

The intense pressure placed on Canada was understandable. After all, Canada and the U.S. had a long-standing agreement to defend North America and the events of September 11 were being seen as nothing less than a direct attack on the U.S. homeland. American government officials were also growing increasingly impatient with what they viewed as Canada's freeloader attitude toward defence.

While Eggleton and his generals had gotten into the habit of claiming that the Canadian military was more capable on the battlefield now than at anytime in the last decade, the numbers told a different story. Under the current Liberal government, the Canadian Armed Forces had been chopped from 80,000 personnel in 1993 to 58,000 in 2001. The defence budget had been cut 25 per cent over roughly the same period. Equipment was old and falling apart. And some NATO allies were openly complaining that the Canadian military was no longer a fighting force but had become a "peacekeeping" army.

In Washington, there was also growing concern that Canada's lax immigration laws had allowed terrorists to infiltrate the country and use it as a staging area for attacks on the U.S. In fact, one terrorist linked to bin Laden's organization had been arrested in December 1999 as he crossed from Victoria, British Columbia, to Washington State with bomb components in his trunk. Ahmed Ressam, a refugee claimant living in Montreal, later confessed he had planned to attack Los Angeles airport and that he had received his training in bin Laden's Afghanistan camps.

In the aftermath of September 11, Prime Minister Jean Chrétien's government had to be seen as doing something substantial to support the Americans and their war against terrorism.

Eggleton didn't disappoint. At the October 8 news conference, he told journalists that Canada would commit six ships to the U.S. war effort, as well as six aircraft to provide surveillance and move humanitarian aid into the region if required. Although it still had to be determined where exactly the Canadian warships would operate from, they would provide support and protection for the American naval battle fleets, the defence minister said.

The announcement, though seemingly a significant military response to the September 11 attacks, would later be viewed by some defence analysts as largely symbolic. Afghanistan was, after all, a landlocked country and neither the Taliban nor bin Laden had the capability to strike out into the middle of the Indian Ocean where the U.S. warships were operating. Later, it would be revealed that military planners saw so little threat to the Canadian naval armada that they decided against outfitting the ships' Sea King helicopters with a full complement of missile defence systems.

But Eggleton wasn't finished outlining Canada's war commitment. He paused for a moment, almost anticipating that his next sentence would catch journalists in the Defence department conference room off guard. "Finally, a component of our specialist force, Joint Task Force Two, has been requested and will contribute to the overall effort," he announced. "You will understand, however, that for reasons of security, no further details will be provided."

The fact that JTF2, the military's secretive counter-terrorism force, was going to war sent a buzz of excitement throughout the usually cynical press corps. This was no naval task group. The inclusion of JTF2 meant that Canadian soldiers could potentially end up on the front lines in the Afghan war. Even Eggleton's brief acknowledgement of JTF2 was a landmark of sorts. It was the first time the government had openly discussed sending the unit overseas.

The last time the military even acknowledged Joint Task Force Two's existence in public was when an opposition Member of Parliament claimed its soldiers had secretly infiltrated Kosovo to gather intelligence and direct aircraft to their targets during the 1999 NATO bombing campaign. At the time, Defence department officials hotly denied anything of the sort had taken place.

Many television viewers watching Eggleton's press conference wouldn't have known what the minister was talking about. JTF2 was so cloaked in secrecy that few outside the military knew it even existed. Besides, most Canadians were under the impression their military only conducted peacekeeping duties. Over the last three decades, the country's successive governments, and especially the Liberals, had hammered home the message that the job of the Canadian Armed Forces was primarily to keep the peace around the world. Even Prime Minister Chrétien referred to Canada's soldiers as "boy scouts" who work oversees helping the United Nations. Any talk of war and training for combat seemed to be discouraged.

By 2001, the ongoing efforts of Defence department bureaucrats, both in and out of uniform, to downplay combat operations had taken its toll. Shortly after the September 11 attacks, young Canadians started walking into recruiting offices declaring they wanted to join the military to be "peacekeepers." The amazed officers on duty gently informed them that they first had to become soldiers, sailors or aviators.

As far as the public was concerned, JTF2 was a mystery unit. Even Canada's lawmakers knew little about the organization that was the country's force of last resort in the event of a terrorist attack. In fact, JTF2 was so low key it only rated a passing reference in a sweeping 1999 Senate report on how Canada should deal with terrorism.

On the rare occasions when the unit was mentioned, the generals went out of their way to downplay what its soldiers had been trained for and what they were capable of doing. During the Kosovo bombing campaign, Brigadier General David Jurkowski, claimed that JTF2 did not usually deploy overseas and, if it did, it would only conduct "very benign observer-type missions."

In reality, JTF2 troops had been on at least a dozen overseas operations since the unit was created in 1993. And there was certainly nothing benign about them. Soldiers talk about "the sharp end" to designate combat troops who do the fighting. JTF2 was the very tip of that Canadian sharp end. Its snipers were trained to stalk and eliminate terrorists and its assault groups skilled in raiding hijacked aircraft to free hostages. Operating behind enemy lines in two or four-man teams, the unit could be the eyes and ears of commanders overseeing a battle.

But over the last decade, JTF2 had yet to be used to its full potential. With the war in Afghanistan, Canada's secret commandos were on the verge of becoming a full-fledged member of the world's elite special forces club. It had been a long road to Afghanistan, one that began with a gun battle in Ottawa 16 years earlier.

ABOVE: *In the 1970s and early 1980s, civilian police SWAT units were Canada's front-line response to terrorism.* (PHOTO BY AUTHOR)

OPPOSITE PAGE: *Officers from the RCMP's counter-terrorist Special Emergency Response Team rappel from a Canadian Forces Twin Huey helicopter at the Dwyer Hill Training Centre in Ontario.* (PHOTO BY AUTHOR)

TWO: "RED CODE, RED CODE"

CLAUDE BRUNELLE WAS nearing the end of a 12-hour shift when he saw a U-Haul rental van pull up outside the Turkish embassy where he worked as a security guard. That was nothing unusual, even so early in the morning. After all, commercial truck traffic was common along Wurtemburg Street, located in an Ottawa neighborhood that was home to many embassies and consulates.

Brunelle, who worked for the private security firm Pinkerton's of Canada, was alone in the embassy guard house. Inside the Tudor-style building, Ambassador Coskun Kirca and fellow Turkish officials were getting an early start to their day. Just a few moments before, at about 7 a.m., an RCMP cruiser had passed by the embassy as part of a routine police patrol of the diplomatic enclave.

But the events that would unfold over the next four hours on March 12, 1985, would forever change the Canadian government's attitude toward terrorism and would set in motion a chain of events that would eventually lead to the creation of Joint Task Force Two.

As the 31-year-old security guard tried to see though the rain-splattered window of his hut, three men jumped out of the van and scrambled onto the truck's roof. Within seconds, they were over the three-metre-high embassy wall. The trio, armed with 12 gauge shotguns, pistols and grenades, were members of the Armenian Revolutionary Army, a terrorist group intent on avenging the 1915 murder of more than 600,000 Armenians at the hands of the Turkish military.

Once inside the embassy compound, the men began firing on Brunelle's guard hut. At Pinkerton's headquarters across the city, radio dispatcher Yves Lavigne could hear Brunelle's frantic call for help. In the first radio transmission, a couple of minutes after seven, the guard sounded frightened and panicked. Lavigne could clearly hear gunshots in the background. "Red code, red code, they're shooting at me," Brunelle yelled into his walkie-talkie.

Shotgun pellets were shattering the windows of the steel-fortified guard house, sending glass raining down on Brunelle's head. He unholstered his .38 calibre revolver and left the hut to confront the terrorists. Brunelle managed to fire four shots, all of which missed their targets. A shotgun blast to the chest knocked Brunelle off his feet, and threw him down hard on the concrete.

As he lay on the ground, one of the terrorists shot him again with a 12 gauge. This time, the shotgun pellets hit him in the groin. As Brunelle lay dying, the trio quickly moved up to the embassy's front door and detonated a powerful homemade bomb. The solid oak door was shattered by a blast so powerful that it sent wood splinters flying across the front yard where they became embedded in a nearby brick wall.

The men then moved through the embassy. One tossed a grenade down a basement stairwell but it failed to detonate. Upstairs, Ambassador Kirca, who had heard the gunfire and explosion, realized what was happening. Figuring he would be a prime target for the terrorists, he jumped from a second-storey window, breaking his right arm, right leg and pelvis as he struck the ground. His wife, daughter and nine other people were still inside the building.

The police response was almost immediate. Within three minutes, officers were on the scene. Brunelle lay dead near the guard hut, his gun and radio beside him. On the side of the embassy, Ambassador Kirca lay crumpled in pain. Risking his life, an Ottawa police constable slipped into the embassy compound and pulled the ambassador to safety.

At first the terrorists seemed intent on a long siege. "We have hostages," one of the men said in a phone call made to the Canadian Press news agency.

"We have demands. And we plan to stay."

But almost four hours after storming the embassy, their determination had evaporated. The terrorists asked police for assurances that they would not be shot if they surrendered. At 11 a.m. the trio emerged from the embassy with their hands over their heads.

The siege had ended peacefully and the hostages had escaped unharmed. Still, the attack was a major international embarrassment for Canada. For years, foreign diplomats in Ottawa had asked the Canadian government for better security, but to no avail. Now, in Turkey's capital city Ankara, politicians declared Ottawa one of the most dangerous cities in the world for Turkish diplomats. Fresh in their minds were the attacks three years before on Turkish officials. In April 1982 diplomat Kani Gungor was shot in the chest and leg as he stepped into his station wagon parked outside his home in a quiet Ottawa neighborhood. The Secret Army for the Liberation of Armenia quickly took credit for the attack which left the attaché paralyzed.

A few months later, Armenian terrorists struck again. On August 27, Turkish military attaché Colonel Atilla Altikat was sitting in his car at a red light on Ottawa's Island Park Drive when a silver Toyota sedan pulled up behind him. A man walked briskly over to the passenger side of the officer's car and pulled a 9 mm Browning handgun from his jacket. He fired 11 shots directly at the military attaché. Ten of the bullets hit Colonel Altikat's head and neck. The assassin then threw the gun into the colonel's car and calmly walked to a nearby parking lot where he jumped back into the silver Toyota driven by an accomplice. The Justice Commandos Against Armenian Genocide claimed responsibility for the hit.

After the Turkish embassy raid, then prime minister Brian Mulroney's Conservative government scrambled to review its counter-terrorism plans, including its ability to respond to hostage-takings. The problem was obvious. The country's federal police, the RCMP, had specialized tactical units, called emergency response teams, situated in each province across the country. But their primary duties involved dealing with domestic situations such as arresting heavily armed criminals or leading raids on illegal drug operations. A separate RCMP ERT unit was based in Ottawa in case of a terrorist attack in the capital city, but it was considered too small to deal with any large-scale embassy takeover or multiple aircraft hijackings. Provincial and municipal police forces across the country also had similar SWAT teams, but again their emphasis was on domestic crime. In Canada, there was not one unit big enough to handle a large-scale hostage rescue.

In the fall of that year, another high-profile terrorist attack overseas drilled home the need for a properly trained hostage-rescue unit in Canada. On November 23, 1985, Palestinian terrorists boarded an Egyptair flight in Athens and quickly took control of the Boeing 737 once it was airborne. From there they had the plane flown to the Mediterranean island of Malta. The terrorists were ruthless, executing several hostages in the first hours after the aircraft landed at Malta's Luga International Airport.

After the death of a fifth hostage, the Egyptian government decided that an assault on the plane was the only way to end the hijacking. Commandos from the Egyptian military's Force 777 were selected to lead the raid. Their attack on the aircraft would become a blueprint for counter-terrorism units worldwide on how *not* to mount a rescue mission. The Force 777 plan called for one team of soldiers to try to enter the aircraft by blasting open a hatch on the Boeing 737. As well, other commandos positioned on the wings would storm the plane from several locations.

But Force 777 was going into the airliner blind. Its operators didn't debrief any of the hostages who had been released to determine where exactly on the airplane the terrorists were located. The assault team didn't even have a blueprint of the large plane to help them study its layout before they entered the aircraft. The explosive charge used by the commando unit to blast open the Boeing 737 hatch was also much too powerful. When detonated, it blew apart the first six rows of seats in the plane, crushing to death 20 hostages. As well, commandos positioned on the jetliner's wings, who were supposed to rush in and overpower the terrorists, were thrown off by the force of the explosion which shook windows of buildings more than a kilometre away. Fifty-seven passengers, including two Canadians, as well as several of the hijackers, died trying to get out of the burning jet. Later, it was learned that not only were hostages killed by the initial explosion, but that some were gunned down by Force 777 commandos who mistook them for terrorists.

The Canadian government didn't want a tragedy of this sort on its soil. Four months after the hijacking, the government announced it would be creating a counter-terrorist unit that would specialize in hostage rescue. Following the lead of Germany, Canada assigned responsibility for creating such a team to its federal police force, the RCMP.

No sooner was the decision made than a debate, which was to dog the new unit for years, began. The question was whether it was appropriate to use police in a counter-terrorism role. Robert Kaplan, a former solicitor general under the Liberal government, argued that the unit should be made up of military personnel because such a force, when used, would almost certainly have to resort to lethal means to deal with hijackers. "Canadian police are peacemakers and conciliators who try to cool people off," Kaplan reasoned. "National defence people are more the ones who are trained to take extreme measures in crises."

The Canadian Association of Chiefs of Police also objected to the proposal that the RCMP take on the role, arguing that the Canadian Army was better suited to the job. Like Kaplan, the chiefs were concerned that law enforcement officers would be put in a situation where they would have to shoot first and ask questions later. Even some retired RCMP officers believed the job should be turned over to the military. John Starnes, former head of the RCMP's security service, noted that the counter-terrorism mission was more akin to war than policing. "The team is meant to be more like a commando unit than a police squad," he argued. "Officers will be trained to kill and destroy."

But the Canadian government dismissed such arguments. On May 12, 1986, it bused a group of journalists to an RCMP training base 50 kilometres outside Ottawa near the small rural community of Carleton Place. There, reporters were introduced to Canada's answer to the war on terrorism: the Special Emergency Response Team - or SERT.

Then solicitor general Perrin Beatty, the politician responsible for setting up SERT, had personally approved the media demonstration, not only to let Canadians know that such a team was on duty, but also to send a signal to terrorists that the country now had the capability to fight back. "I think the message should certainly be sent out that we have a group like this and we're prepared to use it in cases where it's necessary," Beatty said.

Journalists were suitably impressed as members of SERT displayed their firepower and counter-terrorism skills. Armed with German-made MP-5 submachineguns, the SERT officers, their identities concealed by black balaclavas, staged a mock hostage rescue. From a safe distance, reporters watched the counter-terrorism team burst into a room, carefully fire short bursts from their machineguns at nearby targets, while simultaneously pulling a volunteer hostage to safety. In another demonstration, SERT snipers showed off their marksmanship skills while others rappelled from a hovering helicopter.

Government plans called for half of the 49-member SERT team to be on duty while the other half took part in routine RCMP assignments. Every month the two groups would switch roles. SERT could react as a whole or as two separate units. In the event of a major terrorist incident, the team could be backed up by the other RCMP ERT units situated in cities across the country. SERT was to be on call 24 hours a day, but it would only be used as a last resort, brought in after negotiations with terrorists had failed. "We could go this afternoon if we had to," Inspector Al Sabean, the chief trainer of the new unit, told journalists.

Most of SERT's members had been recruited from the Mounties' existing emergency response teams. Before even being considered, they needed a minimum of eight years on the police force. In choosing candidates, the RCMP tried to balance the need for a mature officer with someone who was physically fit, so most team members were about 32 years old. It was determined that SERT officers would serve with the unit for three to five years. In addition to the ERT skills they had acquired before joining the unit, new SERT officers went through a two-week basic training course that emphasized physical fitness and then went on to more specialized training. The elite unit would attract some of the country's most skilled police officers, eager to take on an assignment that was not only challenging but much different from the day-to-day job of regular law enforcement.

SERT members received much of their initial training from the British military's Special Air Service, the world's premier counter-terrorism unit. In fact, the RCMP tried to model SERT on the SAS as much as possible. But the involvement of the SAS once again forced Beatty to defend his government's decision not to use Canadian Forces personnel for such a role. He pointed out that federal law gave the RCMP primary responsibility to deal with acts of terrorism and threats to internationally protected people, such as diplomats. As well, Canada considered terrorism, first and foremost, a criminal act. "If it's a criminal act, it's the role of the police," Beatty asserted.

Besides, the solicitor general argued, SERT members were already better trained in counter-terrorism tactics than Canadian soldiers. The military's role in the new unit would be very limited: SERT would have access to three Canadian Forces Twin Huey helicopters and would also conduct some of its training with members of the Canadian Airborne Regiment.

The day after SERT was officially introduced to the media, newspapers across the country ran front-page stories about the unit. Not surprisingly, perhaps, some of the headlines were a bit over the top. One read, "RCMP killer squad issues warning to terrorists." But the government's message that it was serious about dealing with political violence came through clearly.

Not all Canadians, however, were impressed. Residents who lived near the Carleton Place training facility complained about low-flying helicopters and the constant sound of gunfire and explosions. Some worried that children would sneak onto the site and get injured.

To deal with this problem, as well as recognizing the limited size of the Carleton Place training centre, the RCMP began looking for a larger and more elaborate installation. In 1987, it purchased the 200-acre Dwyer Hill Farms, a former stable for championship horses. For the RCMP's needs the site was perfect. Its location on Franktown Road was relatively secluded but still close enough to Ottawa - some 30 kilometres away - that SERT could respond quickly to any terrorist incident there. The size of the farm also offered the room to expand the training facility.

But it wasn't only neighbors around Carleton Place who were less than impressed with SERT. A year after the team was formed, the Senate's Special Committee on Terrorism and Public Safety recommended the government transfer SERT's duties to the Canadian Forces. What concerned the Senate committee was that SERT didn't have the size or capabilities to deal with two or more simultaneous terrorist attacks. The unit's response time was also an issue. Unless a hostage-taking or hijacking went for days or weeks, SERT wouldn't be able to play much of a role. "A SERT team located in Ottawa would often be unable to arrive in time to have an impact," the Senate report warned.

Despite the criticism, SERT was kept busy. Its members trained with similar units such as Germany's GSG-9 and the FBI's Hostage-Rescue Team. When SERT wasn't training it was providing security to large international gatherings in Canada. SERT officers were on hand for the 1988 Winter Olympics in

Calgary as well as a meeting of economic leaders that same year in Toronto.

But the Senate report was more accurate than SERT commanders would like to have admitted. In April 1989 a Lebanese-Canadian man, distraught about ongoing violence in the Middle East, commandeered a Greyhound bus in Montreal and forced its driver to head to Ottawa. There, the bus drove up on the front lawn of Parliament Hill before becoming bogged down in soggy grass just outside the Centre Block of the House of Commons. The 32-year-old hijacker, armed with a handgun, began firing bullets into the ground to show police he was to be taken seriously. He demanded access to the news media so he could make his request that nations of the world come to the aid of his war-torn Lebanese homeland.

The drama unfolding less than an hour away from SERT's Dwyer Hill base seemed a tailor-made operation for the elite unit. Yet the 60 police officers who surrounded the bus were from the RCMP's regular emergency response teams and the Ottawa Police tactical squad. After eight hours of negotiations, and before SERT could deploy, the hijacker surrendered his busload of hostages.

The Parliament Hill hostage drama did little to boost SERT's prestige within the RCMP. SERT officers, such as Superintendent Jim Quinn, were frustrated about not having a role to play in such a high-profile incident. Quinn likened the unit to a hockey team which continues to practice but never gets to play a game. "It's something you don't want to do but after putting all the resources into the team, you'd like to see how capable you are," he said.

In the fall of 1991, about a year and a half after the Parliament Hill incident, SERT once again invited journalists to watch it perform its hostage-rescue skills. This time, however, the anticipated publicity wasn't about sending a message to terrorists. Instead, SERT was fighting for its existence. Around this time, the Conservative government instituted a new round of budget cuts in an attempt to reduce the country's deficit and all federal departments were expected to come up with some measure of savings. Some officers in the RCMP hierarchy questioned the need for SERT in the aftermath of the bus hijacking. With more than 30 emergency response units nation-wide, the Dwyer Hill team seemed, to some, like overkill. As well, the unit had cost the RCMP some $48 million to train and equip, yet it had never been used in an actual hostage rescue. Every year of SERT's operation was costing the federal police force at least $4 million.

At the same time, the Department of National Defence was quietly pushing to take over responsibility for the national counter-terrorism team. Behind the move was one of Ottawa's most successful mandarins, Robert Fowler. Fowler, serving as the Defence department's deputy minister, had been in the bureaucracy for some 20 years. He had held posts at External Affairs and served at the Canadian embassy in Paris. His political capital grew even further with his work on former prime minister Pierre Trudeau's peace initiative of the early 1980s.

Fowler had an intense interest in military and security matters. While assistant deputy minister for policy for the Defence department, he had been instrumental in developing the Conservative government's 1987 White Paper on Defence. That document had been a grandiose blueprint to substantially increase troop strength and purchase tens of billions of dollars worth of new equipment, including main battle tanks and nuclear submarines. As part of the expansion, some officers had also been advocating the creation of a counter-terrorism squad within the military.

The Canadian Forces already had the elite Airborne Regiment, which trained in counter-terrorism duties. But what some in the Defence department had envisioned was a smaller unit along the lines of the SAS which would not only conduct counter-terrorism and hostage rescue but, as well, special operations missions such as long-range reconnaissance behind enemy lines and hit-and-run commando-style raids.

Shortly after the 1987 White Paper's release, the Canadian military drew up plans to send two soldiers to the SAS base in Hereford, England, for advanced training. One was an officer with the Royal Canadian Regiment, the other a senior non-commissioned officer with Princess Patricia's Canadian Light Infantry. But the men never went. By April 1989, the reality of the government's fiscal problems had set in. Spending billions on expanding the military was not on the agenda and much of what was outlined in the Defence White Paper was scuttled.

Two years later, however, the RCMP's own financial problems presented Fowler and the Defence department with the means to accomplish at least one of their goals - that of creating an SAS-style force. With SERT's job firmly in their sights, the RCMP unit's days seemed numbered.

The second SERT demonstration for journalists was more of the same from

1986 - lots of precision shooting and rappelling from helicopters. By then, SERT was a little less than double its original size and the unit was receiving anywhere from 100 to 300 officers applying annually for a place on the team. Despite the influx of potential recruits, selection standards still remained high. About half of those applying were selected for further evaluation and, of those, only eight to 15 per cent passed SERT's rigorous testing. During the press tour, SERT commanders were upbeat and talked about expanding the unit's role to include dealing with heavily armed criminals. "We're a resource that can be utilized more," Superintendent Quinn said in a message that seemed more for the federal government than for journalists.

But the expansion was never to be. While SERT was making its case to the news media, Fowler had been busy behind the scenes lobbying his political contacts to turn over the country's counter-terrorism mandate to the Defence department. His arguments regarding the military's manpower and resource advantages in filling the role were quickly countered by those RCMP officials anxious to retain the SERT squad. The police team had a solid international reputation among law enforcement agencies with similar duties, they argued. But what the RCMP did not have was Fowler's substantial political clout.

In February 1992, the Globe and Mail broke the story that the RCMP would disband SERT and hand over the role to the military.

SERT's job had been one of hostage rescue, but the Canadian Forces had no intention of concentrating solely on dealing with hijacked aircraft or terrorist-held embassies. The military had finally gotten what it had always wanted - a unit that would not only fight terrorists and rescue hostages but would also eventually branch out into the shadowy world of special operations.

OPPOSITE PAGE: *A member of the Canadian Airborne Regiment on exercises in North Carolina in 1992. CAR soldiers were among the first selected for service in JTF2 during the unit's early days.* (PHOTO BY AUTHOR)

THREE: THE MEN IN BLACK

WHEN CANADIAN FORCES officers arrived at Dwyer Hill to discuss arrangements for the transfer of the SERT base to the military, they were impressed by the scope of the Franktown Road installation. In a few short years, the RCMP had transformed the one-time horse and cattle breeding farm into a state-of-the-art counter-terrorism training centre.

Construction had just been completed on what SERT dubbed its "Method of Entry" building, a four-storey concrete tower that could be used to simulate assaults on high-rises. In another section of the Dwyer Hill Training Centre sat an old Air Canada DC-8, stripped of its engines, as well as a large passenger bus, both used for hostage-rescue scenarios. Snipers could hone their skills on a recently built 300-metre range. The latter, a partially enclosed facility that had cost $1.8 million, gave shooters the luxury of practicing year-round in relative comfort, even through the frigid Ottawa Valley winters. For close-in target shooting there was a 50-metre indoor range. SERT officers had also kept in shape by using the well-equipped, spacious gym and indoor swimming pool. There were even some luxuries, such as a sauna and pool table, so officers could unwind after long days of training.

Perhaps the most important structure at Dwyer Hill was the Close Quarter

Battle House, a large, spacious building where SERT members would practice live-fire hostage rescues. Almost every counter-terrorist team in the world has a similar facility, commonly known as the "killing house" because it is in such buildings that the split-second decisions and precision shooting that mean life or death in an actual hostage rescue are practiced over and over. SERT officers would creep toward one of the rooms, kick in the plywood door and toss in a stun grenade. On the team leader's command, the officers would then charge into the room, opening fire on targets, carefully aiming at those deemed to be "terrorists" while avoiding volunteers playing the role of hostages.

To oversee the transfer of SERT duties to the Canadian Forces, Deputy Minister Fowler and Chief of the Defence Staff General John de Chastelain selected an infantry colonel by the name of Michael O'Brien. Fowler, in particular, liked and trusted O'Brien, who had a track record of getting things done in a fast and efficient manner. The portly officer had been placed in charge of the National Defence Headquarters operations centre and was a key player in the planning of several overseas peacekeeping missions. O'Brien's recommendations on what would be needed for the new Canadian Forces' counter-terrorism unit were readily accepted by the senior military leadership.

The new team was to be modeled on the British Special Air Service. Since its inception during the Second World War, this regiment had earned an enviable, global reputation, both for its battlefield skills, particularly during the 1982 Falkland Islands War, as well as for its counter-insurgency expertise during missions in places such as Northern Ireland, Malaya and Oman. The SAS also enjoyed a large measure of fame for its May 1980 storming of the Iranian embassy in London, viewed by many military professionals as the almost-perfect blueprint on how to end a hostage-taking.

Not only had the unit been successful in operations but it also had led the way in developing new methods to battle terrorism. The SAS became the first counter-terrorist unit to build a "killing house." It was also the first to develop magnesium-based stun grenades or "flash bangs," which give off a blinding blast of light and ear-splitting noise to disorient terrorists during the key initial stages of an assault. Although the SAS was divided into squadrons, each with its own area of expertise, its overall structure was based on a four-man patrol. Such a group was small enough to have good mobility and remain undetected on the battlefield, yet have enough firepower to defend itself. The

Canadian military decided to copy the concept of the four-man teams for its fledgling counter-terrorism unit, and eventually, when the formation was large enough, several squadrons.

Although the basic structure of the Canadian unit had been settled on, there was still the question of what to name it. In late January 1992, O'Brien and Fowler traveled to Key West, Florida, to watch the American government's Joint Task Force 4 in action. JTF4 was a combination military and law enforcement team which focused almost solely on counter-drug operations. The unit specialized in tracking down and capturing drug runners as they tried to slip into Florida aboard light planes or speed-boats loaded with cocaine.

When Fowler returned to Ottawa, he talked at length with colleagues about JTF4 and its exceptional capabilities. At one Defence management meeting, an officer described the deputy minister as being "enchanted" with the American unit. It wasn't long after, that the new Canadian counter-terrorism team was christened with a similar name. Joint Task Force Two had an American ring to it - some of the JTF4 that Fowler found so fascinating - and was just mysterious enough to have people wonder about its origins. (There was never any JTF1 in the Canadian military.)

By the end of February, the selection of key personnel for the new unit was underway. To command JTF2, General de Chastelain handpicked an officer from his own regiment, the Princess Patricia's Canadian Light Infantry. Lieutenant Colonel Ray Romses, a soft-spoken, fit and eminently capable soldier had just given up command of 1PPCLI and was considered one of the top battalion commanders in the army. Captain David Hirter, the son of a former Airborne Regiment deputy commander, was named adjutant of the new unit. Captain R.J. McLean was to command the first troop. Both men were Patricias and both were ex-members of the Canadian Airborne Regiment.

Word went out in the Canadian Forces that JTF2 was recruiting highly motivated and exceedingly fit soldiers. The message outlined the bare minimum needed as a recruit. For starters, they would be required to run one and a half miles in under 11 minutes and bench press 65 kilograms (143 pounds). They would also have to do 40 consecutive non-stop pushups, five consecutive overhand grip straight arm pull-ups and forty sit-ups - each set within a minute. Those who had a fear of heights or confined areas need not apply. The original intent was to have JTF2 soldiers serve two- to four-year tours before returning to their home units. In the beginning, the plan was to recruit enough new members to match SERT, man for man, which by that time had grown to 72 police officers.

More than 1,000 soldiers volunteered for the initial JTF2 recruit course, which ran in August of 1992. Romses decided to use a rigorous selection process based largely on criteria used by the SAS. A grueling five-day test focusing on physical fitness was designed to weed out the weak. Those who passed the initial phase progressed to more advanced testing. Emphasis was placed not only on shooting skills but also on a soldier's ability to operate under extreme stress. Like SERT, the unit used live rounds in its close quarter battle training. Soldiers entering the dark smoke-filled rooms were required to make a rapid assessment of friend or foe and then use their weapons skills to eliminate only the foe. Such shooting was physically and mentally draining. In its training, the SAS suggested that a skilled pair of commandos should be able to identify and kill all the terrorists in a room within five seconds.

Officers vying for a position in JTF2 found it even tougher to make the grade than non-commissioned members. If they successfully completed the first phase, they would get just 48 hours' respite before undergoing a second, four-day test. Even soldiers who sported coveted French Commando badges and U.S. Ranger flashes, awarded in recognition of passing courses held by those foreign military forces, were often RTUed (returned to unit) after just a couple of days in the selection course.

Once selected for JTF2, soldiers and officers would then proceed to advanced counter-terrorism training, including a special operations assault course, in which they learned the intricacies of hostage rescue in buildings, aircraft and vehicles. Others received specialized training as snipers.

Despite its name, in its early days JTF2 was anything but a joint operation. Although it would later be expanded to include navy and air force personnel, initially the unit was almost solely comprised of members from the Canadian Airborne Regiment, 3 Commando in particular, and the PPCLI.

The plan was to have SERT stay in existence until JTF2 was ready to take over its duties. The RCMP officers joined their military counterparts to oversee training, with the Mounties also responsible for screening potential recruits, scrutinizing their personnel files and running background checks on them in the national police force's crime database. In some cases, they didn't like what they saw. More than a few JTF2 recruits seemed to have a "cowboy" attitude, a worrisome finding for the SERT officers, particularly since the counter-terrorism unit would have to adhere to civilian laws during any hostage-rescue operation in Canada. Military attitudes of "destroying the enemy" would not play well in a civilian inquiry into the aftermath of a terrorist attack. Overseas, the SAS was already under scrutiny for several ambushes of IRA terrorists which critics alleged were nothing more than executions. In one attack, three IRA operatives had been shot 117 times, before each was finished off with a bullet to the head.

In a meeting with senior Defence department officials, the Mounties also voiced concerns that the military didn't have the proper safeguards in place to ensure future JTF2 recruits were free from any links to criminal activity. The initial RCMP reviews of military files showed that a few soldiers had had disciplinary problems as well as run-ins with the law. There was also the issue of some Airborne Regiment troopers having links to outlaw motorcycle gangs. The Canadian Forces leadership, however, was not especially worried. JTF2's members were the best the military had to offer and the unit's rigorous selection process would weed out any real troublemakers. Furthermore, the military's justice system would deal harshly with anyone who seriously stepped out of line.

For their part, some of the soldiers had less-than-flattering opinions of the SERT officers' abilities. At times, members of the Canadian Airborne Regiment had been used as an opposing force during SERT training sessions. As the paratroopers told it, they often beat the Mounties at their own game. "We kicked their asses on a regular basis," recalled one officer.

In spite of such internal disputes, JTF2 was unofficially operating by October 1992. It had even planned a full scale counter-terrorism exercise in Toronto with SERT at the end of the month. Ever the cautious bureaucrats, Fowler and General de Chastelain warned that such training should be low-key and, if at all possible, not attract any public attention.

Five months later, Colonel O'Brien and his superior, Vice Admiral Larry Murray, reported that JTF2 was now fully trained and could officially take over from SERT. On Friday, March 26, 1993, O'Brien and Murray briefed the Defence management committee in Ottawa about JTF2's status. Fowler and the new Chief of the Defence Staff, Admiral John Anderson, chaired the meeting and listened intently as the two officers detailed the substantial progress the unit had made in the last year.

O'Brien listed the training that JTF2 had conducted and reiterated the decision by the senior leadership that the unit would be under direct control of the Chief of the Defence Staff. The Deputy Chief would act as the unit's operations officer, relaying the orders from the CDS and advising on how JTF2 should be used.

The joint task force would be unlike any modern-day Canadian military unit. For security reasons, it would be cloaked in absolute secrecy. There would be no meddling journalists asking embarrassing questions, as was now happening regarding the mission to Somalia. Just a week before the Defence management meeting, military leaders had been informed that members of the Canadian Airborne Regiment had tortured and killed a 16-year-old Somali boy. The media reports on the incident were expected any day now.

Almost all details surrounding JTF2 and its deeds - good or bad - would be off limits to the public. In a brief announcement acknowledging that it was taking over SERT's duties, the Canadian Forces would only release the name of the unit and the fact its initial startup cost was $20 million (it was actually $30 million). JTF2's annual budget would be "black," meaning it would not be listed in the federal government's annual financial report. Even Members of Parliament would be left in the dark about the unit.

Admiral Murray told Fowler and the officers at the meeting that JTF2 was now at the same level of effectiveness as SERT. To continue its professional development it would start making contact with similar counter-terrorism and special forces teams such as the U.S. Army's Delta Force, the U.S. Navy's SEALs and Germany's GSG-9. Fowler was delighted. The potential for the new unit was unlimited. "JTF2 constitutes an important resource to the Government of Canada," he told the assembled officers.

Technically, the unit was assigned the role of hostage rescue and counter-terrorism. But in its mandate, Defence planners had added that JTF2 could be used in situations "affecting or potentially affecting the national interest." National interest would, of course, be determined by the generals and Defence department bureaucrats. That all-important wording was carte blanche for JTF2 to begin its eventual expansion into a full-fledged SAS-type formation, carrying out both hostage rescue and special forces operations.

Britain had its "Hereford Boys," a nickname for the SAS, inspired by the name of their home base in Hereford, England. The U.S. Navy's SEAL Team Six had christened their rough and ready counter-terrorist team the "Mob." Now Canada had the "Men in Black," a reference to the black uniforms and Nomex fire-proof balaclavas JTF2 soldiers wore during operations. Five days after the Defence management committee's meeting, Fowler, Colonel O'Brien and a host of generals drove out to Dwyer Hill to watch SERT on parade for the last time. On April 1, 1993, the Men in Black were officially on duty.

For the next year the unit concentrated on training. In the back of their minds, JTF2 operators realized that the Canadian government's policy on terrorism almost guaranteed they would see action in the event of a hijacking or attack. Federal counter-terrorism plans stipulated that every effort would be made to seek a peaceful solution to a hostage incident. But no substantive concessions would be granted and a hijacked aircraft would never be permitted to become airborne except under the most extraordinary circumstances. In short, unless terrorists peacefully surrendered, JTF2 could count on being used to free any hostages.

To prepare for that day, Lieutenant Colonel Romses insisted on continual firearms training. For the reasons behind the need for such precision gunplay, JTF2 operators had to look no further than the lessons learned from the SAS raid on the Iranian Embassy in London on May 5, 1980. During that attack, an SAS sniper positioned across the street from the embassy saved the lives of 15 hostages by killing a terrorist with a single shot through the head. Inside the embassy, SAS trooper Tommy Palmer had used his well-honed shooting skills when he faced off with a terrorist clutching a grenade. After kicking open the door of one of the embassy rooms, Palmer quickly took a shot at a man who was in a corner to his left. The bullet entered the terrorist's skull below the left ear and exited his right temple, killing him instantly. The man slumped to the ground, never having a chance to pull the pin on the grenade.

Developing such precision requires that a soldier fire off tens of thousands of rounds of ammunition each year. For instance, in one 12-month period, the Australian SAS went through the Australian Army's entire stock of 9 mm bullets. British SAS soldiers reportedly use about 3,000 bullets per person for every week they spend in counter-terrorism training. JTF2 was no different in its consumption of ammunition. Its initial ammo budget was set at a little less than $1 million. On the 50-metre indoor range at the Dwyer Hill Training Centre, operators practiced over and over what became known as transition drills, in which a soldier emptied bullets from one weapon into a target and then quickly switched to another firearm.

The 9 mm German-made Heckler and Koch MP-5 sub-machinegun, favored by counter-terrorism units worldwide, was selected as the unit's main firearm. In JTF2's Close Quarter Battle House, the distinctive "pfft, pfft, pfft" sound of silencer-equipped MP-5s became common. For its handgun, the unit dropped the Canadian military's old standby, the 9 mm Browning Hi-Power pistol, for the Swiss-made SIG-Sauer firearms. Snipers used a variety of precision long guns on JTF2's 300-metre range, as well as at the nearby Connaught military range.

To improve their reflexes, necessary for high-speed and accurate shooting, soldiers practiced on a specially designed wall-mounted light board. The system had hundreds of small lights which would continually flash on and off for less than a second at a time. The JTF2 operator would be required to hit with the palm of his hands as many of the flashing lights as he could. A minimum acceptable score was hitting 59 lights in a one-minute period.

In addition, the unit retained some of the same civilian physical fitness consultants that SERT had used. Under their guidance, soldiers trained in hand-to-hand combat, learning varied techniques such as western-style sparring, Thai kick-boxing and Filipino marital arts knife work. The knifefighting was not so much about learning how to thrust and parry with a blade but more to practice the nimble footwork which could be used in a variety of tasks.

Mountain climbing skills, in particular, rappelling, were also key. A JTF2 soldier, pistol in hand, became adept at rappelling off the roof of the Method of Entry building, sliding down the rope and through one of the structure's open windows below. As he slid into a room, the soldier would have his pistol at the ready to begin firing at any targets he encountered.

More specialized training concentrated on "terrorist takedowns" involving aircraft, buildings and vehicles. Attacking a hijacked aircraft or bus is considered one of the most dangerous types of raids because of the narrow and confining area in which counter-terrorism operators have to move around. Most passenger aircraft are about six metres wide, while typical Greyhound buses are even more narrow. Once inside, there is also little protective cover for a JTF2 raiding team. An assault on an aircraft would involve the raiding team quickly entering the plane simultaneously through two or three points. Operators would move down the aisles in single file, each covering a specific area to their right or left.

For a takedown of a passenger bus, three pickup trucks full of JTF2 operators would come to a halt at the front and sides of the vehicle. Soldiers, armed with a collection of MP-5s, handguns and shotguns, would cover the windows and front door of the bus while one of the operators disabled the engine in the rear. In a lighting-quick raid, the commandos would then enter the vehicle, using the same sort of gunplay on the terrorists as in a passenger plane scenario.

Speed and surprise would be the key to a successful mission. JTF2 studied in detail past raids conducted by counter-terrorism units such as the SAS and the French GIGN. The main element common to each successful assault was the speed in which the attacks were carried out. The SAS raid on the Iranian embassy was over in 17 minutes. A GIGN assault on a hijacked Air France A300 Airbus went three minutes longer than the SAS raid because the terrorists on board put up such vigorous resistance.

Outside their Method of Entry building, JTF2 soldiers would practice using explosives to breach, or blow open, doors and windows. The lead soldier, who ignited the charge, would be carrying a heavy ballistic shield for protection. Once the door was blown off, he would throw the shield aside and he and other members of the assault team would rush in to engage their targets.

Each soldier's response time in such exercises was continually tested. What's more, JTF2 operators were provided with pagers and frequently were subject to unscheduled calls - often in the middle of the night. In such cases, the commandos were required to meet at pre-assigned assembly points, never certain if the callout was a drill or a real mission. Instructors meticulously timed how long it took for them to assemble and prepare for action.

JTF2 also had access to the sophisticated surveillance equipment used by the military police's SIU Special Operations Branch. That spy unit had a wide selection of miniature video cameras and electronic bugs which JTF2 made use of during exercises at Canadian Forces Base Petawawa in the fall of 1993.

Such equipment could come in handy, particularly in gathering vital intelligence before an assault. Shortly before launching its successful 1994 raid on the hijacked Air France Airbus, GIGN had placed miniature eavesdropping devices throughout the plane. Unit operatives, disguised as an aircraft maintenance crew, planted tiny closed-circuit cameras and microphones on the windows of the aircraft, allowing the team to monitor what was happening inside as well as determining the locations of the terrorists in the Airbus.

For air support, JTF2 had three Twin Huey choppers from the 450 Tactical Helicopter Squadron. The airmen were a welcome addition to the unit, aggressively flying their helicopters at low levels to land the assault teams accurately on their targets. Some even made suggestions on how to modify the aging helicopters for JTF2's specialized role. For example, Corporal Guy Lavallée improvised a "snipper ring" that could be used as a mooring point by JTF2 members when they were positioned on the skid of a flying chopper. Previous methods of securing the commandos on the skids had proven unstable and obstructed the pilots' peripheral view. As well, while working on JTF2 rappelling operations, Lavallée, a Twin Huey flight engineer, discovered there was no quick method to cut away the ropes in the event of an in-flight emergency. His solution was that flight engineers should carry a special knife from the Twin Huey rescue kit normally used to cut seatbelts.

JTF2 members also learned how to "fast-rope" from the hovering Twin Hueys, a method which involved the commandos sliding down a thick felt rope, similar to the way a firefighter moves down a pole. Fast-roping allowed as many as eight operators to exit a helicopter and be on the ground within several seconds. During fast-roping, unlike rappelling, a climbing harness was not used, so JTF2 soldiers could move quickly into position without having to unhook themselves from ropes. Such methods, however, could be dangerous. In 1985, a member of the FBI's hostage-rescue team fell to his death during a fast-rope exercise from a helicopter.

This rigorous training at Dwyer Hill went largely unnoticed by the news media. When a few journalists did ask about the new unit's activities, they were told that for reasons of national security no aspect of JTF2, except for its name and the initial disclosure of its set-up cost, could be discussed. "Information on the size, tactics, capabilities, equipment, organization, identity of unit members are classified for security reasons," Canadian Army Captain Marc Rouleau told a journalist in what would become a common mantra for the military's public affairs branch on the rare times they were quizzed about JTF2.

Inside the unit, vigilant security precautions were part of day-to-day life. Some JTF2 soldiers let their hair grow longer than regulation length, so they could better blend in with the civilian population. When leaving Dwyer Hill in their personal vehicles, JTF2 commandos would also frequently check whether they were being followed.

With the training regime well underway, Romses, who had since been promoted to the rank of colonel, turned his attention to expanding the size of his fledgling strike force. In that effort, he had the full support of General de Chastelain who, in January 1994, had returned from a brief stint as the Canadian ambassador in Washington to his old job as Chief of the Defence Staff. The general immediately approved increased personnel levels for JTF2 and sought to expand the unit's role from counter-terrorism - the so-called "black operations," named for JTF2's black uniforms - to include special forces operations, such as behind-the-lines intelligence gathering and sniper work. To prepare for that role, known as "green operations," JTF2 would eventually widen its training parameters to include parachuting, the use of improvised explosives, small-unit ambush tactics, scuba diving and other field skills.

In early 1994, a message went out to all Canadian Forces units that JTF2 was recruiting again. Another 40 master corporals and corporals, five sergeants and two captains were needed. Only regular force soldiers with a minimum of four years of service could volunteer. Officers required at least two years' experience.

One day in February, while JTF2 officers worked on expansion plans, the secure communications equipment at Dwyer Hill began transmitting an urgent and secret message from National Defence headquarters. The February 2, two-page "warning order," containing details about worsening violence on three Indian reserves in Quebec and Ontario, put the unit on alert. The crisis had been building since the end of a 1990 standoff at Oka, Quebec, and Akwasasne, Ontario, between the militant native Mohawk Warrior Society and security forces. More than 5,000 soldiers had been brought in to peacefully quell that dispute. Under a deal reached with the Canadian government, many of the Mohawk Warriors were allowed to slip away, taking their automatic weapons and rocket-propelled grenades with them. Over the next four years, the federal government, not keen on another showdown, took a hands-off approach on the native territory and the reserves slid into a state of virtual lawlessness.

The Mohawk Warrior Society, under the guise of a native sovereignty move-ment, had transformed itself into a tightly run, highly successful organized crime group, raking in hundreds of millions of dollars in profits by smuggling cheap American cigarettes and firearms into Canada. The Warriors were firmly in control at the three main reserves, Akwasasne, near Cornwall, Kanesatake, near Oka, and Kahnawake, just south of Montreal. In particular, the Akwasasne reserve had become a major entry point for illegal guns and cigarettes.

The area along the St. Lawrence River at Cornwall had been dubbed "Smug-glers' Alley" because of the large number of high-speed boats crossing the waterway at night carrying contraband. In the fall of 1993, the violence linked to smuggling had escalated. Gunfire could be heard almost nightly on the St. Lawrence as rival native gangs engaged in firefights to control the lucrative trade. At least one person had been killed. Cornwall Mayor Ron Martelle, who had called for tougher police action to end the problem, went into hiding for several days after receiving death threats from smugglers. The movement of contraband cigarettes, already at epidemic levels, was escalating and robbing the federal government of an estimated $1 billion a year in taxes.

Now Ottawa was ready to do something.

Throughout December 1993 and into early January, senior officials from the Defence department, RCMP and Canadian Security Intelligence Service held a series of strategy sessions to determine the best course of action. By the end of January, a plan had been hatched and Cabinet ministers briefed. Put before them was a sweeping operation that would see an assault force of as many as 800 RCMP officers, backed by several thousand soldiers, take control of the reserves. The RCMP would use four military sites, including CFB Trenton, Ontario, as jumping off points for what was essentially an invasion of native lands.

Covert reconnaissance and intelligence-gathering missions would be con-ducted by the military police's SIU Special Operations Branch. In particular, the RCMP needed detailed information on the numbers and types of weapons the Mohawk Warriors might have on hand. JTF2 would be needed to deal with any attacks by natives on key points such as water treatment plants and highways. The unit was told to prepare for multiple native-led terrorist strikes.

A separate message sent to JTF2's intelligence cell outlined the extent of the problem the commandos could face. The government's electronic eaves-dropping agency, the Communications Security Establishment, had been moni-toring radio messages between the various Mohawk Warrior factions. They knew that a large number of automatic weapons were being transported from Akwasasne to other reserves in southern Ontario and Quebec. JTF2 was also informed that the planned RCMP assault was expected to spark country-wide native protests. Military intelligence reports listed a few of the vulnerable ar-eas. For instance, there was potential for natives at the Tyendinaga reserve, east of Belleville, to close down Highway 401, the main transportation artery in Ontario. Mohawk sympathizers might also seize and sabotage a water treat-ment plant at Deseronto, Ontario, releasing toxic waste into the treatment plant to poison the water system. The same scenario might play out at water filtra-tion and pumping stations near Forest, Ontario.

Although there could be attacks across the country, Canada's spy agency, CSIS, informed JTF2's intelligence branch to expect the worst trouble just down the highway from its own Dwyer Hill base. "The MWS (Mohawk Warrior So-ciety) has the capability to rapidly deploy a potent arsenal at Kahnawake and Akwasasne with a more limited capability at Kanesatake," CSIS said in a mes-sage to the unit. "Of the three reserves, the potential for internal faction vio-lence is strongest at Akwasasne."

Other military units across the country, in particular those in Quebec and New Brunswick, were also put on five days notice to move into the volatile areas. The Second Battalion of the Royal Canadian Regiment (2RCR) was to provide engineers with heavy equipment to smash down Mohawk barricades as well handle crowd control. To do its job, the battalion requested seven M113 armored personnel carriers, 13 heavy machineguns, and large stocks of riot gear including face shields and body armor. The 5e Groupe Brigade Mécanisé du Canada, also part of the assault force, asked for an extra $4.2 million worth of ammunition. At CFB Petawawa, the First Battalion of the Royal Canadian Regiment (1RCR) began training for crowd control and dismantling roadblocks. In all, a quarter of the Canadian Army's combat power was at a high state of readiness.

The mission went by two names: Operation Campus and Scorpion-Saxon. Worried that the news media might find out about the plan, the military de-cided to call their assault preparations an "exercise." Canadian Forces public affairs officers concocted a cover story to mislead journalists about the growing movement of troops around bases in Quebec and New Brunswick. Reporters were told that since some units had let their combat skills slide while on peacekeeping duties in the former Yugoslavia, they needed to take refresher training. A few news agencies didn't buy the story. On February 16, Le Journal de Montreal reported that two artillery units from CFB Valcartier, Quebec, had been placed on standby to support some kind of RCMP operation within the next eight days. The next day, La Presse newspaper reported that troops at Valcartier and CFB Gagetown, New Brunswick, were going to take part in counter-smuggling operations.

In the end, cooler heads prevailed and Prime Minister Jean Chrétien's Liberal government backed off the assault plan. With the element of surprise lost, Ottawa would try new, more peaceful methods, such as reducing cigarette taxes, to break the lucrative trade in smuggled smokes. But it would also improve its intelligence-gathering capabilities on the Mohawk crime syndicates, which would result in a series of major arrests over the next several years. JTF2 would play a key role in conducting surveillance on the cigarette and gun smuggling rings, in particular, those operating in Akwasasne and Kanesatake. The commando team's soldiers soon became familiar with the trails and backroads on the native reserves as they spent days hidden in forests, observing smugglers at work and relaying the information to the RCMP and other civilian police forces.

After setting up the counter-terrorist unit and seeing it through its early days of operations, Colonel Romses was ready to move on. On February 23, 1994, JTF2 soldiers stood at attention as their new commander, Lieutenant Colonel J.R. Gaston Côté, reviewed their ranks.

Now, JTF2 turned its attention to security arrangements for the upcoming Commonwealth Games scheduled in August in Victoria, British Columbia. Bob Fowler had been keen to promote the unit's capabilities to senior government leaders, and the Commonwealth Games, an international sports meet expected to draw huge crowds, presented him with the ideal opportunity. On May 27, Solicitor General Herb Gray and Defence Minister David Collenette, arrived at Dwyer Hill to view an impressive display of JTF2 firepower and training. Fowler and Deputy Solicitor General Jean Fournier put on a sumptuous luncheon for the VIP group, which also included high-ranking civilian police and municipal government representatives. The JTF2 demonstration the politicians saw was the forerunner to "Exercise Praetorian," a three-day-long test of federal, provincial and municipal governments' ability to respond to a terrorist attack. During that scenario, terrorists from the "Khalistan National Army" would seize key points in Victoria. Civilian police forces would be the first to respond to the situation but the scenario called for JTF2 to be brought in to conduct a final assault on terrorist strongholds.

Among the VIPs, Deputy Solicitor General Fournier acknowledged that the greatest concern from an operational point of view was the time needed to activate the military counter-terrorism unit. "It is not possible to have troops take over from police and mount an assault in a matter of minutes, because reconnaissance, planning and particularly relief in the line all take time to do properly," he explained. "Exercise Praetorian," to be held in Victoria, hopefully would improve that response time.

In the first week of June, a team of JTF2 operators flew to the British Columbia capital under the command of their new leader, Lieutenant Colonel Côté. The three-day exercise was to be run in different locations in Victoria, but most of the action was centered at the old B.C. Cement Company factory just north of the city. Although the training exercise was supposed to foster co-operation between civilian police and JTF2, the military unit didn't appear terribly keen on breaking the ice. In fact, unit secrecy was so tight that JTF2 operators refused even to give their first names to the police officers with whom they were training alongside. Instead, according to one civilian law enforcement official, the soldiers all used codenames.

Equally bizarre were the reasons the commandos gave for declining invitations from civilian police SWAT officers to have a few beers after a hard day of training. The soldiers claimed they could only go to certain pubs where they could be assured their identities would be kept secret. JTF2's ultra-tight security precautions surprised even those veteran civilian police tactical officers who themselves usually kept a low profile because of their involvement in busting illegal drug operations. "The whole thing was seen as a little extreme to say the least," recalls one police officer.

On June 9, the final training scenario for "Exercise Praetorian" was set to go. In the carefully scripted operation, terrorists were holding hostages on the second floor of a building, in this case, an abandoned warehouse at the B.C.

Cement factory. Negotiations had broken down and JTF2 had been ordered to launch a rescue mission. The plan called for the raiding party to approach the building in a half-ton pickup truck. Once the truck was aligned with the second-storey window, JTF2 commandos would quickly set up a ladder and one member of the team would toss a stun grenade through the window. The remaining members of the assault force would follow the soldier up the ladder and through the window to rescue the hostages.

JTF2 had been briefed on the plan the night before. Rehearsals were conducted using live ammunition and explosives with particular emphasis placed on properly lining up the ladder between the pickup truck and the window. The rehearsals continued until around midnight, after which the soldiers caught a few hours of rest. At 6 a.m. the JTF2 assault team attended its final briefing and went over the plan once again with the civilian police and its own officers.

Almost five hours later, the rescue mission was put into motion. The truck carrying the commandos came to a screeching halt just below the window and the ladder was quickly put up against the warehouse wall. A JTF2 operator pulled the pin of his stun grenade and began scrambling up the ladder. Seconds later there was a violent explosion and the soldier fell backwards on top of the assault team members following directly behind him. On the ground, stunned JTF2 operators began staggering away from the blast area. The non-commissioned officer who had been holding the grenade tightly in his left hand when it exploded was slowly walking toward a picnic table. Only two fingers remained on the shredded lump that was once his hand. "I blew my fucking hand off!" he yelled out. Even though shock was setting in, the soldier still had the presence of mind to use his radio to call in a "no duff" medical emergency. It was a signal to those at the nearby command post that a terrible accident had happened.

Another JTF2 operator grabbed the injured soldier and held him down, injecting 20 milligrams of morphine directly into his right thigh. Within minutes, a Coast Guard helicopter landed at the cement factory as soldiers prepared to load the injured man, and another JTF2 operator who had burns on his arm and a gash on his leg, on the aircraft.

In the emergency ward at Victoria General Hospital, doctors and nurses had been told in advance that two casualties from a military exercise were being flown in. The injured NCO had even brought in the remaining pieces of his amputated fingers in hopes they could be reattached. As a doctor went to work on the man, a nurse asked him for his personal information so she could start the paperwork to admit him to the hospital. She needed his name, address and blood type, for starters. Before the injured man could answer, a JTF2 officer intervened. "That information is considered classified," he told the health care worker. The surprised nurse responded that if that was the case, there was nothing much the hospital could do but give the soldier another shot of morphine and send him on his way. At that point, the injured NCO yelled out his name and the other information the nurse needed.

Despite the best efforts of the medical staff, the soldier eventually had to have his left hand amputated. Shortly after the accident, RCMP Superintendent Kelly Folk, head of the Commonwealth Games security committee, told journalists that "Exercise Praetorian" was an "unqualified success." He labeled the stun grenade accident as bad luck. It was anything but. Military investigators would later determine that the grenade was prone to unexpected detonations and wasn't suitable for anything but the most simple training mission. Defence department lawyers even recommended the federal government sue the company that made the device.

The Victoria incident caused a shakeup in JTF2 tactics and equipment. Orders went out that the grenade was not to be used in any further training and the unit's procurement staff were told to immediately find a replacement. In the meantime, the grenades would stay in JTF2 ammunition stocks but only as a last resort for operational use. The commando team also changed its tactics when it came to storming buildings. There would be no more scrambling from the back of a pickup truck and throwing aluminum ladders up against a wall. JTF2 began to scout around for a proper vehicle assault platform. Such a device could be attached to the unit's GMC Suburban trucks and included a ladder that would not only swing out from the vehicle but also lock into place. Non-slip rungs would give the assault team added safety.

After JTF2's duty at the Commonwealth Games, it was back to more training and promoting the unit within the Canadian Forces. On November 4, 1994, its soldiers staged an elaborate assault demonstration at Dwyer Hill for the benefit of a group of senior air force officers. The "dynamic entry," as it was called, involved blowing off a door of the training tower and having a team of commandos rush in to rescue "hostages."

The countless hours of practicing such scenarios were about to be put to the test. A few weeks after the demonstration for the air force, the unit received an urgent call - its specialized talents were required in Bosnia.

ABOVE AND LEFT: *A large number of Canadian Airborne Regiment soldiers were selected for JTF2 in the summer of 1992.*
(PHOTOS BY AUTHOR)

OPPOSITE PAGE: *A Canadian Air Force CC-130 Hercules aircraft used by JTF2 for transport needs and parachute training.*
(PHOTO BY DND)

FOUR: OFF TO WAR

FOR THE BOSNIAN Serb soldiers milling around the police station in the town of Ilijas, life had become relatively quiet. The country's ongoing civil war, for them at least, had slipped into a temporary lull and, these days, instead of fighting Muslim forces, most of their time was spent standing guard over their Canadian "guests."

Inside the police station and a nearby schoolhouse, 20 Canadian soldiers were being held captive as insurance against NATO air strikes. Other Canadian soldiers were being detained at their observation posts. They had been allowed to keep their weapons, but weren't permitted to leave their bunkers nor to receive supplies from their main base in the nearby town of Visoko.

For the Bosnian Serbs in Ilijas, guarding the Canadians wasn't entirely unpleasant. In fact, they had gotten along just fine with the soldiers from Canada whom - unlike other foreign peacekeepers in the region - they held in high esteem for their military professionalism. For their part, the Canadians passed the hours playing Risk, a board game whose challenge, somewhat ironically, was to conquer the world.

Unknown to the Serbs, their every movement was being closely watched. A well-camouflaged two-man JTF2 reconnaissance team had slipped into the outskirts of the town, located 15 kilometres northwest of Sarajevo, and was scanning its collection of buildings with high-powered binoculars. Photographs of the police station were taken and the Canadian commandos carefully noted the numbers of Serb troops moving in and out of the police complex, the number and type of armored vehicles parked outside, and the presence of any heavy weapons. Also carefully recorded were the locations of nearby Serb bunkers and other strong points. To back up the reconnaissance team's efforts, Canadian military planners also had regular access to U.S. military spy satellite photos which were able to provide a top-down look at each of the locations where the peacekeepers were being held.

It was early December 1994 and JTF2 was preparing for its first hostage rescue.

For more than two years, Canadian peacekeepers, in varying numbers, had been caught in the middle of fighting in the Bosnian civil war. But keeping the peace was no easy task as Serb, Muslim and Croat forces battled each other for territory. Just a little over a week before JTF2 had begun its mission, Bosnian Serb troops had punched their way through Muslim defences in the town of Bihac, a UN-declared safe zone. NATO had retaliated by sending more than 40 U.S. and British fighter jets to attack Serb anti-aircraft missile sites and an airfield.

It wasn't the first time NATO had used its airpower against the Serbs. In April of that year the military alliance had bombed Serb tanks in a failed attempt to force a cease-fire on the warring factions. In retaliation, the Bosnian Serbs temporarily took dozens of peacekeepers hostage, including a group of Canadians, but eventually released those soldiers unharmed.

Once again, it didn't take long for the Serbs to react to the latest round of air strikes. On November 23, their soldiers surrounded United Nations observation posts throughout Bosnia. Roadblocks were set up, sealing off the peacekeepers from their home bases. In other cases, UN soldiers were taken into custody and moved to police stations or schools. In all, some 400 peacekeepers were seized as insurance against further NATO air strikes, among them 55 Canadians in the Visoko area, about 25 kilometres northwest of Sarajevo, including those taken to Ilijas.

The detained Canadian troops were mostly members of the Royal Canadian Dragoons battle group, A Squadron, from Petawawa, Ontario. In Ottawa,

Prime Minister Jean Chrétien tried to put a brave face on the situation. "There is no great need for alarm at this moment and the situation should become normal soon," Chrétien told reporters. "I'm informed by the Department of Defence that we don't see a major problem."

On the ground, the Canadian commander in Visoko, Lieutenant Colonel Bill Brough, didn't see it that way. As soon as his troops had been detained, Brough was in contact with National Defence headquarters requesting tactical support from JTF2. Chief of the Defence Staff General John de Chastelain was keen to deploy a formation of his commandos, and preparations were immediately set in motion at Dwyer Hill. Within hours a group of 32 highly trained JTF2 operators were packing their equipment in preparation for a rescue mission.

This wouldn't be the first time members of the unit had been to the former Yugoslavia. Over the course of several months in the summer of 1994, small groups of JTF2 were already in country cutting their teeth on "green ops" missions, mainly intelligence gathering and sniper work. It was an open secret among Canadian troops that the mysterious two and four-man teams of soldiers who showed up at their observation posts with high-powered sniper rifles were members of the elite commando group. Regular force soldiers were instructed not to ask too many questions of the new arrivals, who came and went from the observation bunkers as they pleased.

Although they may have been co-located with Canadian units, the JTF2 sniper teams operated independently of the chain of command and usually worked more closely with British SAS units in the region. The SAS had been deployed in Bosnia earlier that year at the insistence of UN commander, British Major General Mike Rose. Rose, a former SAS commanding officer, believed special forces could give him an edge in gathering intelligence on the ground. A similar tactic had worked extremely well in the Persian Gulf War where the SAS had been brought in to hunt for Scud missile launchers. In Bosnia, Rose wanted the SAS to conduct covert reconnaissance of Serb and Muslim positions, particularly around Gorazde, a key town that had been the scene of much fighting.

Although the JTF2 teams already in country co-operated with the SAS, for the most part, they concentrated on counter-sniping to protect Canadian troops. Working out of Visoko in the summer of 1994, JTF2's Captain R.J. McLean and

Warrant Officer Gib Perrault would often disappear into the hills around the town whenever Canadian soldiers found themselves under fire from Muslim or Serb snipers. The job of hunting down such gunmen was an exhausting and dangerous mission for the two men who, to outsiders, looked like an odd couple indeed. McLean was a good-looking, blonde-haired soldier of average height and slight build with a reputation in his former PPCLI regiment as being a keener. Perrault, also originally from PPCLI, was seen as rougher around the edges. A former comrade once described the muscular, non-commissioned officer as having the face of a boxer and the grace of a bar room bouncer. McLean and Perrault would position themselves in the hills and sit quietly for days if necessary, scanning ridges or seemingly abandoned buildings for the tell-tale signs of a sniper's nest. In particular, they would look for the slightest movement or glint of sunlight off a gunman's rifle scope or binoculars.

If warranted, additional JTF2 soldiers would be flown into Bosnia from Dwyer Hill for special missions. When Jean Chrétien came to Visoko on June 9, 1994, two teams of JTF2 arrived from Canada to take up positions to provide protection for the prime minister and his entourage. Another JTF2 team, already in the country at the time, was used to gather intelligence and determine the level of threat to the prime minister. The visit went smoothly, though at one point during the afternoon, Muslim gunmen executed a traitor just outside the walls of the Canadian camp at Visoko. Chrétien's entourage could hear the gunfire but had no idea what it was about. The JTF2 snipers, who watched the execution unfold from the their hidden perches, didn't open fire on the Muslims because the gunmen didn't pose a direct threat to the prime minister.

The situation in December 1994 involving the Canadian military hostages, however, presented JTF2 with a greater operational challenge. The Canadian soldiers were scattered, being held in five different locations. There were those in Ilijas, who had been allowed to lock their weapons in an armored personnel carrier as one of the Canadians stood guard over the vehicle. Four of the men, all officers, were separated from the main group. The rest of the Canadians were at their observation posts and allowed to keep their weapons.

CBC Radio journalist Michael McAuliffe, who had already been at the Canadian base in Visoko when the soldiers were taken captive, observed first-hand some of the rescue preparations. McAuliffe wasn't specifically told about JTF2 but it didn't take the savvy reporter long to figure out that the officer attending regular morning planning meetings wasn't just a regular soldier. The CBC reporter had also been told by one of the officers in the camp that a two-man "sniper-scout" team had slipped into the woods near Ilijas and had been able to set up a video camera to provide a live television feed of the police station and school. (According to what McAuliffe had been told, the main rescue force had flown to Italy and was awaiting its orders.)

By mid-December JTF2 was ready to launch "Operation Freedom 55," the rescue of the A Squadron troops. The codename was a reference to a popular insurance company ad that was continually running on Canadian television. For their heavy fire support, the commandos had requested the Royal Canadian Regiment's anti-tank platoon and its TOW-under-armor vehicles. The TOW missiles, contained in a firing pod on top of the M113 armored personnel carriers, had a range of almost 4,000 metres and would be more than a match for taking out Serb bunkers and armored vehicles. As an added benefit, the TOW pods could be reloaded by the crew from a protective enclave inside the armored carrier.

Captain Mike Pennel, the RCR's anti-tank platoon commander, had been assigned as third-in-command of Freedom 55, but he and many of his men had grave doubts about the JTF2-led rescue mission. If the Serbs put up stiff resistance, the Dragoons' battle group was to respond with a column of armored vehicles while U.S. helicopter gunships provided the Canadians with fire support. A group of JTF2 operators, along with their counterparts from the U.S. special forces, would also hit specific Serb targets. It was a risky plan. If it was raining or foggy at the moment the rescue mission was to be launched - which wouldn't be unusual in the hilly terrain of Bosnia during December - Pennel and his platoon would be driving a column of armored vehicles down a solitary access road right into well-prepared Serb defences. The night before Freedom 55 was to take place, the captain and his men wrote out their wills and filed them with a company clerk.

Back in Canada, there was debate inside the military and government as to whether the Canadians could even be considered true hostages. Those in the observation posts had access to their weapons and were in radio contact with their comrades in Visoko. One soldier had even managed to order roses for his wife at the Dragoons' home base of Petawawa after receiving a fax that his son had been born. The Serbs, for the most part, had treated the Canadians quite well, even inviting some of the soldiers to a pig roast. One Serb officer in Ilijas had made a point of leaving a loaded AK-47 in a closet where the Canadians were being held. It was his way of sending a signal that, despite the high-powered political rhetoric, the Canadians would be safe. The cautious Liberal government and, in particular, Defence Minister David Collenette, were also reluctant to approve the Freedom 55 plan. Collenette didn't even like to use the word "hostage" when discussing the predicament of the Canadian soldiers with the news media. He preferred the term "detainee."

But in the end, after all the weeks of preparation and buildup to Freedom 55, the elaborate rescue plan was never needed. On December 8, after a series of high-level negotiations between the Serbs and the UN, the Canadians were released.

After the peacekeepers were freed, a JTF2 team stayed to offer suggestions about how security at Visoko-area observation posts could be improved. They also worked out escape routes for Canadian soldiers in case there was another hostage-taking attempt. But their advice wasn't greeted with too much enthusiasm among the troops of the Royal Canadian Dragoons and the Royal Canadian Regiment. Almost from the start, the arrival of JTF2 had sparked resentment. For trained soldiers, the idea of someone else coming to their rescue or, worse yet, providing protection, was considered the ultimate insult. Others were put off with what they considered the arrogant attitude of the JTF2 commandos, who were easily identified by their low-slung, black cordura pistol holsters. "They were telling us what to do when we had already been on the job for a couple of months," recalled one soldier. "It pissed a few people off."

But ingratiating themselves to other Canadian soldiers wasn't a prime concern for JTF2. The unit had its job to do and such overseas assignments were considered excellent experience for building up green operations skills. To that end, Captain McLean and a small group of JTF2 commandos were already in Rwanda, working with their old comrades in the Canadian Airborne Regiment. The paratroopers, caught up in the fallout of the torture murder of 16-year-old Somali Shidane Arone and repeated calls for a public inquiry into that African mission, had been given one more chance to make good on a foreign operation. The Airborne Regiment had been sent to Rwanda to provide security for aid workers and a Canadian Forces medical unit that was administering to destitute refugees in the country. Once in Africa, JTF2 had set up an advanced operational base near the Ugandan border from where it launched long-range covert patrols into the jungle to gather intelligence.

Every few weeks the Dwyer Hill commandos would be resupplied by a column of trucks from the main Canadian camp in Kigali, Rwanda. It wasn't entirely a hardship post. Every now and then the JTF2 soldiers returned to the Airborne barracks at the Amahoro Stadium in Kigali for beers and barbecue steaks.

Despite the inclusion of such "green operations," back at Dwyer Hill, JTF2 commanders still considered counter-terrorism as the unit's core responsibility. "Our principal focus remains that of ensuring an effective hostage-rescue capability," officers wrote in the unit's 1994-95 training plan. During 1995, emphasis was placed on developing strong leadership and on preventing the erosion of skills already learned. Continual practice in terrorist takedowns was the order of the day. As well, physical fitness needed to be improved. "All JTF2 personnel must be fit as fitness is a down-payment on everything that we do," the training plan emphasized.

Political events would soon place even higher demands on JTF2's specialized skills. Looking for an easy way out of the growing Somalia scandal, the Liberal government officially disbanded the Airborne Regiment on March 5, 1995. Although light infantry battalions eventually would be created to fill the void left by the Airborne's demise, it would be some time before these were operational. JTF2, with its elite soldiers, was now one of the few units in the Canadian military that could quickly respond to a crisis, either overseas or at home.

Shortly after the disbandment of the Airborne, General de Chastelain cryptically referred to JTF2's new status at a luncheon for Ottawa businessmen. De Chastelain told the crowd that the news media, which kept referring to the Canadian Airborne Regiment as the military's elite, "had gotten it wrong." In fact, said the general, the most elite formation in the Canadian Forces went by the name of JTF2. Few of the business people at the gathering had any idea of what the general was referring to.

In that same month, JTF2 branched out to include, for the first time, maritime operations. Three days after the Airborne Regiment was disbanded in

Petawawa, a JTF2 team was aboard a Coast Guard ship in the middle of the Atlantic Ocean on a mission that had nothing to do with the unit's hostage-rescue mandate but did fall under the all-encompassing area of "national importance." Federal Fisheries Minister Brian Tobin had been crusading against foreign overfishing in Canadian waters and the government was keen to make its case, in particular, against the large fleet of Spanish trawlers frequently operating near Newfoundland's Grand Banks.

The Canadian military's high-tech listening post at CFS Leitrim, just west of Ottawa, had already been intercepting the fleet's radio transmissions and knew the Spaniards had far exceeded established quotas. But rather than using this electronic evidence to make their case, Tobin and the federal government staged an elaborate charade to obtain physical evidence from the deck of a Spanish trawler and, in the process, embarrass the Spanish government. Two Fisheries department ships and a coast guard vessel zeroed in on one trawler in particular, the 65-metre *Estai*. It was decided that a four-man JTF2 team would provide backup for the fisheries officers as they boarded the ship.

It wasn't the first time Canada and Spain had clashed over fish stocks. Almost a decade earlier, in May 1986, four Canadian fisheries officers had boarded two Spanish trawlers to look for evidence of illegal fishing. But instead of submitting to the inspection, the Spaniards headed for international waters with the Canadians trapped on board. In hot pursuit was a Canadian patrol boat, the Leonard J. Cowley, carrying an RCMP emergency response unit. The chase went on for three days and covered 540 nautical miles before the RCMP team opened fire with machineguns and tossed smoke grenades onto the deck of the trawlers. The Spaniards surrendered and immediately filed complaints against the RCMP for their aggressive tactics.

In the March, 1995, high seas showdown, JTF2 wouldn't have the same success as its RCMP counterpart. On the first attempt to board the Spanish trawler, the Canadians tried to hook boarding ladders on the *Estai*, but the Spaniards dumped those into the ocean. The trawler then started to move at full speed, with JTF2 in pursuit. A second attempt at boarding the *Estai* was made by the commandos, but high waves hampered that assault. A third try also failed and the *Estai* showed no sign of changing course or altering speed. Finally, a Fisheries department official had to step in and use a .50 calibre machinegun on board one of the patrol vessels to fire a stream of bullets across the trawler's bow. At that point, the Spanish skipper surrendered his boat. The Canadian actions were denounced in Europe, but Brian Tobin had his prize catch - the *Estai*'s illegally-sized fishing net which he put on display. JTF2's participation in the seizure of the trawler was never mentioned. In fact, journalists were told that the RCMP had tried to board the *Estai* without success.

But the iron-clad secrecy surrounding JTF2 wouldn't last forever. On the morning of April 18, 1995, the unit had its first major breach in security when two of its soldiers were approached in an Ottawa parking lot by a man who claimed to be a freelance journalist. The JTF2 operators, both in civilian clothes, had driven to a car dealership to return a vehicle. As one of the soldiers stood near the unit's unmarked GMC Suburban, a man with a camera approached. "Hey, that vehicle's with JTF2 so that must be where you work," said the mystery man. "Can I get a photo of you and the truck?" One of the JTF2 operators led the man away from the Suburban as the other trooper remained unnoticed in the background. The soldier politely asked that his photo not be taken and declined to talk to the journalist. After the man gave him a business card and got into a Black Chevrolet, the JTF2 soldiers discretely copied down the vehicle's licence plate number.

Concerned that information had leaked out about the unit to the news media, the commando team requested the military's Special Investigation Unit be called in. The Canadian Security Intelligence Service also started its own probe but both spy groups determined that the man was harmless. They discovered that he had written a few freelance articles for a variety of military vehicle publications and had simply recognized one of the unit's Suburbans as he passed the car dealership parking lot. Police weren't overly surprised that the man knew about the counter-terrorism team. Despite all of its secrecy, JTF2 operators and their vehicles were well known in the Dwyer Hill area, according to investigators.

A month later, details about JTF2's covert operations were, for the first time, widely available for Canadians to read about after the Ottawa Citizen newspaper broke the story about the aborted Freedom 55 raid in Bosnia. Defence Minister David Collenette was visibly taken aback when asked by a Citizen journalist why JTF2 operators, supposedly to be used only for domestic hostage-rescue and counter-terrorism duties, were roaming around the former

Yugoslavia. "JTF2 is involved in very secret missions," Collenette responded testily. "It has very difficult responsibilities it has to perform in exceedingly dangerous situations. Therefore, we don't talk about it."

But, the Defence minister added, even if JTF2 had been in Yugoslavia, it wouldn't be violating its mandate. Although he didn't get into details, Collenette was obviously referring to the unit's all-encompassing mandate which allowed it to be used in any situation involving "the national interest."

A few weeks later, the satirical political publication, Frank Magazine, reported that the Defence department had launched a spy operation against the Citizen to try to ferret out who had leaked the Freedom 55 information. Military commanders had to reassure Collenette that, contrary to Frank's assertions, its spies were not running amok but they did acknowledge that Royal Canadian Dragoons commander Lieutenant Colonel Bill Brough had launched his own probe to determine which soldiers talked to the newspaper about the rescue plan.

The Citizen article also created problems for the Canadian government in New York after UN officials started asking embarrassing questions about the Freedom 55 operation. Not only had the UN not approved of such a risky plan, but it didn't even know that JTF2 was in Bosnia until its officials read about it in the press.

It wasn't only in the pages of daily newspapers that JTF2 was having trouble adhering to its policy of air-tight security. The commandos weren't even supposed to tell their wives about some of their missions, but more than a few found it impossible to keep secrets from their spouses. In the summer of 1995, details of some of the unit's training and operations came out in a messy public divorce proceeding in Petawawa. After a two-week investigation, military police confirmed that a JTF2 soldier had indeed breached operational security. He was summarily tried, found guilty, and sentenced to 14 days in jail.

Divorce court, aside, JTF2 was about to get more unwelcome attention, this time on a national level. In the early morning of August 9, 1995, military helicopters carrying a JTF2 assault force lifted off from a base in St. Hubert, Quebec, and headed towards Anjou, an east-end Montreal suburb. Using night vision goggles, the pilots from the 450 Tactical Helicopter Squadron began circling over an industrial park. The mission was to land a JTF2 team outside an abandoned warehouse for a simulated raid on a terrorist stronghold.

Such secret operations in urban areas could be fraught with problems. In April 1992, SERT and the Ottawa Police almost got into a firefight after the RCMP counter-terrorism unit conducted secret training at a downtown office building under construction. An alert security guard phoned 911 after he saw a group of men, dressed in black and carrying sub-machineguns, enter a high-rise building in the city's core. SERT had received permission from the building contractor to practice rappelling down the sides of the tower but no one had bothered to inform Ottawa police of the exercise. Thirteen police cars responded to the emergency alert about armed men in the downtown area before realizing the group was made up of SERT's Mounties.

Complaints about such clandestine training were even more common in the U.S., where Delta Force had become notorious for conducting mini-wars in abandoned buildings and not informing local police and government officials. These night-time raids had been conducted in Houston, New Orleans, Miami, Pittsburgh and Des Plaines, Illinois, not only terrifying the unsuspecting citizens in those cities but often causing a great deal of property damage. The American commando team dealt with the problem by having its officers dole out wads of cash to placate angry residents, but by the early 1990s the situation was at a point that some communities, even when approached in advance by Delta Force, were declining to allow the unit to practice in their cities.

The JTF2 mission to Anjou would be even more controversial. Not only had military commanders failed to inform local authorities about the exercise, but had planned for it to take place just months before the citizens of Quebec were to vote in a referendum on whether their province should begin the process to separate from the rest of Canada. The entire country was tense as federal politicians warned about the consequences of Quebec sovereignty and some commentators were openly talking about the potential for some francophone units in the Canadian Forces to break away and form a separate Quebec army.

The first explosions - the JTF2 flash-bangs detonating in the warehouse - started going off at about 4 a.m. and woke scores of people in Anjou and across the St. Lawrence River in Boucherville. Residents rushed out to their front yards where they were confronted with a scene that seemed to be taken right out of the popular war movie, Apocalypse Now. Helicopters circled the industrial park; bright flashes lit up the skyline from the explosions; machinegun fire could heard for another 30 minutes; and police and 911 emergency lines were jammed with panicked callers.

The next morning a furious Quebec Premier Jacques Parizeau held a press conference to accuse the federal government of deliberately conducting a scare tactic campaign to dissuade people from voting for separation. The Liberals, he said, were creating a "climate of crisis" on the eve of the referendum. "That makes a hell of an impression on the civilian population to drop a couple of grenades and make a lot of noise without warning," he fumed.

Inside the military, some officers wondered if Parizeau was right and the JTF2 raid was perhaps designed to send a less-than-subtle signal to the people of Quebec. They knew that three years earlier, during a referendum on the Charlottetown Accord, the federal government had put a halt to all military exercises so as not to upset Quebec citizens. This time, with the province teetering on leaving Canada, the stakes were much higher and the political tension in Quebec much greater. Some officers found it simply unbelievable that the JTF2 mission hadn't been approved at the highest levels of government.

But when asked about the early morning raid, Prime Minister Chrétien responded that he had never heard of JTF2 and knew nothing of the exercise. "Nobody is even aware of this," shrugged the prime minister. If Chrétien truly was unaware of JTF2's existence, his Cabinet ministers were not. Less than two weeks after the Anjou raid, the RCMP was requesting, through Solicitor General Herb Gray, that the counter-terrorism unit take a lead role in a stand-off between natives and the Mounties in the small British Columbia community of Gustafsen Lake.

The handling of a land-claims dispute at Gustafsen Lake, 350 kilometres northeast of Vancouver, had been botched almost from the start by the RCMP. A small group of Shuswap natives had occupied a section of a rancher's property, claiming the private land to be a sacred ancestral burial site. Some Mounties had been in contact with the protesters over several weeks and peaceful negotiations were underway. But all that was scuttled when an RCMP emergency response team, decked out in camouflage uniforms, tried to infiltrate the native encampment on an intelligence-gathering mission. Believing the intruders to be local rednecks, the natives fired over the heads of the men and frantically called police for help.

In response, some 400 RCMP officers from ERT teams throughout the province surrounded the encampment. From the start the Mounties portrayed the natives as "terrorists." Journalists were told by officers that the protesters were heavily armed and had a vast arsenal that included AK-47 assault rifles and home-made bombs. Reality was a little different. In fact, there were just 18 people in the camp who were led by a 64-year-old native elder. Among the "heavily armed terrorists" who confronted the RCMP was a 24-year-old mentally handicapped man. Although there had been an AK-47 in the encampment, most of the weapons the natives had were common hunting rifles.

As the weeks dragged on, the animosity between police and protesters got out of control. The RCMP claimed the natives had fired at a police helicopter and tried to ambush two ERT officers. The natives accused the Mounties of being intent on provoking a confrontation and alleged the tactical officers had opened fire on them at random. RCMP ERT squads, hidden in the forests and bush around the encampment, were starting to feel the pressure as the siege went from days into weeks. It was almost impossible to monitor all of the rugged terrain around the camp and the Mounties knew the protesters were being resupplied at night by sympathizers using mules and, at times, even trucks, to bring in food and water. Tired and overworked, RCMP commanders requested that the military provide them with armored personnel carriers and a contingent of JTF2.

On the afternoon of September 11, the Gustafsen Lake confrontation boiled over into a wild shootout between protesters and police. A red pickup truck, with two armed natives in the back, was spotted leaving the camp by a surveillance aircraft. It wouldn't get far. A short distance down the road the truck exploded after hitting an RCMP landmine. The natives, stunned by the blast but uninjured, leaped from the heavily damaged truck and began firing at an approaching Canadian Forces Bison armored personnel carrier. Inside the Bison, panicked RCMP ERT officers returned fire, shooting out of the gunports of the armored vehicle with their automatic weapons. Some 2,000 rounds were fired at the aboriginals, who wisely turned and fled into the forest. Another RCMP tactical squad situated across a lake from the Bison opened up on the natives with their M-16 assault rifles. RCMP bullets pinged off the thick skin of the APC as those inside mistakenly thought they were still under fierce attack by the Indians.

Inside another Bison several hundred metres away, RCMP ERT officers heard the initial explosion and figured their tactical squad comrades had just been blown up by a homemade native landmine. "Get this machine moving now," ordered one of the police officers to the Bison crew. The armored vehicle roared off in the direction of the gunfire, but in their haste to get to the scene, the APC crew drove the vehicle straight into a tree. Police would later claim it was disabled by native gunfire.

The RCMP officers escaped injury in the largely one-sided gun-battle in which they fired off thousands of rounds into the surrounding forest. But the morale of the ERT units was broken. At 7:40 p.m. that same night, the RCMP requested that a JTF2 liaison officer proceed immediately to Gustafsen Lake and that the counter-terrorism unit begin a reconnaissance in preparation to take over duties from the exhausted police tactical squads.

But Canada's generals weren't rushing to take a lead role in the Gustafsen Lake siege. The military's standoff with natives at Oka was still fresh in the minds of many senior officers and although the Canadian Forces had received public kudos for its role in that 1990 siege, there was the potential at the time for the siege to turn into a bloodbath. In addition, a standoff between police and native protesters who had occupied a military base in Ontario had already resulted in the death of one aboriginal man. A week before, an Ontario Provincial Police tactical sniper shot and killed an unarmed native, Dudley George, at Ipperwash. With the ongoing tension at reserves near Cornwall and Oka, along with the Ipperwash killing, the last thing the country needed was a JTF2-led commando raid on Gustafsen Lake.

Military planners also didn't believe that JTF2 would be enough to handle the situation. The area surrounding the native encampment was some 25 square kilometres in size and Brigadier General Robert Meating, the Canadian Forces liaison officer for Gustafsen Lake, determined that the military would need as many as 4,000 troops for any operation. But as the Defence department tried to avoid becoming further embroiled in the standoff, the situation defused when, on September 17, the natives peacefully surrendered.

The military had been wise to steer clear of granting the RCMP's request to have JTF2 take over at Gustafsen Lake. Almost two years later, the protesters' civilian trials would end up damaging the RCMP's reputation when it was revealed that the Mounties had engaged in a deliberate smear campaign against the aboriginals. One officer had even joked about killing the natives' lawyer. The court also heard how RCMP snipers violated standard police policy by opening fire, without warning, on one of the aboriginal men as he walked to a lake one day to retrieve water. During the trials, defence attorneys were highly successful in portraying the RCMP as an aggressive force that had turned a simple land dispute into a 36-day siege. The serious charges of attempted murder originally laid against the protesters were dropped and, in the end, only a few of the natives were found guilty of trespassing.

JTF2's exact role at Gustafsen Lake is still shrouded in secrecy. Officially, the unit wasn't deployed to the standoff. But civilian police officers privately confirm that JTF2 operators were at the siege, helping them in covert intelligence gathering as well as determining the lay of the land in case the entire unit was needed for an assault on the native encampment. Some of the native protestors also insist that it was members of JTF2, and not the RCMP, who engaged them in a gun battle in early September.

In response to an Access to Information request, the Department of National Defence declared that all files related to JTF2's operations at Gustafsen Lake were off limits for reasons of national security - a strange response if the unit was truly never sent to British Columbia.

But even as the Mounties picked up the pieces at Gustafsen Lake, JTF2 operatives were busy packing their bags again for a new overseas mission. They would put the dense, dark forests of B.C. behind them, and head into the humid, foul-smelling slums of a troubled Caribbean city.

ABOVE: *JTF2 commandos providing security advice for Haiti's president René Préval had the backup of a Canadian military quick-reaction force which stayed at the National Palace in Port-au-Prince. (PHOTO BY AUTHOR)*

OPPOSITE PAGE: *Canadian diplomat Raymond Chrétien in 1996 with two of his JTF2 bodyguards in Zaire. (AP PHOTO)*

FIVE: "BODYGUARDS INC."

IT WAS A typically muggy night in July 1996 when the Haitian police SWAT team smashed down the door of a house in Port-au-Prince and stormed into the building. The team's mission was to find illegal arms being hidden by right-wing extremists who were determined to undermine the Caribbean island's fledgling democratic government. Weapons drawn, the heavily armed SWAT officers cautiously moved from room to room, handcuffing suspects and searching for guns and explosives.

In the background, a group of Canadian soldiers observed with approval as their Haitian students used the tactics they'd been taught just weeks earlier with almost perfect precision. No one was injured during the raid. No shots had been fired. Although no firearms or explosives were recovered, the JTF2 team considered the mission a success. Before their training with JTF2, the Haitian police likely would have shown less restraint in such a raid, indiscriminately opening fire on anybody unfortunate enough to be in the building at the time.

Across the city at the presidential palace, two other JTF2 operators were advising on security arrangements for Haitian President René Préval. The Canadian commandos were giving Préval valuable advice on how to avoid assassination by the former Haitian army officers who had vowed to kill him. But the destitute Caribbean island, with its vast slums and stifling 40°C temperatures, was also helping to give JTF2 what it needed to ensure its own survival. By 1996, Canada's counter-terrorism force had become a multi-million-dollar operation with more than 100 soldiers. But the overall Canadian Forces budget was in the process of being reduced by 25 per cent and tens of thousands of troops were being cut from the ranks. Units across the country were canceling training because funding had been so severely reduced. Fighter aircraft were being mothballed. Equipment programs were being scuttled.

JTF2 was in a potentially vulnerable position. The Canadian Forces had spent almost $40 million so far on the unit. It had even gone as far as creating a new organization within National Defence Headquarters. The Counter-Terrorism Special Operations (CTSO) branch, staffed mainly with former JTF2 officers, was designed to act as a liaison between the unit and the senior military leadership. But, as the RCMP had discovered, the need for hostage rescue was becoming rarer in a world where terrorists more often relied on bombs and assassinations. A country's counter-terrorist team - fortunately or unfortunately, depending on one's point of view - would be used for a hostage-rescue mission perhaps once every 10 years.

Although JTF2 was keen to expand into the so-called "green" operations, there were limits on the number of missions it could undertake. Canada didn't have the vast economic and military interests of the United States so it had little need for a special operations team to be roaming the world. Canada also didn't have the terrorism problems that Britain faced with the IRA, which required that the SAS operate continual domestic covert missions.

JTF2's leadership realized it needed something more than hostage rescue to justify the team's existence to the government and promote itself in front of the generals. As part of their solution, unit commanders decided to branch out into two areas: foreign training and close personal protection for VIPs. JTF2 senior officers felt the team had developed sophisticated counter-terrorism skills that could be shopped around to smaller undeveloped nations in a similar fashion as the U.S. had used its Green Berets to teach foreign armies. While JTF2 received valuable overseas experience, Canadian interests would presumably be well served by the goodwill generated among foreign governments and armies who received such training.

Close personal protection - or bodyguard work - for overseas operations had usually been performed in the Canadian Forces by military police, while the RCMP most often handled any such assignments at embassies. But JTF2 leaders felt they could make the argument that their unit should take over the roles. JTF2 operators, they reasoned, were better trained and better armed than both military and civilian police officers. Standing guard over generals and politicians would have the added benefit of exposing senior officials to the unit's capabilities, thereby further promoting the commando team.

Some of JTF2's counterparts, such as the U.S. Army's Delta Force and the SAS, did close protection work on a limited basis. The SAS had guarded then British prime minister Margaret Thatcher when she came to Toronto in the mid-1980s. SAS members blended into the background and were indistinguishable from the regular British police who surrounded the prime minister. The SAS had also been involved in protecting foreign leaders on their own turf, in particular, the Sultan of Oman in the early 1970s.

Delta Force had also been on close protection assignments, for instance, guarding U.S. General Norman Schwarzkopf during the Persian Gulf War. But like the SAS, much of Delta's bodyguard work was in the shadows. They were so low-profile, that few people outside the U.S. military knew that eight Delta operators had been killed during the 1984 suicide bombing of the U.S. embassy in Beirut. The soldiers had been in the city to guard American diplomats taking part in sensitive political negotiations.

For JTF2, the tiny and unstable island of Haiti offered the opportunity to engage for the first time in both new roles of close protection and foreign training. Ruled for decades by a corrupt dictatorship supported by an equally corrupt military, Haiti seemed ready to disintegrate into chaos when, in 1994, the U.S. military invaded the island to restore law and order and install a democratically elected government. Five months later, the United Nations had taken over from the Americans, and peacekeeping troops patrolled the dangerous streets of Port-au-Prince. It wasn't long before Canada became involved. In November ,1995 Prime Minister Jean Chrétien, as a favor to the U.S., committed 750 Canadian soldiers to support the island's new democratic government.

Other special operations teams had already been in Haiti. Delta Force and SEAL Team Six operators were brought in after former Haitian army soldiers, opposed to the return of a democratic government, vowed to gun down American soldiers and high-ranking officials. Those units provided protection for American generals and State Department officials. The mission was later taken over by a 50-man squad from the Polish special forces unit, known by the acronym GROM. The Poles handled security for a host of VIPs visiting the island, including UN Secretary General Boutros Boutros-Ghali and U.S. Defense Secretary William Perry.

When a group from JTF2 arrived on the island in the summer of 1996, its members were assigned two missions. A four-man team would teach the newly formed Haitian police SWAT unit various tactics, while a team of two men would act as security advisors to President Préval.

The JTF2 soldiers teaching the Haitian tactical squad had their work cut out for them. The Haitian police force had earned a reputation for being more dangerous than the island's criminals. Poorly trained, thoroughly corrupt, they had been involved in extortion, beatings, torture and murder. Police were killing about 20 people a year, many in highly suspicious circumstances. In April 1996, they had stormed the slum of Cité Soleil and executed six people on the spot. In another questionable incident, police shot and killed five men on a busy downtown street. One of the victims had been in handcuffs.

JTF2's job was to train Haitian police officers in the art of "door kicking" and building takedowns. Hostage situations weren't all that common on the island so the SWAT team would be used to hunt down and seize arms caches held by extremists and former army officers intent on overthrowing the Préval government. Under JTF2's tutelage, the SWAT unit began a series of successful raids throughout Port-au-Prince and the surrounding area. JTF2 commandos accompanied the Haitian SWAT officers on numerous raids, three in the first couple of weeks of July alone. But the Canadians were there as advisors only. "They went out with them but only in a backup role," said one Canadian Army officer in Port-au-Prince. "Our guys would observe from a distance. It wasn't a case of our guys doing any shooting."

The team at the presidential palace had its own challenges. The National Palace, a large estate in the middle of Port-au-Prince, was a nightmare to properly secure. It wouldn't be difficult to slip into the compound, and the palace itself was a labyrinth of rooms and wide hallways that would have been hard to defend. Préval's own security detail was a motley collection of police and ex-army officers who packed Uzi sub-machineguns under their cheap suits.

The JTF2 security team was backed up by a 30-member quick-reaction force of regular Canadian soldiers who were housed in a white stone barracks behind the palace. The platoon of A Company, Royal 22nd Regiment, had stationed a Bison armored personnel carrier in a garage on the palace grounds in case at some point Préval needed to be whisked away to safety. For added security, the platoon's commander, Major Dan Ménard, had stationed his snipers on the palace roof where they had a commanding view of the sprawling city. "If something is going to happen in Haiti, it will probably be at the palace," Ménard explained. His men, equipped with C7 rifles and Minimi machineguns, patrolled the palace grounds and accompanied Préval in a convoy of motorcycles and four-wheel drive trucks anytime he left the walled compound.

The mission was high-profile. It was only the second time Canadian troops had been responsible for protecting a foreign head of state in that leader's own country. The first time was in Britain during the Second World War when Canadians guarded Queen Elizabeth, now known as the Queen Mother. Besides providing security, the JTF2 soldiers and the quick reaction platoon were also training Préval's 190-member palace security force, showing them how to handle weapons and instructing them in close protection tactics.

The threat to the president was real enough. Although the Haitian military had been disbanded after U.S. troops invaded in 1994, some former soldiers wanted to overthrow, or at least disrupt, the new government. Uniformed commandos had attacked a police station just behind the National Palace with grenades and automatic weapons, killing one person, before being driven off by police. Shortly after, Haitian officers arrested 20 people involved in an assassination plot against Préval.

As the months wore on, JTF2's job of protecting Préval became increasingly difficult. On one presidential visit to a Port-au-Prince slum, one of Ménard's men was pepper-sprayed by a member of the crowd, though Préval escaped unharmed. In another particularly tense showdown, more than 1,000 people stormed the palace grounds demanding to see the president. Two of Préval's Haitian guards were stabbed when they waded out into the angry mob. Canadian soldiers appeared on the palace steps armed with C7s and C8 carbines while the Van Doos' snipers on the rooftop scanned the crowd in an attempt to target its leaders. Faced with this show of force, the mob backed off and left the compound. Later, in September 1996, it was discovered that some of Préval's own Haitian guards had been involved in the assassination of one of the president's political rivals. The president expressed disbelief that anyone from his hand-picked group could be involved in such a crime and quickly ordered a revamping of his security force.

But the situation went from bad to worse. Months later, the Canadian soldiers who eventually replaced Ménard's platoon as a quick reaction force found that the Haitian president regularly ignored their advice. Although they were in charge of a counter-ambush team to protect Préval, he kept the Canadian security team in the dark about any of his travel plans and last-minute unscheduled trips were common. The Canadians were also prevented from conducting routine security checks on those coming into the palace. And not much seemed to have changed as far as the presidential guard went - they were still the collection of ex-soldiers and police officers with dubious backgrounds. To make matters worse, if anything were to happen to Préval, the blame for poor security would likely fall on Canadian shoulders. "You put yourself in danger and they don't care," Warrant Officer Jean Boivin, a member of the palace quick reaction force told Toronto Star reporter Linda Diebel. "For our men it's not a good situation."

Canadian generals didn't want to hear about the problems. After the Toronto Star article appeared, the soldiers who spoke with the journalist were removed from palace duty. The fact that JTF2 had been at the presidential compound was never revealed in the article. That wasn't surprising. Even among fellow Canadian soldiers, the commandos kept up their high level of secrecy and security. When an administration clerk at the Canadian camp began processing paperwork so that the JTF2 operators could receive peacekeeping medals, she naturally asked for the men's names and military identification numbers. They politely refused. "We can't tell you any of that because it's classified," one of the commandos told the disbelieving clerk.

Ultimately, the mission to Haiti was considered by JTF2 to be a success. Despite its problems, the operation was an important step in the unit's objective to continue branching out into new roles.

No sooner was the Haiti mission complete than another foreign operation required JTF2's new-found skills in close protection. In September 1996, fighting between rebels and Zaire's army flared up once again along Zaire's border with Rwanda. Trapped in the middle were several hundred thousand Rwandan refugees, who had earlier fled their own country to escape civil war. Ottawa had approved a UN request that Raymond Chrétien, Canada's ambassador to the U.S. and the prime minister's nephew, fly to the region to meet with African leaders and try to negotiate an end to the fighting. The air force's 412 Transport Squadron was tasked with providing Chrétien a "white non-threatening" Challenger aircraft and crew so he could whisk between cities in Central Africa. The military also offered a team of JTF2 bodyguards to stand watch over the ambassador.

In the second week of November, Chrétien and his Dwyer Hill commandos found themselves jetting between Rwanda and Zaire. In the Zairian capital of Kinshasa, the ambassador held a press conference to provide an update on how peace negotiations were proceeding. As he spoke, two JTF2 soldiers, clad in safari-type photographers' vests with portable radios attached, stood near Chrétien scanning the crowd for any threats.

Shortly after, Ottawa announced the Canadian Forces would lead a multinational rescue mission to ensure food and relief supplies reached refugees trapped by fighting in eastern Zaire. Canadian Army commander Lieutenant General Maurice Baril had been selected to lead the mission, codenamed "Operation Assurance." But even as Baril outlined his plans, the raison d'être for the mission evaporated. After a major battle on the morning of November 15, tens of thousands of refugees were able to flee the area and a 40-kilometre-long line of men, women and children began working its way towards the relative safety of the Rwandan border. The fact that the refugees appeared to be successfully escaping the fighting on their own had some Rwandan government officials questioning whether the international rescue mission was needed at all. At the same time, the U.S. government started hedging on its promise to provide combat troops and attack helicopters for the Canadian-led force.

But the Liberal government, buoyed by positive publicity at home, wasn't ready to shut down "Operation Assurance" just yet. A small number of Canadian troops had already arrived in the region to begin the mission and several days later Baril headed to Africa to assess the situation for himself. On the ground, with the state of affairs still highly volatile, the general met with a new team of JTF2 soldiers who would guard him over the next several weeks.

Baril was faced with two problems. Although thousands of refugees were now streaming home to Rwanda, there was concern that some 200,000 were still missing somewhere in the forbidding jungle and mountainous terrain of eastern Zaire. Secondly, if the international community still wanted "Operation Assurance" to continue, Baril would have to meet with rebel leaders in Zaire to negotiate some kind of cease-fire so relief supplies could be delivered.

On November 24, Baril and his JTF2 bodyguards boarded a Canadian Forces Hercules aircraft and went looking for the missing 200,000 refugees. For three hours, the plane scoured the dense jungle and rugged mountains as Baril peered out of the cockpit. American intelligence officials had given the Canadians details about the locations of rebel anti-aircraft sites on the ground and for added protection the Hercules had been outfitted with armored floors and chaff dispensers to launch decoys for any heat-seeking missiles. As well, Baril and those on board were bundled up in body armor. "We took fire but we didn't get hit," recalls the general. "We were too low for missiles and we knew where the ground fire was coming from." Within three hours, Baril had found the missing refugees moving en masse through the jungle.

Now the focus of "Operation Assurance" shifted to helping those still trapped in Zaire. On November 28, General Baril accompanied by several JTF2 soldiers, crossed the Zaire-Rwandan border to do his own reconnaissance and establish contact with rebel leader Laurent Kabila. Baril's convoy headed west to the village of Sake where some 30,000 refugees had set up camp. At Sake, rebel soldiers stopped journalists from following the general any further. The situation was tense. When some reporters began interviewing the refugees, the soldiers opened fire over their heads as a warning. Baril's JTF2 bodyguards instinctively reached for their pistols and quickly moved the general away from the area.

Baril's convoy continued onward to Goma, which had just been captured by Kabila's Congolese Liberation Army. There, the rotund guerilla leader greeted the Canadian general at a ransacked mansion that had once belonged to Zaire's president. With the JTF2 team standing guard and Kabila's own rag-tag army of guerrillas nearby, the two men met for 50 minutes to try to work out some kind of compromise to allow international aid to be brought in to the remaining refugees. After the meeting, the rebels took the general and his Canadian commandos for a guided tour of war-torn Goma. Baril's five-hour reconnaissance trip to meet with Kabila was highly dangerous and criticized by some back in Canada who wondered what the head of the Canadian Army was doing running around the jungles of Zaire. But Baril was unrepentant: "I had to reassure the government of Canada that the situation had changed and we could go home."

"Operation Assurance" didn't officially end until, Friday, December 13, when General Baril, now back in New York, announced that the situation in Africa had changed for the better and a large military force was no longer required. The mission paid off rich dividends for the senior officer. Impressed by his take-charge attitude, the Canadian government would later name him Chief of the Defence Staff.

For JTF2, the Zaire mission was also a resounding success. It presented the unit's operators with more valuable experience in close personal protection - and for no less than the future Chief of the Defence Staff and the prime minister's nephew. The mission spoke well of how JTF2 was starting to be viewed in the Canadian bureaucracy. In previous years, the job of guarding a diplomat such as Raymond Chrétien on an overseas trip normally would have gone to the RCMP.

At home, while some people still debated the pros and cons of the Zaire rescue mission (nicknamed "the Bungle in the Jungle" by more than a few cynics in the military), a different kind of conflict had been unfolding in south Asia that would require the Canadian military's newly developed counter-terrorism expertise.

The once peaceful kingdom of Nepal was in the midst of a worsening guerrilla war with Communist rebels who were threatening to overrun several of the country's remote provinces. The year before, Nepal's security forces launched an attack they had hoped would snuff out the then small group of Communist extremists whose aim was to overthrow the country's monarchy and replace it with a socialist regime. The operation, codenamed Romeo, backfired terribly. The heavily armed police force sent into several provinces in the impoverished northwestern part of Nepal brutalized the peasant population, arresting more than 1,000 people, many of them with no links to the Communists. This ill-planned offensive created an even more radical and larger rebel force. On February, 13, 1996, the guerrillas struck back, firebombing and attacking police stations in northwest Nepal. Guns were snatched from remote outposts and the insurgency quickly spread to other districts. The "people's war" had begun. In a few short months, a relatively small collection of guerrillas armed with hunting rifles and homemade pistols had proven more than a match for the country's 51,000 police officers.

In the capital of Kathmandu, government officials were demanding that the Royal Nepalese Army join the battle. The 47,000-member force traditionally avoided internal security duties and was content to guard the country's borders and take part in overseas peacekeeping operations. As it prepared for a potential civil war, the Nepalese military turned to Canada for help.

On August 22, the Canadian Forces Adviser's Office in New Delhi, India, relayed details of the Royal Nepalese Army's request to National Defence Headquarters and JTF2. The RNA wanted Canadian military advisors to oversee its counter-terrorism plans and suggest how best to fight the Communist guerrillas. Members of the Canadian Defence department's recently created Counter Terrorism and Special Operations (CTSO) branch, most of them former JTF2 officers, would oversee the mission.

The small Canadian team which visited Nepal in November quickly understood that the RNA was in a tough position. The Nepalese military's total annual budget was a paltry $52 million (U.S.). According to a CTSO analysis, Nepal's army had neither combat aircraft nor armed helicopters - two necessities for conducting a counter-insurgency campaign in a mountainous country. Spare parts for its existing aircraft, three fixed-wing transport planes and one transport helicopter, were also in short supply. True, the guerrillas were still armed mostly with a collection of hunting rifles and homemade weapons, such as land mines built from kitchen pressure-cookers. But modern military small arms, such as AK-47s, were being smuggled over the border from India and the guerrilla army had increased its ranks from several hundred to about 1,000 fighters.

The Canadian training team went to work advising the RNA on tactics and the best use of its forces against the guerrillas. Two Royal Nepalese Army soldiers were also sent to Canada to attend mountain instructors' courses - excellent training for the battles in which they would later take part. Another RNA officer was selected for Canadian military flying training while six others attended courses at Pearson Peacekeeping Centre in Nova Scotia. For Colonel John Bremner, the Canadian Forces Adviser in New Delhi, the training team's visit in November and the movement of RNA troops to Canada for advanced training was a success that paid off in improved relations between the two countries. Canada's advisory role had been well-received in Kathmandu and Bremner informed National Defence headquarters in Ottawa that Nepal was "extremely well disposed toward Canada and the Canadian Forces."

In case any journalists got wind of the mission, military public affairs officers were instructed not to acknowledge the CTSO role or the numbers of soldiers who made up the Canadian team. They were to release just enough information to satisfy the media's curiosity. "The visit was conducted at the request of the Nepalese government and dealt with the Royal Nepalese Army counter-terrorist posture," was the line they were to recite to journalists. "No further details will be provided." The media response lines were never needed because no journalists ever found out about the Nepal mission.

As Canadian counter-terrorism specialists were training the Nepalese Army, an incident was unfolding half a world away in Lima, Peru, that could require JTF2's hostage-rescue skills. On the night of December 17, 1996, a group of guerillas belonging to the Tupac Amaru Revolutionary Movement, or MRTA, had captured much of Peru's ruling elite in a daring raid on the residence of Japan's ambassador. More than a dozen MRTA guerrillas had used explosives to blow a hole in the back wall of the Lima mansion while others had posed as servants catering to the 380 guests who were attending a lavish party.

The raid was well planned and executed. In one bold stroke, the MRTA had captured 30 foreign ambassadors, two Peruvian cabinet ministers and six members of the Peruvian congress, as well as other dignitaries and their families. Among the hostages were four Canadians, including Ambassador Tony Vincent and his wife.

The guerrillas treated their hostages well but were insistent that their demands be met. They wanted economic reforms, the release of MRTA prisoners, and sweeping changes to Peru's brutal prison system. The MRTA had formed in 1983 with the goal of establishing a Marxist state and throughout the rest of the decade it conducted an unrelenting campaign of assassinations, bombings, kidnappings and ambushes against government forces. But by the time of its raid on the Japanese ambassador's residence, the guerrilla group had been all but written off as a serious threat. Peruvian special forces had conducted several successful operations that had significantly weakened the rebel army and resulted in the arrests of many of its leaders. Now the MRTA had struck back with a vengeance that surprised even Peru's counter-terrorism specialists.

The presence of Canadian hostages, including a senior diplomat, was enough to put JTF2 on high alert. The Foreign Affairs department was preparing to send a team down to Lima to bolster its embassy staff there. The military's Challenger jet was on standby to transport the group, which included an RCMP bodyguard and a hostage negotiator. At National Defence headquarters, military officials recommended an intelligence operative be included in the team to pave the way for the possible deployment of JTF2.

As a sign of goodwill, the guerrillas almost immediately released 170 hostages including Vincent's wife and the other Canadians. The ambassador was set free a couple of days later and promptly agreed to act as an intermediary in trying to resolve the crisis. Still holding more than 200 people, the MRTA warned it would start executing the VIPs if its demands weren't promptly met. As the hostage-taking dragged on, special forces soldiers from foreign countries began to arrive in Lima. Delta Force was the first on the scene. They were joined by a British SAS team on December 20 which was to help advise the Peruvian government. A small group of JTF2 operators also flew into Lima.

For the next month, negotiations between the Peruvian government and the MRTA continued with neither side getting what it wanted. The guerrillas had not harmed their captives but nor had they succeeded in forcing Peru's president, Alberto Fujimori, to accede to any of their demands. Relations between the hostage-takers and the police who surrounded the ambassador's residence had reached a crisis point. The MRTA guerrillas had fired several gunshots after dozens of Peruvian police paraded around the residence trying to unnerve the terrorists by playing loud music and making obscene gestures.

In the first week of February 1997, the Canadian government stepped up its role as an intermediary in the siege by agreeing to act as host for a high-level meeting between Japanese and Peruvian officials. At the meeting in Toronto, Japanese diplomats convinced Peruvian authorities to make sure security forces outside the mansion toned down their confrontational behavior. In return, Japanese Prime Minister Ryutaro Hashimoto agreed to support Peruvian President Fujimori's position not to give in to the main MRTA demand for the release of 400 of their imprisoned comrades.

The two leaders discussed giving the MRTA asylum in a foreign country, possibly Cuba. Originally the terrorists wanted safe passage into the jungle but they had since been convinced that sanctuary in another country might be the best alternative. Rumors started circulating in Toronto that Canadian soldiers would be involved in guaranteeing safe passage for the guerrillas, but a top advisor to Prime Minister Chrétien quickly denied such an offer had been made. Ambassador Tony Vincent also claimed he knew nothing about any Canadian guarantee.

At National Defence headquarters, military planners had come up with a decidedly risky and, in the eyes of some officers, unworkable scheme. According to the plan, a main force of JTF2 would be flown to Peru by a Canadian Forces aircraft as a kind of modern-day Trojan Horse. The plan called for the Canadian commandos to ambush the rebels if and when they agreed to vacate the ambassador's residence in return for passage out of the country. JTF2 operators, who had just spent a month training on a jetliner at Toronto's Pearson Airport in hostage-rescue techniques, were pumped and ready to go.

But Foreign Affairs diplomats took one look at the Defence department plan and quickly overruled the idea that JTF2 be used. Canadian officials in Lima had been predicting that while negotiations would be lengthy, there likely would be a peaceful ending to the hostage-taking. "Peruvian authorities are not presently accepting offers of assistance from foreign countries," Canadian diplomats in Lima had tersely reported back to the Defence department, shortly after the hostage-taking had begun.

Behind the scenes, Peruvian commandos, under the tutelage of the SAS, were busily practicing their own rescue mission. They had built a full-scale model of the Japanese ambassador's residence and had began running through different assault plans. Another team of commandos had been tunneling under the mansion to position itself for the attack. Peruvian intelligence officials had also successfully smuggled in a miniature radio receiver to one of the hostages, retired naval officer Admiral Luis Giampietri Rojas.

On the afternoon of April 22, the Peruvian assault force was ready to go. At 3:17 p.m., President Fujimori personally gave the order to attack. The radio transmitter in the possession of Admiral Rojas crackled with a message. "We'll free you in three minutes," the voice on the other end said.

In another room of the mansion, a group of terrorists was playing soccer with a makeshift ball of rolled-up duct tape. As they kicked the ball around, the floor beneath them suddenly exploded and a commando team emerged from the gaping hole. The terrorists were immediately gunned down. Outside the mansion, another assault force used explosives to blast open the front door, quickly tossing in stun and smoke grenades. At other entrances, soldiers used sledgehammers to bash down doors and rush inside. The MRTA, taken completely by surprise, was overwhelmed by the 140-member assault team. A few of the terrorists managed to fight back and one was able to throw a grenade, killing two of the raiders.

Outside the ambassador's residence, the special forces soldiers from several other countries could hear the shooting reach a crescendo and then quickly subside. A few minutes later, some of the hostages were seen scrambling out of a skylight on the roof as Peruvian commandos directed them to safety. Another 10 minutes passed before more soldiers appeared on the roof waving their arms and holding MRTA flags they had torn down from inside the residence. The raid was an outstanding success. All but one of the captives, a member of the Peruvian Supreme Court who died of a heart attack, survived. All the terrorists had been killed and, although there would later be allegations that some had been executed as they tried to surrender, the assault was hailed around the world as the equivalent of the SAS's famous 1980 Iranian embassy attack in London. Casualties for the Peruvian assault force were light considering the danger the soldiers faced: along with the two commandos who had been killed by a terrorist's grenade, half a dozen had been injured.

While they hadn't taken a direct role in the assault, the JTF2 officers in Lima also considered their mission a success. A lengthy list of "benefits to government of Canada" and "benefits to Canadian Forces" was filed by the JTF2 operators and promptly classified "secret."

OPPOSITE PAGE: *Chief of the Defence Staff, General Maurice Baril, is accompanied by JTF2 bodyguards (third and fourth soldiers behind him) as he tours Canadian operations in Eritrea.* (COURTESY DND)

SIX: THE WAY AHEAD

BY THE TIME JTF2 was in its fourth year of existence, it had run into major problems in attracting the high-calibre soldier needed for counter-terrorism and special operations duties. The flow of new recruits had almost stopped at Dwyer Hill by early 1997 and unit commanders were scrambling to keep those soldiers already on the team.

At the heart of the problem was the federal government's plan to shrink the size of the Canadian Forces from 80,000 in 1993 to 60,000 by 1999. Already by 1997 the military had been reduced to around 70,000 soldiers, sailors and air force personnel. Although JTF2 now recruited from all three services (the unit's main karate/self-defence instructor, for example, was from the navy), it was the army that the commando team still relied on as its main source of recruits. But the army had only 22,000 members and, of those, less than half were seen as front-line soldiers. That relatively small pool of potential recruits, plus JTF2's rigorous physical fitness standards, meant that there were simply not enough soldiers for the unit.

JTF2 was also finding itself penalized under the military's heavily bureaucratic system. Soldiers who served with the team still remained in their specific military trade category - for example, as a weapons technician or radio operator - and were technically still part of their original parent unit while on a temporary assignment with the counter-terrorism force. But some trades and units weren't recognizing a soldier's service in JTF2 or, in some cases, the promotions he received while at Dwyer Hill. As well, some trades were insisting their soldiers return as soon as their time in JTF2 was up, even though most of the operators wanted to stay because they enjoyed the challenge of counter-terrorism duties.

Salaries had been another point of contention among the troops. In November 1995, JTF2 officers pleaded their case to the Deputy Chief of the Defence Staff to approve a "special operations allowance," but by 1997 this still hadn't materialized. JTF2 members, they reminded the DCDS, were required to pass a tough physical and mental screening process in which only 10 per cent of the applicants were successful. Once on the job the work was dangerous, with long hours spent training with live explosives and ammunition. What's more, members were on call 24-hours a day.

According to JTF2 officers, their salaries paled in comparison to the RCMP's now-defunct Special Emergency Response Team. The annual pay of a SERT officer, augmented by a generous overtime package, totaled around $64,000 a year. On top of that, from 1988 to 1990, SERT members had received "standby" pay. In contrast, JTF2 members received the standard pay allocated to their rank but nothing more. The officers were also requesting that soldiers be given a civilian clothing allowance since JTF2 members could be used on covert missions and, in order to blend in, they often wore their own street clothes.

It was a bad time to be without recruits. Just months before, JTF2 commanders had received approval from the Chief of the Defence Staff General Jean Boyle and Defence Deputy Minister Louise Frechette for the unit's future strategy document, "The Way Ahead." In July 1996, JTF2 officers had gone to National Defence headquarters to make their pitch for "The Way Ahead" blueprint, which called for the commando team to be significantly expanded. Senior Defence officials at that briefing listened intently as the officers reviewed the major global terrorist strikes of the last several years. The Israeli embassy had been attacked in Buenos Aires in 1992. A year later a truck bomb had exploded in the underground parking lot of the World Trade Center. An Air France passenger jet had been hijacked in 1994. In an attack on the Tokyo subway system, terrorists had used crude chemical weapons. And Timothy

McVeigh had used a fertilizer truck bomb to kill 168 people in Oklahoma City. "The threat has dramatically changed," a JTF2 officer told senior Defence department officials. "It is more and more volatile, hitting indiscriminately often without clear political motives."

The officers were also told that the 130-member JTF2 would have trouble conducting an assault on a large target or handling multiple terrorist attacks (the briefing would be somewhat prophetic as less than a year later Peruvian special forces used a 140-man assault team for its attack on the Japanese ambassador's residence in Lima).

What was needed, according to the JTF2 leadership, was a change not only in numbers of commandos, but in how the unit was structured. "The Way Ahead" report proposed a gradual increase in the size of JTF2 in several stages, with the expansion finished by 2001. By that point, roughly 300 soldiers would make up the unit. Three squadrons of around 70 men each would form the main force. Those squadrons would be subdivided into smaller groups called "troops" and further divided into the four-man teams, known as "bricks," for work in the field. The small training cadre, already in existence, would be expanded. Additional categories of soldiers would also be created. There would be new support personnel as well as specialists called "mobility operators" who would handle the job of getting the assault teams to their targets. At the end of it all, the unit would have a "general purpose capability," according to the JTF2 presentation to Defence leaders.

More equipment and facilities would also be required: new individual radios would have to be purchased; some 24 new trucks would be bought; Dwyer Hill was to be expanded. At present, JTF2's annual budget was around $14 million. Under "The Way Ahead" plan, that would jump to somewhere between $17 million and $21 million a year. The JTF2 officers reiterated to senior leaders that the unit's mandate had been deliberately left vague so just this type of expansion could be undertaken. Boyle and Frechette readily approved "The Way Ahead" plan.

Their support was a welcome sign to those serving at Dwyer Hill that the senior Defence department hierarchy was firmly behind the unit at a time when other regular force formations were being reduced. Considering the significant down-sizing going on across the Canadian Forces, JTF2 had done well in establishing itself during a time of such uncertainty. In comparison to other commands, it had access to large amounts of money. The unit was also well on its way to developing the regalia that accompanied a military formation. For example, it had selected a unit crest. The design featured half a globe on one side, half a maple leaf on the other and a commando dagger in the centre. (The partial globe on the left indicated JTF2's ability to respond in support of a Canadian presence worldwide. The maple leaf represented allegiance to Canada. And the dagger centered vertically and pointing upwards indicated the profession of arms and an association with other special operations units worldwide.) As well, a unit coin had been issued to JTF2 members and a motto selected. "Facta non verba" (deeds not words) would be the code that JTF2 lived by.

With "The Way Ahead" approved, all the unit had to do was find the manpower for the expansion. As a first step, it decided to open up employment to reservists. JTF2 staff also made the rounds to the military's leadership schools, visits which were seen as an important method of advertising the unit and expanding its recruiting base.

But what was needed most, according to JTF2 officers, was the creation of a unique "Special Operations Assaulter" trade within the Canadian Forces so that JTF2 would have control over its own soldiers. By creating a unique trade, a soldier could serve the rest of his career in JTF2 without having to worry about whether he would be called back to his parent trade or unit. A JTF2-specific trade would also cut down on poaching by civilian police forces, in particular, SWAT teams. Since their tactical training was extensive, JTF2 soldiers found they were much in demand in civilian law enforcement. Police emergency response units offered better working conditions and stability as well as a chance to continue in hostage rescue for a longer period than JTF2 could hope to match under the present conditions.

Just as important, believed JTF2's senior leadership, was marketing the unit within the Canadian Forces. For a continual supply of quality recruits, as well as for the newly required support personnel, JTF2 would have to become more dependent on servicemen selected not only from the army, but also the air force and navy. "Unit members can boost recruiting by being proactive in identifying prospective candidates as well as always representing the unit in a positive manner when working alongside senior members of the CF," JTF2 senior commanders reminded their operators.

As part of its recruiting efforts the unit produced its "Dare to Be Challenged" video and pamphlet. The slick promotional material showed potential recruits the exciting world of counter-terrorism and special operations. JTF2 snipers and assault teams were prominently featured in thrilling action scenes. Emphasis was placed on the unit's daring and unusual training; one photo in the recruiting brochure showed a masked soldier climbing the outside of a high-rise building, without ropes. Another, depicting the grueling nature of JTF2 training, showed a soldier in scuba gear and armed with a rifle struggling to pull himself along a thick rope.

Recruits were told that the average JTF2 operator was 28 years old and had been in the regular forces for at least nine years. Characteristics that contributed most to a recruit's selection for the unit included a high level of maturity and a strong sense of responsibility in both his professional and personal lives. Besides excellent fitness and top-notch agility and reflexes, the qualities sought in a recruit were his ability to work independently, as well as being a team member.

New personnel, according to the promotional material, would be trained in handling special weapons, explosives, fieldcraft, patrolling and navigation as well as insertion and extraction techniques using numerous means of transportation. A JTF2 soldier would also be well versed in survival and medical skills and the use of advanced communications equipment and computers. Significantly, the training regime had more of an emphasis on green operations than it did on hostage rescue.

As the leadership worked on attracting quality recruits, JTF2's pilots and aircrew were dealing with their own set of problems. The unit's three CH-135 Twin Huey choppers had since been retired and JTF2's pilots from 427 Tactical Helicopter Squadron/B Flight were putting the new CH-146 Griffon through its paces. Things were not going well. Some of the generals and, in particular, the new Defence Minister, Art Eggleton, spoke in glowing terms about the Griffon, insisting it was a state-of-the art helicopter and the envy of Canada's allies. It wasn't. Chief of the Defence Staff General Maurice Baril was more accurate when he labeled the Griffon, a version of the Bell 412 chopper which had been in production since the 1980s, as simply a civilian helicopter painted khaki. The $1-billion contract for the 100 Griffons (of which JTF2 would receive three) was viewed by many in Canada's defence community as nothing more than a politically inspired purchase with the primary aim of creating jobs at Bell Helicopter's assembly line in Quebec.

The Bell 412 may have been adequate for use by civilian logging companies, but as a counter-terrorism aircraft it had definite drawbacks. High on the list was the intense electrical charge the aircraft generated, zapping soldiers as they jumped from the hovering chopper. It posed a particular threat to JTF2 soldiers, according to air force reports, since the charge was potentially high enough to detonate the specialized explosives they might be carrying. Special forces missions were dangerous enough without having the added deadly potential of being blown up by one's own helicopter.

The electrostatic discharge, or ESD, was a generally well known phenomenon in the helicopter world. ESD occurs naturally during flights as the result of the frictional contact between the surface of the aircraft and airborne particles such as dust, sand, snow or rain. As well, a helicopter will generate a charge itself because of its moving components such as rotor blades. The level of ESD varies from helicopter to helicopter and it was hardly noticed in the JTF2's Twin Hueys.

The Griffons, however, were another matter. One military rescue technician was zapped after the electrical charge from the helicopter traveled from the aircraft down a cable to the ground. At the time, the man had been hooked onto the cable and instantly became a lightening rod for the electrical charge. Other soldiers were receiving shocks as they piled in or out of the choppers when they were in a hover. The high ESD levels in the Griffons weren't detected before their purchase because in order to satisfy the government's desire to acquire the choppers quickly, the aircraft never received any proper testing.

Shortly after the Griffon's purchase, the federal government's Auditor General, Denis Desautels, highlighted the ESD problem in one of his reports. To counter the auditor's claims, senior military officials simply stated that ESD was common among all helicopters and Desautels' staff had misunderstood and overstated the phenomenon. Behind the scenes, however, air force officials knew they had a major problem on their hands. "The significant charge generated by the aircraft currently presents a hazard to personnel and ordnance carried by JTF2 team members," warned one air force report.

There were also numerous warnings of ESD interfering with the Griffon's navigation and communication systems during low-hover insertion and extraction missions, the staple of JTF2 operations. To counter the problems, air force planners suggested that all movement in and out of the Griffons be done only after the helicopter landed, a definite limitation if the aircraft needed to fly into a landing zone under fire. In such operations, every second counted and standard practice usually involved soldiers leaping from a low-hovering helicopter. This tactic meant that both soldiers and helicopter crews were exposed to the dangers of enemy fire at a landing zone for the minimal amount of time.

The ESD problem was eventually solved by using specialized wicks sticking out from under the Griffon, allowing the electrical charge to dissipate after the stick-like devices came in contact with the ground. The wicks were long enough that they touched the ground even as the chopper hovered about a metre in the air.

Other Griffon problems also had the potential to limit JTF2 operations. Each of the chopper's landing skids could only handle 414 kilograms (920 pounds) of weight resting on them. But when four JTF2 soldiers stood on each skid in preparation to rappel, that limit was exceeded, causing the aircraft to become unstable. To solve the problem 427 Squadron used a special metal step attached to the side of the Griffon which provided a temporary 540-kilogram (1200-pound) load limit.

Griffon limitations and recruiting issues aside, the unit was ready in the fall of 1997 to provide security for the Asia Pacific Economic Conference, a gathering of 18 world leaders in Vancouver. The security precautions for APEC 97, scheduled for the end of November, were extensive, involving some 2,800 civilian police alone. Two RCMP aircraft, equipped with closed-circuit TV cameras, would provide a command post with a live video feed of each leader's motorcade after its arrival at the Vancouver airport. RCMP teams were assigned to bolster each leader's own security detail and the federal police force had its emergency response teams stationed near the various locations where the politicians were scheduled to meet. JTF2 and the military's Nuclear, Biological and Chemical Response Team were to be stationed at CFB Chilliwack, some 90 kilometres from Vancouver, in case their specialized skills were needed.

In preparation for the international meeting, JTF2 and the RCMP conducted "Exercise Shield" in mid-September in Vancouver. Almost 400 officers and government officials were involved in practicing Canada's national counter-terrorism arrangements, using scripted scenarios involving multiple attacks. Specifically, "Exercise Shield" called on the government to respond to a terror-ist group that had hijacked an aircraft loaded with foreign VIPs in Vancouver while another terrorist group exploded a chemical weapon in the city's down-town core. As the Canadian Forces Nuclear Biological Chemical Response Team dealt with the chemical weapon scenario, JTF2 prepared to strike at the "ter-rorists" (actually volunteer military personnel) who were inside a Canadian Airlines passenger jet at Vancouver airport. At 2 a.m. on September 11, the assault team stormed the aircraft, freeing the hostages and "killing" all the terrorists.

"Exercise Shield" wasn't without its problems. For starters, RCMP hostage negotiators were poorly prepared for their roles and it would take several days before they gained control of the situation. As well, when the training scenario first began, senior RCMP officers were no where to be found and the initial "command response" to the terrorist attack at the airport was in the hands of a lowly corporal. From JTF2's point of view the assault on the aircraft went smoothly. Its operators quickly accessed the plane from several entrances and methodically moved down the aisles using precision shooting to kill the hi-jackers.

What wasn't going smoothly for JTF2 were the medical preparations re-quired for APEC. Canadian Forces doctors wanted the commandos to sign a consent form that would allow them to be injected with an experimental drug in the event they were exposed to a nerve agent during the economic summit. Each soldier was to carry a special injector containing a nerve gas antidote known as HI-6. In the event of an attack, the soldiers would inject themselves with the HI-6 as well as any disabled comrades nearby.

Although they had been assured by Defence department medical staff that the untested HI-6 was safe, one of the JTF2 non-commissioned officers balked at signing the consent form. The Canadian Forces didn't have the best reputa-tion when it came to administering untested medicines. Some Canadian Air-borne Regiment paratroopers sent to Somalia still complained of strange side effects from an experimental malaria drug administered to them. Other sol-diers who served in the Persian Gulf War were seriously ill, and some had died. They blamed the chemical and biological warfare vaccines administered to them by the Canadian Forces.

More disturbing for some of the JTF2 soldiers was the disclaimer handed out with the HI-6. Not only was it not approved for use in Canada but there was a possibility the drug could alter their DNA structure. Military doctors reluctantly admitted to the counter-terrorism team that they really didn't know the long term effects of having the nerve agent antidote injected into a human being.

The HI-6 issue was the tip of the iceberg of a long-standing dispute with military brass about the nature of JTF2 operations and their aftermath. At the heart of the problem was the unwillingness by the Defence department to accept that operations within Canada could be classified as a legitimate "area of conflict." If a regular force soldier was injured in a war zone, then a government system of compensation kicked in. But Canada wasn't considered such an area of conflict and if a JTF2 soldier got hurt in any domestic mission, such as during a hostage rescue, he could face an uphill battle in trying to receive any benefits.

During "Exercise Praetorian," JTF2 operators had already been given a preview of what would happen to them if they were injured in Canada. The non-commissioned officer whose hand was blown off by the faulty stun grenade in Victoria during the "Praetorian" incident had since been booted out of the Canadian Forces. Even though the military had decided the soldier was no longer of use, the Ontario Provincial Police quickly hired the JTF2 operator to instruct its emergency tactical teams. As well, a regular force sergeant who had part of his hand blown off at the Gustafsen Lake siege by a malfunctioning stun grenade had been subjected to similar callous treatment. He had been given a small pension and was now trying to sue the federal government for compensation for his injuries.

JTF2 officers had attempted to convince the Defence department's lawyers of the unfairness of the system, arguing that the unit should be given special duty status while it was serving in Canada. "I feel this would serve to protect my soldiers who are subject to extremely hazardous conditions in support of 'real' operations," one officer tried, unsuccessfully, to explain to the military lawyers. By 1997, JTF2 soldiers had had enough of the National Defence headquarters' unrealistic view of military operations. They had already started talking to a private firm, Great West Life Insurance, in an effort to obtain group medical coverage for the unit. An internal Defence department study of the military's failing health-care system noted that the JTF2 soldiers were more than willing to bear the cost of the group plan if it meant their families would be taken care of in the event they were injured or killed.

In the end, the commandos never had to take the HI-6 antidote and the private insurance plan scheme was eventually abandoned.

Three months after APEC, JTF2 operatives found themselves back in their old stomping grounds of Africa. In February 1998, a team was dispatched to Arusha, Tanzania, to protect Canadian Major General Romeo Dallaire. In the aftermath of the Rwandan genocide, in which Hutu extremists slaughtered more than half a million people, the international community had set up a war crimes court and had charged some of the more high-profile perpetrators involved in the slaughter. Dallaire, in charge of the small UN contingent stationed in Rwanda during the massacres, was to testify at the trial of a Rwandan government official charged with genocide.

Although Arusha was thousands of kilometres away from Rwanda, JTF2 was not taking any chances. During the Rwandan mission, it was believed that Hutu extremists had plotted to assassinate Dallaire. It wouldn't be beyond the realm of possibility that the senior officer might be targeted again. Particularly dangerous was a Hutu guerrilla group known as the Army for the Liberation of Rwanda. The ALR was intent on toppling Rwanda's Tutsi-dominated government, reinstating Hutu control and, possibly, completing the genocide. In 1996, it threatened to kill the U.S. Ambassador to Rwanda and other U.S. citizens in the country. (The group would later take part in the killings of foreign tourists along the Congo-Uganda border.) Although the ALR tended to operate in the Congo and Rwanda, it was also active in Burundi which bordered on Tanzania.

"Operation Sphere," as the unit called its bodyguard mission, involved eight JTF2 operators assigned to Dallaire. The team worked with him in two four-man shifts, forming a protective bubble around the general and reconnoitering routes in advance as he moved throughout Arusha. In contrast, the alleged mass murderers on trial only had two guards to watch over them. Close personal protection duties were becoming so entrenched that JTF2 commanders believed it was time to meet with the RCMP and military police to decide just who was responsible for what. "Close personal protection is an important part of our job and we are ready to formalize our position with the RCMP (and MPs, whose mandate includes CPP, I believe)," one JTF2 officer wrote.

Six months later, another JTF2 team was back in Central Africa to help with "force protection" for a UN mission. Following two years of civil war in the Central African Republic, the UN had agreed to a 1,300-strong peacekeeping force, made up almost entirely of troops from the region. The force would secure key areas in the country, particularly around the capital of Bangui, and help maintain security so elections could be held. Defence Minister Art Eggleton had given approval for a small contingent of Canadians, mainly radio operators and staff officers for the peacekeeping force's headquarters in the capital. Nothing was said, of course, about the JTF2 squad. A "technical assistance team" from the unit's 1 Squadron flew to the Central African Republic in the summer of 1998.

When the unit wasn't overseas on missions, it was keeping up its strict training regime at Dwyer Hill and demonstrating its expertise for VIPs. Generals and high-ranking government bureaucrats were all regular visitors to Dwyer Hill as JTF2 built up the political capital it needed to survive and expand. The unit gave each group a thrilling display of hostage-rescue techniques, complete with gunfire, rappelling from helicopters and "dynamic demonstrations" in which explosives were used in assaults on the Method of Entry building. Dozens of other observers, including officials from Canadian Security Intelligence Service, members of the Defence department's Bosnia planning cell and RCMP criminal intelligence directorate, also toured the Dwyer Hill compound. "The demonstrations eat up valuable training time and take a considerable amount of resources," wrote one officer after a two-day series of VIP shows, "but the dividends have proven this venue to be worth the costs to the unit."

The unit was also holding week-long familiarization meetings for civilian police agencies to enable the two groups to get to know each other better in the event that they would one day have to work together. Particularly close ties were being developed with the Ontario and Quebec provincial police forces. JTF2 was also keen to arrange secondments of its soldiers to civilian police forces, in particular, SWAT units. As a morale booster for the troops, JTF2 also created an "Assaulter of the Year" award.

Besides the strong support of Defence Minister Eggleton, the counter-terrorism team also had other political allies. Bob Fowler's old friend, Liberal Senator Colin Kenny was selected as JTF2's honorary colonel. Kenny, was a member of the 1987 Senate Committee on Terrorism and a key political proponent of transferring the national counter-terrorism role from SERT to the Canadian Forces.

More important than VIP recognition was the expansion of the unit as directed by "The Way Ahead" study. In late 1998, the unit issued a message across the Canadian Forces that it was creating several new categories of soldiers. The main special operations assault teams would now have backup, particularly of two groups, the "mobility operators" and selected technical specialists. These soldiers would be known as "Category B" troops.

The mobility operators would be responsible for getting the assault teams to and from their targets. At the same time, they would provide fire support during missions and would be trained to handle a variety of vehicles and boats as well as crew-served and personal weapons. Ranks designated for mobility operators would range from privates to warrant officers.

The tough selection process for mobility operators, who if successful would be given a four-year stint with the unit, was essentially the same as that of JTF2's "assaulters." A minimum of three years' service would be required. The positions were also open to reservists, but the part-time soldiers had to be prepared to commit to a four-year period of full-time service.

A second Category B group involved specialists who would provide direct tactical support to JTF2 operations. Among that group were explosives technicians, radio operators, medics and scuba divers. They would serve four to six years with JTF2.

A "Category C" group consisted of soldiers in support trades such as administration clerks, mechanics, weapons technicians, supply and equipment personnel, and military police. Those in Category C positions were considered non-combatives and would be expected to serve four to six years with JTF2. Screening for all of the new positions began in November 1998.

The expansion of the Dwyer Hill compound was also well underway. Eggleton had already approved $11.8 million for the construction of a new squadron building and other facilities. The new structures would include a barracks with more rooms to house the operators who stayed at the compound while on alert, storerooms, offices and four classrooms. The unit's map room was also being expanded, and its military police, who had been operating temporarily from a trailer at Dwyer Hill, would get their own building. Even the weight room would be redesigned and a new acoustic system installed. The base's communications systems was also upgraded and a large number of computers installed. A new kitchen was built to handle the expected influx of new soldiers and a modern garage with three work bays, including one to handle five-ton trucks, was constructed.

Also high on the Dwyer Hill expansion list was a new training building. JTF2 needed a large spacious centre in which various layouts could be arranged to accommodate training scenarios. If hostages were to be rescued from an embassy, for example, the unit could construct an exact copy of the floor plan to practice its attack. At first, JTF2 believed it could use a building at Uplands air base in Ottawa but substantial renovations would be needed. So, instead, the unit ordered a pre-engineered steel warehouse where soldiers could practice in the large expanse whatever scenarios a situation might dictate.

By early 1999, the commando team had successfully pushed military police out of their close personal protection role and was now being used on a regular basis to guard Canadian VIPs overseas. JTF2 operatives were also a fixture on every major peacekeeping mission, acting as advisors to contingent commanders. An assignment such as the one in Bosnia, for instance, had become so part of its routine that JTF2 had regular rotations to the former Yugoslavia just like other Canadian Forces units.

With the situation deteriorating in the Serbian province of Kosovo in January 1999, special forces would once again be called upon to play a key role in the former Yugoslavia. Intense fighting had broken out between Serb police and members of the Kosovo Liberation Army, whose aim was to create a separate country in the Serbian province. Atrocities were being committed by both sides but the Western countries, especially the United States, put most of the blame on the Serbs. The Yugoslav government was given an ultimatum: sign a peace agreement with the KLA or face NATO airstrikes. The Serbs, who believed they had the right to deal with internal security matters in one of their own provinces, refused to comply.

On March 24, NATO struck. U.S., British and Canadian aircraft began pounding Serb positions in Kosovo, with the bombing raids eventually spreading to Belgrade and other cities throughout Yugoslavia proper. Days later,

NATO military commanders decided special forces units were needed on the ground to help gather intelligence and guide bombers searching for well-camouflaged Serb tanks. Teams from France's 13 Regiment de Dragons Parachutistes, the British SAS and the American Central Intelligence Agency slipped over the border into Kosovo. The SAS had also set up camps near Trinia, Albania and along the Kosovar border, to instruct KLA officers in hit and run tactics and how to conduct intelligence-gathering missions on Serbian positions.

It wasn't long after the SAS and other NATO special operations troops were on the ground in Kosovo that speculation began circulating in Canada about what JTF2 was up to. On April 19, an opposition MP announced in the House of Commons that he had it on good authority that JTF2 operators were in Kosovo. Conservative MP David Price said a "very, very solid" military source with "direct involvement" in JTF2 operations told him that some unit members were helping train the KLA as well as gather intelligence for NATO about targets to bomb. He "guesstimated" that about 50 JTF2 members were involved in the mission. Price didn't have a problem with JTF2 being used in the former Yugoslavia, but he believed that Parliament should have at least been informed that Canadian troops were at war.

Caught off guard by the claims, Defence Minister Eggleton was furious. Facing a horde of curious journalists he dodged questions about whether JTF2 was actually in Kosovo but his answers suggested there was a possibility that Price's information was correct. "I'm not going to tell you they are there, and I'm not going to tell you they're not," Eggleton blurted out. That less-than-authoritative answer was enough to prompt front-page headlines the next day about Canadian commandos in Kosovo.

As Price continued with his claims about JTF2, Eggleton accused him of endangering the lives of Canadian soldiers. But that prompted the inevitable question from both Price and journalists: If JTF2 wasn't in Kosovo then how was the Conservative Member of Parliament endangering lives? Eggleton didn't have an answer. "I've been prepared to say that we don't have such forces, the JTF2 in the Federal Republic of Yugoslavia which includes Kosovo, Serbia, and Montenegro, that we don't have them there today," he angrily responded.

At National Defence headquarters, Brigadier General David Jurkowski,

Chief of Staff for Joint Operations, found himself facing a mob of reporters anxious to only talk about one thing - JTF2. Jurkowski claimed that Price was ill-informed. JTF2's role, the general lectured journalists, was in hostage res-cue and domestic counter-terrorism, not overseas missions. It was conceiv-able, Jurkowski admitted, that the unit could be used on foreign assignments but only in "very benign observer-type" missions.

With little actual evidence that he could present to reporters, Price eventu-ally started backing away from his claims. JTF2, while not in Kosovo at that moment, may have been there once, he backtracked.

What the Conservative MP didn't know was how close to the truth he was. Eggleton was indeed right in his carefully worded, but ultimately deceptive, denials. JTF2 wasn't in Kosovo at that moment. But one of the unit's close personal protection teams was in Albania, guarding Canadian Brigadier Gen-eral Michel Maisonneuve who headed a refugee task force there and who had earlier been in Kosovo as part of a multinational observer mission. There was no way, of course, the Defence department was about to reveal this informa-tion publicly. Not only would that give credibility to Price's other claims but it would likely lead to new questions from Parliament about what a domestic hostage-rescue force was doing in Albania.

On May 12, Lieutenant General Raymond Henault, the Deputy Chief of the Defence Staff, put the whole matter finally to rest. JTF2 was not involved in Kosovo - period, the media-savvy officer told journalists. "Nor do we have plans to engage them in any way, shape or form," he added.

Less than two months later, JTF2 was in Kosovo. On July 13, Canadian judge Louise Arbour, the chief prosecutor for the International War Crimes Tribunal, flew into the province to visit forensic experts working on mass graves of suspected massacre victims. Accompanying her was a JTF2 bodyguard team. According to the information already collected by JTF2's CTSO counterparts, the potential for "terrorist" paramilitary units to still be operating in Kosovo would be high.

Such threats might also explain why Governor-General Adrienne Clarkson needed a JTF2 bodyguard when she visited the Canadian military base in Donja Koretica in November 1999, although it's debatable whether most Kosovars, friendly or not, would even recognize who she was. As Clarkson clambered out of a Griffon helicopter, a giant of a JTF2 soldier, armed with a C8 carbine, stood guard. The man's size, specialized targeting sight on his weapon, and wraparound Gargoyle sunglasses - the shades of choice of North American SWAT officers - pretty much gave him away.

But while JTF2 soldiers were busy taking care of security for VIPs in Kosovo, a civilian police investigation unfolding in Canada was gathering the momentum to potentially put their unit's own security and future in jeopardy.

OPPOSITE PAGE: *Sergeant Darnell Bass in custody in the back of a police van. (CALGARY HERALD PHOTO)*

SEVEN: SHOOT-OUT IN CALGARY

SERGEANT DARNELL BASS cradled the Steyr Aug assault rifle and glanced down at his watch. It was shortly before midnight, March 19, 1998 and Bass, a muscular Canadian army paratrooper and failed JTF2 recruit, was holed up in a small filing room in a north-end Calgary bank.

If everything went as planned, Bass and his partner, former reserve soldier Patrick Ryan, would soon be rich men. Within the next 15 minutes Bass expected two Brink's security guards carrying bags of cash to come through the bank's sliding doors. A couple of hours earlier, Bass and Ryan, themselves disguised as Brink's guards, had slipped into the bank using a key obtained from an accomplice at the security firm. Their fake uniforms were good enough to fool a janitor who was just finishing up cleaning the bank's restrooms. After the janitor left, Bass and Ryan took up their positions to ambush the Brink's guards. Bass had even written down some instructions for the guards on an easel and finished off the list of demands by drawing a happy face at the bottom.

As Bass double-checked that his Austrian-made .223 calibre assault rifle was loaded, he heard the click of the bank doors being opened. The soldier cursed under his breath; the Brink's guards had arrived a few minutes earlier than expected. Nevertheless, it was time for the paratrooper to make his move. Bass walked out of the filing room and immediately found himself staring at guard Paul Bisson. For a moment, Bisson appeared startled, his eyes wide as he tried to grasp what was happening. But the guard, a former Canadian Army veteran, quickly recovered. Bisson had been pushing a metal trolley loaded with money, which he now shoved towards the gunman, while at the same time pulling out his revolver. Bisson then jumped for cover and, as he flew through the air, opened fire.

For the next 10 minutes, the inside of the Canadian Imperial Bank of Commerce at North Hill Mall resembled a war zone. Bisson's shots had missed and Bass, with his Steyr Aug, and Ryan, armed with a Chinese AK-47 assault rifle, quickly returned fire. But Bisson, a former corporal with the Lord Strathcona's Horse regiment, was no stranger to gun battles. While serving in the former Yugoslavia he was credited with saving the life of a fellow UN soldier, whom he dragged to safety under fire. Across the room, Bisson's partner, who had thrown his gun away in panic, had also scrambled for cover.

Ryan and Bass were shooting at the two men relentlessly. Bass's Steyr Aug spit out spent cartridges onto the floor and the paratrooper paused only briefly to slam in a new ammunition magazine. Ryan had also changed magazines as he fired at Bisson who had taken refuge in one of the bank's offices. More than 80 rounds were fired at the Brink's guards to keep them pinned down.

From where they were shooting, the two would-be robbers could see the money piled tantalizingly close in the grey bags the guards had abandoned when scrambling for cover. But to get to the $385,000 in cash, they would have to expose themselves to Bisson's gunfire. Even though the bandits were wearing bullet-proof vests, it was too much to risk. Bass decided it was time to cut and run. "Gas, Gas," he yelled out to his boyhood friend, Ryan. It was the former reserve soldiers' cue to detonate a military tear gas grenade. The two men moved out under the cover of the acrid gas and fled through an emergency exit. Jumping into their getaway van, they sped off to a nearby hotel where they destroyed their Brink's uniforms and packed up their guns.

A few days after the botched robbery attempt, Bass returned to his unit, the Third Battalion, Royal Canadian Regiment, at CFB Petawawa. The Calgary shootout had left him shaken but he believed himself home free. The police, he thought, wouldn't have a clue who had hit the bank. Ryan decided to stay in Calgary.

Their luck wouldn't hold out. Suspecting almost from the beginning that Ryan a former Brink's guard, was somehow involved in the attempted heist, police began monitoring his movements and listening in on his telephone calls. Based on a tip they had received, police also suspected Ryan had been involved in stealing $134,000 from an automated teller machine several months earlier.

It wasn't long before the trail also led to Bass. On the morning of July 16, 1998, a team of heavily armed civilian and military police arrested the 31-year-old soldier at CFB Petawawa, charging him with attempted murder and armed robbery. Ryan had already slipped out of the country and was wanted by police.

At the Defence department, senior military leaders, informed in advance by Calgary police that Bass would be arrested, had approved a set of "media response lines" to be read to journalists. The lines acknowledged that military police were helping in the investigation and that Bass was a member of 3RCR. No other information would be given out. The generals at National Defence headquarters expected to see the stories detailing Bass's arrest and the charges he would face. What they read, however, in the Calgary Herald newspaper the next day caught them completely off guard. A front-page Herald article claimed that Bass was a member of JTF2, "an anti-terrorist squad so secret that its existence is acknowledged but little else is known about it." The article also suggested that Bass had put the specialized skills he learned with JTF2 to use in the commando-style attempted bank robbery.

For the senior Defence department leadership, the Herald report had the makings of a potential disaster. The military had just been through five years of the so-called "Somalia affair" which had resulted in the disbandment of the Airborne Regiment and the exposure, by the civilian-run Somalia Inquiry, of a litany of mistakes by the Canadian Forces' leadership. Over the last six years, military officials had, for the most part, successfully protected and kept JTF2 out of the headlines. Now the Calgary bank robbery threatened to drag the most secret unit in the Canadian Forces into glare of the media spotlight.

The day the Calgary Herald article appeared, journalists at several major newspapers received unsolicited phone calls from military public affairs officers. Officially, the reporters were told that the Herald article was wrong and that Bass was never a member of JTF2, although he may have tried out for the unit at one time. Unofficially, they were told to check out a relatively obscure document that had been presented to the Somalia inquiry almost three years earlier and an equally obscure transcript from a House of Commons Defence committee.

The first document was a military police report from early 1990 that detailed how Bass, then a member of the Canadian Airborne Regiment, had been taken into custody after he was discovered loading a large number of guns into a car at Petawawa. During his interrogation, Bass told police he needed the weapons and ammunition to protect himself when the world's food supply ran out and society collapsed. A review of the separate Commons Defence committee transcript showed that Bass had testified to Members of Parliament just weeks after the Calgary robbery, complaining that the army's ability to wage war was dwindling. He eagerly told the federal politicians that Canada needed fighting soldiers who were willing to go into combat at a moment's notice, "guys that are ready, you know, to get it on." Tipping off journalists to both documents was a clever strategy to discredit Bass. The next day, newspaper reports citing the two documents portrayed the soldier as a mentally unstable survivalist fixated with firearms and warfare. At the same time, journalists dutifully reported that Bass was never a member of JTF2.

Despite the successful ploy by public affairs officers to head off any further attempts to link Bass to the counter-terrorism unit, the leadership at Dwyer Hill was starting to realize the sergeant's connections with JTF2 could prove damaging. In November 1996, Bass had passed the initial JTF2 interview and strict screening process, which was supposed to subject a soldier's personnel file to intense scrutiny. Somehow, the JTF2 reviewers had missed the 1990 report on Bass's desire to be prepared for the coming "food crisis." Having successfully completed the initial selection process, the sergeant had been invited to Dwyer Hill for a tryout with the unit. According to JTF2's files, Bass completed that phase, which took place from March 10 to April 5, 1997, but was ultimately rejected because he was not physically fit enough.

After making additional inquiries, JTF2 officers also discovered that Bass had friendships with - or connections to - three, if not more, serving or retired JTF2 members.

A report produced by senior JTF2 leaders determined that Bass had stored personal weapons (later revealed to have been used in the robbery) in the Smiths Falls, Ontario, home of Brent Countway, a serving JTF2 member. Sergeant Countway himself was no stranger to controversy. During the Somalia mission, he was one of a group of Canadian Airborne Regiment soldiers who had chased two Somali men on the night of March 4, 1993, at the unit's base in Belet Huen. One of the Somalis died after Countway and another soldier opened fire. Several years later at the Somalia Inquiry, it was alleged that Airborne Captain Michel Rainville had ordered that food and water be put out as "bait" for Somalis. The inquiry also heard testimony that the dead Somali had been shot at close-range, execution style, an accusation Countway and the other soldier denied.

Another serving JTF2 soldier linked to Bass was Sergeant Darren Armes. It would later turn out that Armes had accepted almost $2,000 from Bass to be the getaway driver for the Calgary heist but backed out at the last moment. Also as part of their investigation into Bass's activities, civilian police had raided an Orleans, Ontario, home, later questioning Thomas Koch, a retired member of JTF2. Koch, Armes and Countway were never charged with any crime.

After the initial flurry of publicity, public discussion about JTF2 and Bass had all but dried up. The paratrooper had quickly cut a deal with prosecutors and pleaded guilty to conspiracy to commit robbery, prompting Reform Party MP Art Hanger, a former Calgary police detective, to question whether the Defence department had made some kind of deal with the soldier to keep the JTF2 name out of the courts.

Bass's guilty plea in November 1998 had indeed spared JTF2 adverse publicity, at least initially. It wasn't the first time a deal with prosecutors had helped the unit avoid being dragged into an embarrassing court case. In 1995, JTF2's founding father, Colonel Mike O'Brien was court martialed for inappropriate use of public funds and fined $1,500. The legal proceedings were over quickly and the colonel retired to his rural home outside Ottawa with a full pension. With O'Brien's guilty plea, the military also closed the file on a series of allegations involving the officer and JTF2. Previously, military police had investigated the colonel's 1992 visit to Joint Task Force 4 in Key West and allegations that he stayed in Florida afterwards on vacation at taxpayers' expense. But police were also probing O'Brien's use of JTF2 equipment in his home-based real estate and investment company. The Defence department had installed a secure telephone in the colonel's house for JTF2 and other military business but O'Brien was also using the scrambling device, designed to prevent anyone from eavesdropping on conversations, for his real estate dealings. As well, when customers couldn't reach him at home, they were referred to the colonel's JTF2 pager.

O'Brien didn't see that he had done anything wrong. Just because a JTF2 pager and security phone were being used to sell real estate didn't mean the unit's ultra-tight security had been compromised. The secure phone was essentially a regular telephone with added security features and O'Brien was using his own money to pay for the phone line. Those calling up the pager service didn't even know it was for JTF2 use, the colonel reasoned. Military police, however, saw the issue differently. They concluded in their report, released under the Access to Information law after O'Brien's court martial, that JTF2 security had indeed been compromised when the colonel used his pager number for personal business use. Police had also alleged that their probe into some of the colonel's activities had been purposely derailed by the senior military leadership.

That the JTF2-related allegations never made it into O'Brien's court martial was not unusual in the world of special operations. Secret units are often beyond the usual scrutiny that regular military formations can expect, ostensibly for reasons of national security. But such secrecy also works in the unit's favor by allowing it to avoid any public embarrassment. In the early 1980s, U.S. Army auditors discovered that members of Delta Force had been pilfering taxpayers' money for years in an elaborate scam involving the unit's equipment purchases. Delta commandos had bought hundreds of expensive items, including a hot air balloon and a Rolls Royce Sedan, supposedly for covert operations. Instead, the equipment was sold and the money funneled into soldiers' private bank accounts. Hundreds of thousands of dollars were drained from Delta's "black" budget before auditors caught on to what was happening. For the most part, the unit avoided any embarrassing publicity by reprimanding dozens of Delta Force soldiers and transferring them out of the organization. By handling the situation itself, the unit prevented court martials from being held and any embarrassing details emerging from those public legal proceedings.

JTF2's links to the Calgary robbery probably would have gone largely unpublicized too if it hadn't been for Ottawa Citizen police reporter Gary Dimmock. In a series of articles that appeared in April 2000, Dimmock outlined the connections between the counter-terrorism unit and Bass. He also reported on Patrick Ryan's claims, contained on an audio-tape obtained by the RCMP, that Bass had asked the former reserve soldier to gather information on Liberal government politicians involved in the disbandment of the Airborne Regiment. "I was asked to provide information on residences, out-of-town cottages, places of work, family," Ryan says on the tape. "Anything I found." While it's unclear why the two men would be interested in such information, former defence minister David Collenette was reportedly concerned enough about the contents of the tape to ask law enforcement officials whether they thought he needed police protection.

Dimmock also reported on an underground arms network in which Canadian Forces soldiers collected and traded stolen government weaponry. (Bass, it would later turn out, had pilfered explosives and tear gas grenades from a military training site in Ontario). The Ottawa Citizen journalist also revealed that a pistol had gone missing from JTF2's arsenal even though officers at Dwyer Hill claimed that all firearms assigned to the unit had been accounted for. The gun mysteriously turned up months later at the base.

When Dimmock's articles appeared, Defence Minister Eggleton dismissed them outright and labeled them as nothing more than unsubstantiated allegations. The Defence Minister's quick rejection of any JTF2 links to Bass was typical of how he usually dealt with negative or embarrassing media reports. When faced with any type of potential scandal or controversy, Eggleton usually declared that journalists or critics such as opposition Members of Parliament had exaggerated or misrepresented the facts.

A former JTF2 officer also took the highly unusual step of publicly discussing the unit, albeit in a limited fashion, by denouncing the Ottawa Citizen series. In a letter to the newspaper, Mike Rouleau, who had served as a tactical squadron commander with JTF2 for five years, claimed that Bass had only spent 40 hours at the Dwyer Hill Training Centre before failing the selection course. "While I'm certain Joint Task Force 2 captures headlines, you do a tremendous disservice to both the outstanding troops in the unit and the public, who are unaware of the facts," he admonished the newspaper. "The people of our great country should take pride in knowing that the members of JTF2 are world-class operators and should not be discredited by association."

Retired Major Rouleau's spirited defence of his former unit was understandable. But in less than a month, the full extent of JTF2's links to Bass would become public at Ryan's trial. Bass's former partner in crime had been extradited from France, where he had fled after the robbery, and while he sat in jail, Calgary police had built their case around the scenario that the former part-time soldier was the real brains behind the heist. Bass, the hard-core career sergeant, they concluded, was simply following orders issued by Ryan, the army reserve private. Their investigation also determined that Ryan had pulled off the earlier robbery from the automated teller machine in Calgary and that some of the $134,000 stolen had been shipped to Bass in Petawawa.

To lead his courtroom defence, Ryan had hired a highly capable Calgary attorney named Balfour Der. As part of his strategy to prove Ryan's innocence, Der was preparing to focus on the key role Bass had played in setting up the robbery attempt as well as his links to JTF2.

When the trial began in May 2000, one of the first people to testify was JTF2 Sergeant Darren Armes who admitted to the court he had been recruited by Bass to be the getaway driver for the heist. On the witness stand, Armes also acknowledged that he decided not to go through with his part in the robbery and had backed out at the last minute.

Retired JTF2 soldier Thomas Koch testified that, at Bass's request, he shipped heavy "metallic" items to Ryan in Calgary, but that he never knew what was inside the package. When asked whose return name and address he used when sending the box, Koch testified he couldn't remember. "I used an alternate name," he told Balfour Der. "I don't know if that's forgery."

"Take it from me, that's forgery," Ryan's lawyer responded.

Koch also said he exchanged bundles of Canadian $20 bills for U.S. currency at Bass's request but didn't ask his army buddy where the money had come from. The former JTF2 operator also testified he had purchased airline tickets, in his own name, for Bass to fly to Calgary on two different occasions. One was a ticket for Bass to travel to the city in March 1998, shortly before the bungled heist, but Koch emphasized that he had no idea his friend had been planning to rob a bank.

The former JTF2 soldier also admitted giving a false statement to police investigators when they asked him about Bass's whereabouts the day of the robbery. Koch had told officers that his friend was in Ottawa. "Darnell asked me to reinforce his story that he was in Ottawa in March of 1998," Koch testified. "He said he was extremely distressed that the police were accusing him of being in some sort of criminal activity." Koch's lawyer had made a deal with police so he wouldn't be charged for the providing Bass with a false alibi.

JTF2 Sergeant Brent Countway also testified he knew nothing about Bass's illegal activities. Although Bass had talked about the robbery after it happened, Countway said he didn't believe the story because Bass was always making outlandish statements. The two men were such good friends that Countway had given Bass a key to his house so his army buddy could come and go as he pleased. He also allowed Bass to store guns in a hidden room at his Smiths Falls home but Countway testified he didn't know that the weapons Bass stashed there had been used in the Calgary bank job.

Balfour Der's strategy was to suggest that Countway, and not his client Ryan, was Bass's cohort in the crime. To do that, the lawyer wanted to question the JTF2 sergeant about his involvement in the March 4, 1993, Somalia killing in an attempt to "establish that he is the type of person who would pick up a gun and start shooting at people."

"The defence theory is that if Mr. Ryan was not the second person that was in the bank - this person seems to fit the description," Der told the court.

But Justice Peter Martin ruled that the questions Der wanted to ask about the Somalia killing had no relevance to the Calgary case and the issue was dropped. Besides, Countway had denied any involvement in the attempted robbery and had an air-tight alibi. When the bank raid was unfolding, the JTF2 soldier and his wife had been in Halifax at his parents' home. Countway's wife had also provided a statement to police attesting to that fact.

Bass also denied Countway had anything to do with the robbery and he continued to name Ryan as the mastermind behind the heist. But Bass did contradict some of Koch's and Countway's testimony. He told the court that he informed Countway about the robbery and asked him whether the military tear gas canister used in the raid could be traced back to him. Bass claimed that Countway told him not to worry. The paratrooper also testified that Countway agreed to obtain more gas canisters for him. Bass also contradicted Koch's testimony, alleging to the court that the former JTF2 soldier was supposed to get a share of the money from the robbery for purchasing the plane ticket that Bass used to travel to Calgary.

For his part, Eggleton shrugged off the information coming out of the Calgary trial, including Bass's allegations that he was promised a supply of military gas grenades. Weapons security was tight at all Canadian Forces installations, including Dwyer Hill, Eggleton claimed.

In June 2000, Patrick Ryan was sentenced to 12 years for masterminding the commando-style bank raid and the ATM robbery. Bass, who had been given seven years for his part in the bank heist, later applied for parole in 2000, but was turned down because of fears he would re-offend. Particularly worrisome, according to the National Parole Board, was Bass's "training in the field of counter-terrorist activities" and his other military skills which the board felt made him an extreme risk to the public. The Parole Board, after reviewing psychological and case management reports, labeled Bass a "walking time bomb" who was full of resentment against the federal government, in particular, for the disbandment of the Canadian Airborne Regiment.

A year and a half later, the board reversed its position and the so-called walking time bomb was granted parole, largely because a Calgary police detective vouched that the former paratrooper felt remorse for his role in the Brink's raid.

While Bass's links to JTF2 and the testimony at the Ryan trial had brought unwanted publicity, the unit had emerged relatively unscathed from the whole episode. During the trial and afterward, JTF2 officers had decreed that the unit would adhere to its secrecy policy and not acknowledge any of the information that came out of the court case. "I see no advantage to drawing attention to and provoking interest in this issue," one officer wrote in a secret May 24, 2000, report. The JTF2 approach paid off. Few journalists questioned why the unit's much-vaunted screening process had broken down. Officially the rigorous selection system weeded out "Rambos" and those with questionable backgrounds before they could even get through Dwyer Hill's gates.

With that in mind, Darnell Bass's 1990 encounter with military police and his desire to get prepared for a post-Apocalyptic society should have set off all kinds of warning bells. Bass had even been fined $200 for keeping his arsenal of guns in the Petawawa barracks. Not only were those records readily accessible to JTF2, they were even made public in November 1995 by the Somalia Inquiry which openly questioned Defence department officials why Bass wasn't subjected to further disciplinary action. The concerns the inquiry raised about Bass came a year *before* he applied to JTF2 but it's likely the unit, in its rush to expand, missed such critical information.

As it turned out, the counter-terrorism unit's screening process was not nearly as rigorous as it was reputed to be - in fact, it was haphazard at best. The Defence department acknowledged that as late as 1995 it had never compiled any psychological assessments of JTF2 soldiers. Just as troubling was a confidential report detailing a list of soldiers with disciplinary problems who had been accepted into JTF2 in its early days. The concerns of the RCMP's SERT officers about the questionable backgrounds of some JTF2 candidates, and the lack of a proper screening process on the part of the military, turned out to be correct.

Darnell Bass wasn't the only soldier linked to JTF2 who found himself in the courts. In the fall of 1999, Captain Michel Rainville was charged with torture, kidnapping, extortion and assault in connection with a brutal February 7, 1992, military raid on the Quebec Citadel. During that incident, Rainville led a group of soldiers, dressed in civilian clothing, their identities concealed by balaclavas, in an attack against the military installation. The raid was supposedly conducted to test the security of the weapons vault at the Citadel but no one had bothered to tell the soldiers on duty there and, not surprisingly, the men believed they were being attacked by real terrorists. Rainville's troops quickly overpowered the guards and began to beat them. One of the masked soldiers shoved a police baton into the anus of one of the guards so hard that he was almost lifted off the ground. Later, the guard was bound with duct tape and forced to lie down, while another soldier inserted a gun barrel into his anus. Eventually, one of the captives managed to escape and alerted city police to what he believed was a terrorist attack. By the time Quebec police arrived at the Citadel, Rainville had called off the operation and his men had taken off their ski masks. After the fiasco, Rainville was reprimanded and the incident was hushed up by the Defence department.

But due to the diligence of civilian prosecutors and the perseverance of one of the guards who had been terrorized, Rainville found himself in a Quebec City courtroom seven years after the Citadel incident had taken place. Some in Canada's defence community suggest that the 1992 raid was a JTF2 mission gone wrong, not unlike the violent and realistic operations that a secretive

U.S. Navy special operations unit had conducted in the mid-1980s to test security at American military installations. Responding to an Access to Information request, the Defence department acknowledged that documents regarding Rainville's JTF2 "service and training" exist, but that those records cannot be released due to federal government privacy rules and for reasons of national security.

Although Rainville would later be found guilty of torture by a civilian court in connection with the Citadel raid, a review of available military documents makes it highly unlikely that the attack was a JTF2 mission. Defence department records show that at the time of the Quebec City raid, the Canadian Forces leadership was still in the early stages of setting up the counter-terrorism unit and had not yet even selected Lieutenant Colonel Romses as its first commanding officer. Personnel selection for JTF2 soldiers and officers wouldn't start until several months after the Citadel operation.

While Captain Rainville's Quebec City mission wasn't a JTF2 operation, the same can't be said definitely about the March 4, 1993, killing of the unarmed Somali man at the Canadian Airborne Regiment base in Belet Huen. There have been allegations that the mission, led by Rainville, was JTF2's first overseas operation and, while technically the unit didn't come into official existence until April 1, 1993, it was, indeed, well established in March of that year.

What exactly happened the night of March 4 in Somalia is still steeped in controversy and uncertainty. The engineers' compound at the Canadian base in Belet Huen had become a regular target for Somalis hoping to steal food, fuel, equipment and soldiers' personal items. Normal security precautions were failing to prevent the Somalis from entering the compound and some soldiers worried about sabotage. Captain Rainville volunteered his reconnaissance platoon to boost security at the site and he and his men made plans for a stakeout that evening. The captain ordered that food and water be placed in the back of a trailer, visible from a path used daily by Somalis to go to a river to get water. Some members of the reconnaissance platoon believed the items were "bait," but Rainville later would say the food and water would attract thieves, not saboteurs, enabling his men to distinguish between the two.

Equipped with night-vision goggles, the reconnaissance platoon lay in wait in the compound. Shortly after 8 p.m., two Somali men were seen approaching the wire that surrounded the engineers' base. The two looked inside the Canadian camp and pointed in various directions while talking to each other. There has been disagreement among soldiers involved in the mission about the Somalis' exact movements after that, but at one point the two men became frightened and started running, ignoring demands from the paratroopers to stop. The soldiers then began to pursue the men, firing warning shots from their C7 assault rifles into the air. One of the paratroopers, Sergeant René Plante, realized he wasn't going to be able to catch the pair, so he aimed and fired his 12 gauge shotgun at the legs of one of the men, Hundebei Sabrie Abdi. The pellets tore into the Somali's buttocks and legs but he managed to run for 10 more metres before collapsing in the dirt.

The other, Ahmed Afrahow Aruush, 50 metres away, stopped briefly to see what was happening to his 30-year-old cousin. At that point, Rainville turned to his soldiers. "Go, go get him," he ordered. A hundred metres away, Master Corporal Brent Countway, Corporal Terry Smetaniuk and Master Corporal Roch Leclerc heard the shots and yelling. Suddenly Aruush burst out of the darkness, veered away and continued running. Corporal Smetaniuk started after the Somali, but when he heard yelling and a gunshot from behind him he threw himself to the ground. Master Corporals Leclerc and Countway had dropped to kneeling positions and one of the soldiers had fired a warning shot. After the fleeing Somali ignored their demands to halt, both soldiers opened fire. One bullet hit Aruush in the small of the back, ripping through his stomach and leaving a gaping hole as it flew out of his body. Countway and Leclerc watched as the Somali, about 75 metres away, tried to get up. His back was facing the two soldiers and both paratroopers would later say they thought Aruush could have had a weapon. They were also not sure if the Somali had been hit and feared he would head towards Corporal Smetaniuk so they opened fire again.

One of the bullets slammed into Aruush's shoulder, metal fragments ricocheting off the bone and blowing open the side of his face. The unarmed Somali slumped to the ground, dead. Inside a tent in the Canadian compound, a radio crackled, a Somali had been shot. "They got one," someone said and several soldiers cheered. An entry was later made in an Airborne Regiment logbook: One Somali "killed in action" and another wounded.

Later, a Canadian Forces doctor, Barry Armstrong, would allege that the dead Somali appeared to have been shot at close range, execution-style. Both Countway and Leclerc, who were not charged in the shooting, would deny such allegations, testifying at the Somali Inquiry that they opened fire because the Somali man still posed a threat to them and other Canadian soldiers. Rainville was charged with negligent performance of duty in connection with the incident but was acquitted by a court martial. The March 4 shootings became a centrepiece at the 1995-97 Somalia Inquiry, amid allegations that senior military officials tried to cover up the incident and the later torture-killing by other soldiers of a Somali 16-year-old in a bid to protect the political career of then defence minister Kim Campbell.

The Defence department still declines to discuss, or deny, whether JTF2 was involved in the Somalia killing. But a review of military records points to intriguing links that suggest the March 4 incident could have been the counter-terrorism unit's first foray into missions affecting "the national interest." There is, of course, the mysterious connection Rainville had to JTF2 and the acknowledgement by the Defence department that records exist concerning his training and service with the unit. Shortly before he left for Somalia, Rainville was also quoted in a Montreal newspaper saying he had received special forces training and the news report featured a photograph of the officer with commando knives strapped to his body. It also mentioned how he had been taught assassination techniques. In Somalia, the job of Rainville's reconnaissance platoon included special operations missions such as long-range patrols and the setting up of covert observation posts to gather intelligence. The unit also reportedly worked closely with U.S. special forces in Somalia, namely a Green Beret contingent that had disguised itself by wearing Canadian uniforms. That U.S. special forces team, which had come to Belet Huen for a five-day period, specialized in long-range intelligence missions along Somalia's borders.

Another interesting link between JTF2 and the Somalia mission is the presence of the unit's founding father, Colonel Mike O'Brien, who had arrived in Belet Huen the afternoon of March 4. O'Brien had traveled from Ottawa to Somalia to prepare for a visit of the Chief of the Defence Staff in the coming week. As well, there is the involvement of JTF2 soldier Brent Countway, one of the two men who opened fire on the unarmed Somalia man.

Was the controversial March 4 killing JTF2's first foreign mission? If it were, then certainly the Canadian Forces would have plenty of reasons to try to ensure such information never reached the public. The Canadian Airborne Regiment had already borne the brunt of the fallout from the Somalia mission, its soldiers the designated fallguys, taking the heat off the military leadership in Ottawa. For Defence department officials to admit that its most elite unit was involved in a contentious killing on its first overseas deployment would have been enough to destroy JTF2 in its infancy.

Whatever the truth, it is unlikely that the full story of any JTF2 involvement in Somalia - or, for that matter, in any of its more controversial episodes, including the Darnell Bass affair - will ever see the light of day. In 1997, the Liberal government shut down the Somalia Inquiry when the civilian panel started probing too deeply into the actions of senior political and military officials. Inquiry officials have since said they were never told of Rainville's JTF2 training and that such records were never turned over to the panel.

Three years later, in December 2000, MP Art Hanger's renewed calls for an inquiry into the Darnell Bass affair and the bank robber's links to JTF2 were ignored by Defence Minister Art Eggleton. In any case, nine months later any nagging questions about the commando team's alleged links to bank robberies or shootings in Somalia would be long forgotten. An anxious public, worried about the threat of terrorism in the aftermath of the September 11 attacks on the U.S., was keen to embrace this secretive unit called Joint Task Force Two.

ABOVE: *An RCMP SERT team member enters the Method of Entry building at the Dwyer Hill Training Centre by rappelling through a window.* (PHOTO BY AUTHOR)

LEFT: *Defence Department Deputy Minister Robert Fowler, one of the key figures responsible for the creation of JTF2.* (DND PHOTO)

TOP LEFT: *General John de Chastelain, who supported the creation and expansion of JTF2.*

TOP RIGHT: *Corporal Guy Lavallée modified some of JTF2's helicopters to improve rappelling operations.*

MIDDLE: *Lieutenant Colonel Ray Romses, JTF2's first commanding officer. (PHOTO BY SCOTT TAYLOR)*

RIGHT: *Colonel Barry MacLeod, JTF2's commander from 1997 to 2000.*

LEFT: A JTF2 assaulter, outfitted for a "black ops" mission, aims his MP-5 sub-machinegun.
(PHOTO COURTESY DND)

OPPOSITE PAGE, TOP: Two JTF2 operators position themselves on the skids of a Canadian Forces helicopter at CFB Petawawa.
(PHOTO COURTESY DND)

OPPOSITE PAGE, BOTTOM: A four-man JTF2 assault team, armed with different models of MP-5 sub-machineguns, ready to enter a building.
(PHOTO COURTESY DND)

TOP: *JTF2 assaulter, wearing scuba gear and armed with an MP-5 sub-machinegun, emerges from the water. (PHOTO COURTESY DND)*
ABOVE: *JTF2 bodyguards stand behind General Maurice Baril during the 1996 "Operation Assurance" in Zaire. (ASSOCIATED PRESS)*
OPPOSITE PAGE TOP and BOTTOM: *A JTF2 assault team enters an aircraft during a hostage-rescue training exercise. (PHOTOS TAKEN FROM DND TRAINING VIDEO)*

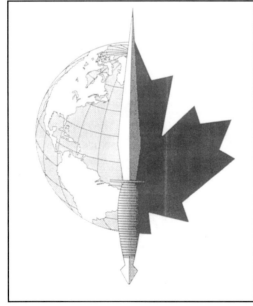

ABOVE AND LEFT:
JTF2's crest and logo.
(*PHOTOS COURTESY DND*)

THIS PAGE: General Maurice Baril on his 1996 reconnaissance in Zaire accompanied by a JTF2 bodyguard. The top photo, clearly showing the JTF2 soldier's face, was originally released by the Defence department. After it realized its mistake the department reissued the same picture with the soldier's face digitally altered (bottom). (PHOTO COURTESY DND)

OPPOSITE PAGE, TOP: A JTF2 team "takes down" a terrorist-held bus during an exercise at Dwyer Hill. (PHOTO COURTESY DND TRAINING VIDEO)

LEFT: *Chief War Crimes prosecutor Louise Arbour and JTF2 bodyguard in Canadian helicopter about to fly to Kosovo in 1999.* (AP PHOTO)

BOTTOM: *Canadian Governor-General Adrienne Clarkson steps out of a Griffon helicopter in Kosovo in 1999 under the watchful eye of a JTF2 bodyguard.* (AP PHOTO)

OPPOSITE PAGE: *JTF2 soldiers rescue a "hostage" held in the Dwyer Hill close quarter battle room.* (PHOTOS TAKEN FROM DND TRAINING VIDEO)

ABOVE: JTF2 recruiting poster. (*COURTESY DND*)

THIS PAGE: *Some of JTF2's weapons.*

TOP LEFT: *The 9 mm SIG-Sauer P228 used by JTF2.*

TOP RIGHT: *A collection of stun and CS gas grenades.*

MIDDLE: *MP-5 sub-machinegun with silencer.*
(PHOTO COURTESY HECKLER AND KOCH)

RIGHT: *JTF2 uses weapons available to regular Canadian units such as the C6 machinegun seen here.*
(PHOTO COURTESY DND)

OPPOSITE PAGE: *Recruiting poster for JTF2.*
(PHOTO COURTESY DND)

LEFT: JTF2 uses weapons available to regular Canadian units such as the C7 assault rifle seen here.
(PHOTO COURTESY DND)

MIDDLE: The CH-146 Griffon helicopter used by JTF2.

BOTTOM: Another aircraft used by JTF2, the CC-150 Polaris.

OPPOSITE PAGE: JTF2 operators on overseas "green" operations will wear the new Canadian Forces camouflage uniform.
(PHOTO COURTESY DND)

ABOVE: *Members of the Ontario Provincial Police Tactics and Rescue Unit, one of the civilian SWAT teams that JTF2 trains with, are shown here about to enter a room during an exercise.* (PHOTO BY AUTHOR)

OPPOSITE PAGE: *Special forces troops, likely American, on the hunt for Osama bin Laden in Afghanistan.* (REUTERS PHOTO)

EIGHT: AFGHANISTAN

THE AFGHAN WAR had been raging for a little more than two months when, in late December 2001, the first JTF2 soldiers began unloading their equipment in the former Taliban stronghold of Kandahar. The city had fallen to anti-Taliban tribal fighters a week earlier and the 40-man Canadian team was there to help weed out any remaining pockets of resistance in the region. American special forces troops were searching caves throughout the area and near Tora Bora where Osama bin Laden had taken shelter before fleeing, many believed, across the border to Pakistan.

Taliban leader Mullah Mohammed Omar reportedly had fled to a mountain village northwest of Kandahar with about 400 fighters. It was an area full of caves and tunnels where the remnants of the Taliban could hole up for weeks, if not months.

JTF2 wasn't alone in Kandahar, which over a couple of weeks had turned into a nerve centre for the American war effort. The U.S. Marines had set up a base outside the city and FBI agents were at a makeshift prison interrogating Taliban soldiers captured by U.S. and British special forces. A week earlier, the first of 150 Australian SAS had arrived in Kandahar, along with members of the elite German Kommando SpezialKraefte (KSK).

The Canadian deployment had been a stop-and-start affair right from the moment that Defence Minister Art Eggleton had announced on October 8 that the unit would be committed to the war effort. Canada's generals were enthusiastic about the opportunity to deploy JTF2 on such a high-profile mission. Not only was this the unit's chance to enter the big leagues of special operations - its first actual war - but such a mission would put an end to the constant debate over whether Canada was pulling its weight in military matters. The JTF2 operators were confident in their abilities, both to respond to a terrorist attack at home and in support of the American offensive overseas. As was the standard operating procedure, pallets of equipment and weapons were prepackaged at the Dwyer Hill Training Centre, ready for the order to move out. But that order took some time in coming.

What delayed the deployment, in part, was that JTF2 didn't have the ability to operate on its own in Afghanistan. Unlike the U.S. Delta Force and the British SAS, it had no long-range helicopters for insertion behind Taliban lines. More importantly, however, the American and British commanders were too busy directing their own special operations troops to deal with newcomers.

The Afghan campaign was nothing like the sniper work and intelligence-gathering missions that JTF2 had been involved with in Bosnia and Rwanda. Several hundred Delta Force and SAS operators were on the ground, conducting hit-and-run raids against Taliban and al-Qaeda forces. Both special forces groups had teams involved in the fighting at the Mazar-e Sharif fortress, helping put down an uprising by Taliban fighters who had originally surrendered peacefully but then began a revolt. The SAS was also conducting raids against al-Qaeda command centres located deep inside mountainous caves. In one particularly bloody battle, four SAS soldiers were wounded and dozens of Taliban and al-Qaeda fighters killed.

American special forces were also conducting attacks on fuel trucks crossing over from Pakistan into Afghanistan. Even though such supplies weren't likely destined for the Taliban, U.S. commanders were not taking any chances. More than a dozen fuel trucks were hit by commandos during the last two weeks of November. Green Berets were also working with local tribes to push the Taliban from towns around the besieged city of Kandahar. The Americans would leap-frog from village to village, pushing the Taliban back by calling in massive airstrikes and then allowing Northern Alliance troops and Pashtun tribes supportive of the U.S. to occupy and hold the area.

But it wasn't just JTF2's deployment that had been delayed by the intense pace of British and American operations. The first troops of the Australian SAS and the German Kommando SpezialKraefte didn't arrived in the Afghan city of Kandahar until December 4.

The delays in JTF2's deployment didn't stop Defence Minister Art Eggleton from seeming to hint for almost two months that the unit was on the front lines of the Afghan war. When first asked if Canadian troops were operating in the country, Eggleton had responded with a cryptic, "None that I can talk about." On November 20, during a trip to Washington, the Defence Minister all but came out and said JTF2 was in Afghanistan. He wouldn't confirm nor deny that the unit was already overseas but added, "Aside from JTF2, which I will not comment on because of the security nature of that entity, I couldn't tell you that there are Canadians in Afghanistan." Journalists were left with the impression that the force was indeed on the frontlines and subsequent news coverage reflected that belief.

In fact, JTF2 appeared to have become an unwitting pawn in the Chrétien government's agenda to show it was an international player in defence matters. Eggleton and Liberal MP David Pratt, the chairman of the Commons Defence committee, had even gone as far as comparing the unit to Delta Force and the SAS. Such talk incensed actual SAS veterans, who noted that JTF2 had yet to prove itself in combat. Some, like retired SAS soldier Alan Bell, a Toronto-based security consultant who was well aware of JTF2's capabilities and missions, wondered how Eggleton could compare the unit to the SAS, which had been on combat operations over the course of almost 50 years. Delta Force, Bell noted, had been involved in similar missions for some 20 years including service during the Persian Gulf War. JTF2's experience in countries like Rwanda and Bosnia didn't even come close to these types of operations, according to the soldier, who had helped train the Afghan Mujaheeden in the 1980s and who had fought during the Falkland Islands War.

After almost two months of vaguely suggesting that JTF2 members could be on the front lines, Eggleton finally admitted on November 26 that the commandos were still at the Dwyer Hill Training Centre. But politics would soon put an end to that. Both Prime Minister Chrétien and Eggleton were being pilloried in editorial pages, on radio talk-shows and by opposition MPs for comments they had made about a 1,000-member Immediate Reaction Force, made up mainly of the 3PPCLI, which was on standby for Afghan duty. Those troops, to be part of an international contingent also involving British and French commandos, were to secure airports and other key points to ensure humanitarian relief supplies could be distributed. But Eggleton was featured on the front page of The Globe and Mail newspaper saying that the Immediate Reaction Force would be pulled out of Afghanistan if it faced heavy fighting. Chrétien seemed to support that view, echoing his earlier comments about Canadian soldiers being like "boy scouts." "Of course, we don't want to have a big fight there," the prime minister told reporters. "We want to bring peace and happiness as much as possible."

At about that time, Defence department officials were expecting the government's Auditor General to release a damning report on the state of the Canadian Forces. The generals had already been briefed about the Auditor's study, which openly questioned claims by the government and military leadership that the Canadian Forces was more combat capable than it had been in the last decade. Auditor General Sheila Fraser had discovered a litany of problems resulting from the Liberal government's decision to cut back on military spending. There was no money for army units to train. The Hercules transport and Aurora patrol aircraft fleets were falling apart. And Sea King helicopters were prone to continual breakdown.

The Liberals needed something to divert attention from the bad press they had been getting - and JTF2 seemed just the answer. The day after the Auditor General's report was released, several journalists in Ottawa received phone calls from their military public affairs contacts. They were told that if they phoned the Defence department and asked whether JTF2 was being sent to Afghanistan that such information would be confirmed. No other details would be given out for "operational security reasons." Technically, the phone calls violated the Defence department's stated policy of not discussing JTF2 operations, but the government was anxious to deflect attention away from the Auditor General's report.

The diversionary ploy worked. The headlines about broken down military equipment were quickly replaced with those about "crack JTF2 troops" being sent off to war.

Five days after leaking that JTF2 would soon be in Afghanistan, the Liberals announced they would double the overall size of the unit. Since the mid-1990s, JTF2 had been slowly increased from around 130 soldiers to the current 300 operators. Now Finance Minister Paul Martin was freeing up money to expand the unit even further, presumably to about 600 soldiers. The government earmarked $119 million to be spent over the next five years for the expansion. Again, the announcement was followed by positive headlines and editorials.

But few commentators raised the most fundamental question about the government's expansion plans. Where would the extra elite soldiers come from?

The Canadian Forces was already in the middle of a recruiting crisis and regular force units were under-strength themselves. JTF2 had already experienced recruiting problems in 1996 and 1997 when the Canadian Forces was 70,000 strong. How would it find the qualified troops for this latest expansion with the military ranks hovering at around 58,000?

For JTF2 to expand it would have to pick off the top soldiers from other units in a situation similar to what happened shortly before the 1992 Canadian Forces mission to Somalia. In his 1995 presentation to the Somalia Inquiry, retired Major General Herb Pitts suggested that part of the Canadian Airborne Regiment's problems in the African country could be traced back to a lack of quality soldiers. In particular, he noted that many of the officers and non-commissioned members that could have strengthened and improved the regiment had instead been transferred to JTF2. All this took place in 1992 when JTF2 was still numbering less than 100 operators. Clearly, the government's 2001 expansion plan meant regular force units would ultimately suffer because of the drain of quality soldiers to the commando formation.

For the government, JTF2 had become the almost-perfect solution to help deflect criticism that it wasn't doing enough on defence. While neglecting the rest of the Canadian Forces, it could build up one small component to be used on a regular basis. What's more, with the intense secrecy surrounding JTF2, the government could pick and choose which details it wanted to release. The Afghanistan war had forced the military to open up a little about the unit, mainly because other countries such as the U.S., Britain and Australia were openly discussing in detail the involvement of their special forces. For the first time in a decade Canada's Defence department acknowledged sending the commandos overseas, the number of soldiers involved and the general area they were operating in. But the information appeared to be released whenever the government needed to be seen as doing something significant in the area of defence. Inevitably, such announcements resulted in positive headlines trumpeting that Canada's "elite" commandos were being sent into combat.

Behind the headlines, however, the expansion of JTF2 was a decision fraught with the danger that in order to increase its numbers so dramatically, its training and selection standards would have to drop substantially. Special forces units, by their very nature, tend to be small to ensure quality control and the best professional development for soldiers in those units. At the same time, successful units carefully cull from a large pool of recruits. Delta Force, with its estimated 800 soldiers, has some 45,000 special forces soldiers, including Green Berets and U.S. Army Rangers, from whom to choose when selecting candidates. And those soldiers, in turn, come from an overall army recruiting pool of a little more than one million troops. For its part, the SAS has around 300 soldiers, selected from an effective army strength of just over 100,000.

As well, the push to expand JTF2 in the mid-1990s had already led to breakdowns in the screening process in which a soldier such as Darnell Bass was allowed to come through the gates of Dwyer Hill. If Bass had been more physically fit, arguably, he would have become a member of the unit.

The main concern is that the government's proposal to transform JTF2 into a 600-member formation will put the unit on the road to becoming similar to the U.S. Army Rangers - a tough and well-trained rapid-deployment combat force, but certainly not one on the same level as the SAS, Delta Force or a host of other special forces teams around the world. And one could certainly argue that if the government wanted a version of the Rangers, it should never have disbanded the Canadian Airborne Regiment.

Even before the 2001 plan to double the size of the unit was announced, there were already concerns inside JTF2 that the expansion that began with "The Way Ahead" study in 1996 had already led to a lowering of some of the capabilities and skills of its soldiers. During one rock-climbing training exercise in Alberta, a JTF2 instructor complained that the soldiers he was to teach were lacking in some basic mountaineering skills and he questioned the use of such an exercise unless those basic training deficiencies were rectified.

In "Exercise Quadrant Brief," an assault on a "hijacked" Canadian Forces Polaris aircraft, other problems were noted. "The operational planning process is not well understood in the unit and therefore contributed to many short-falls in our BP (battle procedure) process," wrote one JTF2 officer in an after-action report. "Therefore major education is required of how we should be doing business." As well, there was confusion during that exercise on what JTF2 soldiers should do if radio communications between unit medics and soldiers were not functioning, prompting officers to recommend the development of standard operating procedures for such an eventuality. But such plans, as well as the knowledge of battle procedures, should be second-nature to any counter-terrorist/special forces unit.

Aside from unit numbers, another major problem in transforming JTF2 into a full-fledged special forces formation, according to foreign veterans of such units, is its lack of access to combat situations. It is difficult to develop the same skills that the Australian SAS learned in the jungles of Vietnam or the British SAS acquired in the frigid mountains of the Falkland Islands from the peacekeeping operations on which the Canadian military finds itself continually deployed. "You can't get those skills on a peacekeeping tour in Rwanda or Bosnia," says SAS veteran Alan Bell. "These are hard-core skills that you don't learn through training. You learn through constant operations, being subjected to all of the problems you get while you are operating as a special forces unit in a hostile environment."

As the U.S. military settles in for the long haul in its war on terrorism, a battle some are predicting will go for the next decade, the role of JTF2 in that conflict remains to be defined. At this point, the unit is at a crossroads. It will undoubtedly play a key role in whatever military operations Canada undertakes in the future. But whether that is as a full-fledged special forces/counter-terrorist unit or a robust light infantry unit similar to the U.S. Army Rangers is still open to question.

ABOVE: *U.S. Marines stand ready to board a waiting helicopter near Kandahar to continue the search for Osama bin Laden. (AP PHOTO)*

OPPOSITE PAGE: *A Barrett .50 calibre sniper rifle used by JTF2.*

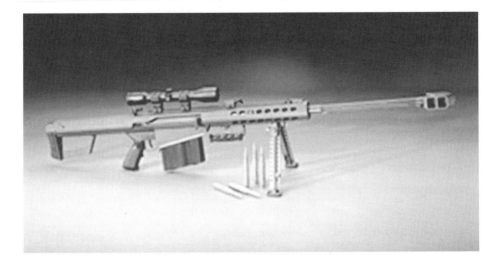

NINE: WEAPONS and EQUIPMENT

JTF2'S SELECTION OF weapons is based not only on the personal taste of individual soldiers but also on what the Canadian Forces has in its small arms arsenal. Also heavily influencing the unit's selection of such equipment are the experiences of other more established counter-terrorism/special operations units such as Delta Force and the British SAS.

Individual JTF2 members are issued a selection of firearms which are all carried in their "load out" gear, the equipment that is ready to go at a moment's notice. All of the weapons are sighted in by the individual member and are configured to the soldier's specific likes or dislikes. For example, some JTF2 operators prefer laser-targeting systems while others use devices such as the Surefire Weapon Mounted Light.

A typical JTF2 assaulter is issued a rifle for "green ops" or "black ops" close quarter battle perimeter security tasks as well as a sub-machinegun or shotgun for black operations close quarter battle work. A pistol is issued as a secondary sidearm but JTF2 tactics often involve using such a weapon for room entry and clearance when rappelling is involved and only one hand is free for a firearm. Some operators also prefer to use a handgun when taking part in an assault on an aircraft.

Sub-machineguns - Like many special operations units, JTF2 relies heavily on the Heckler and Koch family of MP-5 sub-machineguns. The German-made 9 mm weapons have a well deserved reputation for reliability. Designed in the 1960s, the MP-5 allows the operator to fire semi-automatically or full auto simply by flipping the selector switch on the receiver. The 9 mm bullet is considered easier to handle than the 5.56 mm or .45 ACP calibres as the recoil is very moderate. As an added feature, Heckler and Koch also has a twin magazine clamp that allows the shooter to carry two magazines on the gun to enable quick magazine changes in a combat situation. MP-5s have either a 15 or 30-round magazine and can be field-striped in matter of seconds without tools. Unlike most sub-machineguns, the MP-5 fires from a closed bolt position. This helps increase accuracy as there is no forward movement of the bolt when the trigger is pulled (which in other sub-machineguns can put the weapon slightly off target).

JTF2 uses the MP-5A2 (fixed stock), MP-5A3 (collapsing stock) and the MP-5SD (suppressed, either fixed or folding stock). The standard weight of the MP-5 is three kilograms and it has a cyclic rate of fire of 800 rounds per minute. The SD version uses a built-in suppressor or "silencer" to muffle the sound of the gun's report. In that system, the barrel is encased in a suppressor tube; escaping gases are diverted through the aluminum ports inside the suppressor, causing a drop in the bullet's normal velocity. As a result, when the bullet leaves the muzzle it is travelling at a sub-sonic speed and the sound being emitted is similar to a loud hiss of air. Maintenance for the silencer is simple and involves using a cleaning agent to rinse out the gunpowder residue that has built up in the device over time. The other MP-5 variant commonly used by counter-terrorist teams is the MP5K, a shortened, easily concealed machinegun. It is not known if that weapon is in JTF2's arsenal.

Handguns - The unit relies on the SIG-Sauer family of 9 mm pistols including the P-225, P-226, P-228 and P-229. SIG-Sauer handguns, while expensive, are considered among the best weapons available for counter-terrorism and special forces work. Depending on the specific models, SIG-Sauer have ammunition magazines with 13 and 15-round capacity. The SIG-Sauer P-226 is the wide-frame version of the P-225 and comes with a 15-round magazine. All SIG-Sauers, with the exception of the steel-framed P-229, feature lightweight aluminum alloy frames. The SIG-Sauer P-228 is the compact version of the P-

226 and comes equipped with a 13-round magazine.

The decision to adopt SIG-Sauer handguns was made after JTF2 evaluated the 9 mm Browning Hi-Power pistol in the Canadian Forces arsenal. One of the reasons JTF2 selected the SIG-Sauer line was because of the significant safety improvements built into the gun. Unlike the Browning, JTF2 operators can safely carry a chambered round in their SIG-Sauers.

Rifles - The C7 family manufactured by Diemaco Ltd., of Kitchener, Ontario, provides the basis for JTF2's assault rifle arsenal. Among those firearms in the Dwyer Hill weapons vault are the C7, the C7 flat-top variant and the C8, both regular and flat-top and all in 5.56 mm calibres. The C7 is identical to the C7 flat-top (FT) except the FT is outfitted with an optical sight. The C7 has a firing mechanism that permits either single shot or full automatic firing. A three-round burst option is also available. The rifle is capable of firing 700 to 900 rounds per minute and weighs 3.7 kilograms when loaded. All user maintenance is performed without tools, and all armorer maintenance can be performed at the unit level, with a minimum of special tools and gauges. The rifle has a hammer forged barrel and a 30-round magazine.

The British SAS has ordered a limited number of C7s for its inventory after tests showed that it was more reliable than the British SA80 and the U.S. versions of the M-16. The British order from Diemaco was for around $5 million but details on the actual numbers of weapons purchased were not released. The C7 is considered to have a longer barrel life than the American M-16s and reportedly performs better in mud and poor climate conditions.

The C8 carbine used by JTF2 is a lightweight, short version of the C7. The C8 incorporates an integral carrying handle and a two-position iron sight. The flat-top version has the optical sight. The rifle is configured for either single shot or full automatic firings, again with a three-round burst option available. The C8 carbine has bullet accuracy and striking energy 90 per cent of that of the C7 rifle, in a weapon that is 24 per cent reduced in overall length and 20 per cent reduced in weight, according to Diemaco's statistics. The C8 has a collapsible buttstock that reduces the overall length for storage and carrying. It uses more than 90 per cent of the same parts as other C7 family members, resulting in commonality of use, training and maintenance.

JTF2's firepower is greatly increased by the addition of the Diemaco M-203A1 grenade launcher, installed under the forward stock of its C7 family of rifles. The launcher is capable of firing 40 mm grenades out to 400 metres. The launcher's sight was designed and made in Canada and is graduated from 50 to 400 metres. SNC in La Gardeur, Quebec, makes the 40 mm grenades.

Another seemingly natural fit for JTF2 is Diemaco's new Special Forces Weapon. The military will not confirm whether the unit uses the SFW but Diemaco has sold an undisclosed number to the Norwegian Army's special forces. The 5.56 mm special forces weapon looks similar to the C8 but has an enhanced high-performance barrel chamber configuration and a high-endurance long-life barrel. It also has a three-position telescoping buttstock and an ambidextrous fire control selector. A cleaning kit is stored inside the pistol grip. The SFW comes with a 30-round magazine but has an optional 100-round magazine.

Machineguns - The C9A1, equipped with an optical sight, provides JTF2 the firepower it needs, particularly in green operation roles. The C9 is based on the Minimi machinegun manufactured by Fabrique Nationale Herstal S.A. in Belgium. The C9A1 is a fully automatic, gas operated, belt, or magazine-fed weapon. It comes in 5.56 mm calibre and has a 200-round ammunition belt or C7 30-round magazine. This dual feed system is unique to the C9 and it allows for the use of either belts or the C7 magazines interchangeably without the use of any other parts or tools. The ammunition belts are stored in reusable green plastic containers. The C9A1 is capable of firing 700 to 1,000 rounds per minute with an effective range at about 600 metres. The optical sight is 3.4 power.

Also believed to be in JTF2's inventory is the 7.62 mm calibre General Purpose Machinegun (GPMG) C6 (FN MAG 58). The C6, developed in Belgium, is a fully automatic, belt-fed and gas-operated weapon. This versatile air cooled machinegun is used by the Canadian Forces as a fire support weapon. In a sustained fire role, the C6 is mounted on a tripod. The C6 can also be fired from its bipod. The C6 is equipped with a 220-round belt. It only comes in automatic fire mode and has a cyclic rate of 650 to 1,000 rounds per minute. It has an effective range of 800 metres when used on a bipod and 1,800 metres on a tripod. For night image intensification sight, it is equipped with the MaxiKITE sight. The C6 is considered heavy but reliable and comes with a quick-change barrel.

Shotguns - JTF2 uses a modified Remington 870 pump action shotgun and the Heckler and Koch Benelli Super 90 shotgun. The Remington 870 is one of the most widely produced shotguns of all time and is in use among many other armed forces and police agencies. It carries seven rounds in a tubular magazine, is pump action, and weighs 3.6 kilograms.

The Heckler and Koch Benelli Super 90 Police Tactical Shotgun is a slightly heavier shotgun in semi-automatic mode with a capacity for seven shells. It is equipped with a comfortable pistol grip to aid in shooting. The Benelli Super 90 had been adopted by the U.S. Marine Corps as its M1014 shotgun with the first such weapons fielded in April, 2001.

JTF2 would use shotguns mainly in hostage-rescue scenarios because, unlike high-velocity bullets, shotgun pellets do not travel as far and have less potential to injure bystanders. Additionally, the stopping power provided by a shotgun at close-range is almost unequalled by any other weapon. Shotguns are also used with specialized ammunition to blast open locked doors by blowing off the hinges.

Sniper Rifles - The unit has a selection of sniper rifles in 7.62 mm, .300 Winchester Magnum and .338 Lapua Magnum calibres. Its snipers employ the Accuracy International AW or AWP sniper rifle, a favorite of the British SAS. These bolt action guns have a reputation for great accuracy and are available in a model with a silencer/suppressor. Accuracy International sniper rifles are available in a variety of calibres including .338 Lapua Magnum, .300 Winchester Magnum and 7 mm Remington. All three offer greater range than the standard 7.62 mm. The AWP rifle has a stiffer and shorter 610 mm (24 inches) barrel to maximize precision. JTF2 snipers would use match-grade ammunition which is specially designed based on the best performance characteristics (grains of gunpowder and bullet) determined in various tests. Accuracy International recommends the ideal sight for the AWP as the 3-12x50 Variable scope due to the need for both long-range precision shooting and a short-range wide field of view. The AW/AWP sniper rifles weigh around 6.2 kilograms.

Another precision rifle available to JTF2 is the Heckler and Koch semi-automatic PSG-1 sniper rifle. The rifle is 7.62 mm calibre and has either a five or 20-round detachable box magazine. It has a heavy barrel and adjustable butt. The PSG-1 is based on the HK G-3 design but is manufactured as a dedicated sniping system with a heavy barrel, adjustable butt and cheek-piece as well as trigger. The PSG-1 is heavy, weighing 7.5 kilograms. It comes with a Hendsoldt six-power scope which has an illuminated reticle with six-sight settings. Those are set from 100 to 600 metres.

In designing its sniper rifle, Heckler and Koch consulted with the German GSG-9 and the British SAS. The PSG-1 is considered one of the most expensive weapons of its kind on the market, costing an estimated $16,000 per copy. This semi-automatic rifle has the advantage of being able to engage more than one target over a shorter period of time than a bolt-action rifle. The other advantage over a bolt-action is that the sniper does not have to cycle the bolt, potentially giving away his position with his body movement.

The unit also uses McMillan's .50 calibre sniper rifles and the M-82A1 Barrett .50 calibre system. During the 1995 siege at Gustafsen Lake, RCMP officials requested the use of JTF2's .50 calibre McMillan rifles to disable the vehicles driven by native protesters. JTF2, however, declined to send the rifles to the RCMP's Emergency Response Team.

One of the most devastating firearms in JTF2 arsenal is the M-82A1 Barrett .50 calibre sniper system. Ronnie Barrett, a shooter and gun designer from Tennessee, revolutionized the world of military sniping when in 1981 he laid down plans for a rifle chambered for the .50 calibre Browning Machine Gun cartridge. Today counter-terrorism units and armed forces in more than 35 nations use the Barrett rifles, mostly the M-82A1 and M-82A2. The semi-automatic Barrett is extremely heavy, weighing in at 13.4 kilograms. Even though it is equipped with a muzzle brake system to absorb most of the recoil, shooting the weapon is reportedly quite an adventure. Some snipers have suggested it is akin to firing a 12 gauge shotgun while others claim it far exceeds that recoil. The weapon, when used with the Roufess multi-purpose ammunition, gives snipers the capability to engage targets at ranges of 1500 metres as well as provide harassment fire up to 2000 metres.

Contrary to popular belief, the most standard use for the rifle is not for sniping at personnel but in disabling high-value enemy equipment, such as parked aircraft, radar systems, surface-to-air missiles, electrical generators and vehicles. During the Persian Gulf War, U.S. Marine Corps scouts operating in Iraq used the Barrett to damage the control boxes of Iraqi artillery batteries. There have been reports from the Persian Gulf War that the M-82A1 semi-automatic Barrett was used for anti-personnel kills at 1,093 metres and for disabling equipment such as armored personnel carriers at 2,400 metres. In 1995 the SAS received the Barrett M-82A2 before it deployed to Bosnia.

JTF2 usually employs the standard two-man sniper team, with one soldier as the shooter, the other providing protection and handling target-spotting duties. Unit snipers spend long hours practicing on the Dwyer Hill ranges or waiting during scripted exercises for the "go" signal to eliminate a "terrorist." The boredom of such long waits is sometimes taken into consideration by the trainers. During one JTF2 exercise the planners insisted that actors playing the terrorists have a minimum of one person patrolling at all times and that activity be conducted near windows, on occasion, to give snipers something to look at through their scopes. JTF2 marksmen also practice shooting from hovering Griffon helicopters.

Sanitized Weapons - JTF 2 maintains an extensive inventory of "sanitized" foreign weapons - firearms that can't be traced back to the Canadian military, let alone a specific unit. Such weapons, including AK-47s and AK-74s, are also used for familiarization training. Many of these guns have been confiscated during peacekeeping operations. During the Somalia mission, for instance, some two dozen captured weapons, everything from AK-47s to HK G-3s, were distributed to units for "operational use."

WEAPON SIGHTING SYSTEMS

SureFire Weapon Mounted Light -This light, which attaches to the end of a firearm, is considered an excellent tool for counter-terrorism and fighting in built-up areas. It allows a JTF2 soldier to see potential targets in low-light conditions such as inside a building or aircraft and can also be used to temporarily "blind" an enemy when the light is shined in his face.

The CLAM - Used both by JTF2 and the FBI's Hostage-Rescue Team (HRT), this weapon sight is also employed in low-light conditions. For Canadian purposes it can mount on the C7 or C8 in a similar fashion to the Surefire light. The CLAM has a small but powerful white light as well as a laser which projects a red dot on to the target. It also has an infrared pointer and an infrared floodlight. Those two options, for use at night or inside a darkened building, allow a soldier to project an infrared beam that is invisible to the eye. The soldier is equipped with specialized goggles allowing him to see the beam, which he can then use to target the enemy.

Laser Range-Finders -These devices, about the size of an average pair of binoculars, can determine the specific range of a target up to six kilometres away. The ranger-finders are accurate within several metres. There are several models available but one of the best, according to Canadian Army snipers, is the Rockwell Viper Laser Range-Finder Binoculars. Snipers will combine laser-range finders with a Global Positioning System to pinpoint the exact range and location of the enemy. With that information already computed in advance, a sniper team can fire on their target without having to expose themselves for a long period of time.

MUNITIONS AND AMMUNITION

Stun Grenades - Although there are various types, these devices are all essentially designed to blind and disorient terrorists at the beginning of an attack. Royal Ordnance first developed stun grenades, also known as "flashbangs," for the British SAS in the early to mid-1970s. They were first used during a raid on a hijacked aircraft at Mogadishu in 1977 by SAS and German GSG-9 operators. When detonated, the stun grenade lets off an extremely loud bang and an intense, but brief, blinding light. The devices contain a mixture of magnesium powder and fulminate of mercury. To minimize injury to hostages, the grenades are constructed with as few metal parts as possible. Earlier models used a cardboard wrapping but now some stun grenades are made of light plastic. Other specialized munitions used by JTF2 include CS grenades, which once detonated, produce an instantaneous buildup of the irritant CS agent. The CS smoke cloud will hang in a room for several minutes allowing commandos to overpower a hostage-taker. JTF2 also uses hydrocut breaching demolitions and shotgun breaching rounds to gain entry through doorways and windows.

Simulation ammunition - Also widely used by JTF2, such cartridges, which allow soldiers to conduct what is known as force-on-force training, are quite similar to civilian "paint-ball" ammunition. The main difference is that the cartridges are more accurate and can be fired from MP-5/C7/C8/SIG-Sauer firearms with simple modifications made to those weapons. Those modifications include a special barrel for pistols and a replacement bolt to be installed in sub-machineguns. Another type of simulation ammunition, again for use in a converted firearm, is ideal for the close confines of buildings, buses and aircraft. Known as a safety blank, this ammunition will bounce harmlessly off walls and furniture. Because of that it can be used at close ranges to simulate realistic, but safe, assault scenarios. Another useful simulation ammunition for JTF2 is a 9 mm Close Quarter Combat Safety slug made by a Canadian company. The round can be used in an unmodified weapon but only has a maximum range of 100 metres. It can be used in the Dwyer Hill Close Quarter Battle rooms without penetrating the plywood walls there.

OTHER EQUIPMENT

Night Vision Goggles - The upgraded AN/PVS-504 NVGs are standard issue, in small quantities, for the Canadian Army. JTF2 reportedly uses the more advanced AN/PVS-7D Night Vision Goggles and AN/PVS-14 Monocular system. The Defence department has also purchased three-power optical magnifiers designed for use with the AN/PVS-7D. The magnifier effectively doubles the range of the goggles.

JTF2 also has access to the MaxiKITE sight, a third-generation night vision sight that performs extremely well in low-light conditions. The MaxiKITE can be installed on a C6 general purpose machinegun, and has a range out to 800 metres. As well, there is the PAQ-4 Infrared Pointer which is mounted on the C7A1 rifle. This device projects a beam, invisible to the eye, but which can be seen by soldiers who are wearing night vision equipment. It can be used to target an individual enemy or by a commander to "highlight" a target for soldiers using night vision equipment.

Radios - Special operations forces depend on reliable and light radio systems as their lifeline. Such systems can be used for everything from calling in air strikes to requesting a helicopter for extraction from behind enemy lines. During the Persian Gulf War, it wasn't unusual for an eight-man Green Beret team, sent behind Iraqi lines, to carry five radios so team members could talk among themselves and to air force support crews. In its early years, JTF2 appears to have used some radio systems that were of non-Canadian military issue. In its "The Way Ahead" - which would guide, among other things, equipment purchases for the future - JTF2 commanders stressed the need to purchase personal radios for assaulters that had a "compatibility with CF radios."

As a result, it would make sense that JTF2 will have adopted the new Canadian Forces IRIS system, a family of combat net radios. The system has embedded voice and data encryption, a fixed or frequency-hopping mode, as well as air-to-ground, ground-to-air transmission capabilities. The IRIS system also includes long-range and satellite communications, ground stations, portable data terminals and an information distribution system for headquarters. At the small unit or individual soldier level, there is the CNR (P) - combat net radio (primary) - which has either fixed or frequency-hopping capabilities. As well, there is the LAR, or lightweight assault radio, which is fixed-frequency.

There is one drawback, however, to IRIS. While some senior Defence department officials have declared the system the most advanced in the world, Brigadier General Glenn Nordick has noted that there is growing evidence that the VHF-based system will encounter serious problems when used in built-up areas such as in cities. As proof of that concern, he noted that during Urban Ram, an exercise where soldiers and police tactical teams operated in an urban setting, many of the troops went out and bought their own handheld UHF systems to use.

Global Positioning Systems - JTF2 teams are all outfitted with global positioning systems to aid in navigation. These small hand-held devices pick up signals from a number of GPS satellites and, using that information, are able to compute a soldier's location within a few metres. GPS devices are also widely used by special operations teams to better co-ordinate air strikes.

Assault ladders -These are specialized ladders for quick access to buildings and aircraft. They are made of lightweight aluminum so they can be easily managed and placed up against the fuselage of an aircraft, for instance. Exposed faces on the ladders are coated with rubber to cut down on noise and the rungs have a non-slip material on them. JTF2 also has a vehicle-mounted assault platform. The platform, installed on the roof of a GMC Suburban truck, can hold up to six men with equipment. During an assault on an aircraft, the vehicle would be driven up to the plane in line with the passenger doors. Once there, a ladder attached to the platform would be unfolded, allowing the assault team access to the aircraft doors.

Anti-tank Weapons - For its green operations, JTF2 would also have access to the full complement of weapons from the Canadian Forces arsenal such as the Eryx. Eryx is a short range anti-armor weapon that can be fired from the shoulder or from a tripod. It is a portable system effective against armored vehicles or bunkers. Eryx has a range from 50 to 600 metres and is equipped with optical or thermal imagery sights.

Miscellaneous Equipment -The storage lockers at the Dwyer Hill Training Centre have a wide selection of gear, much of it bought from commercial stores such as Mountain Equipment Co-Op in Ottawa. The unit has purchased everything from rock climbing shoes and backpacks to computer laptops and toboggans for hauling equipment. Specialized tactical equipment includes battering rams and other breaching devices.

JTF2 is constantly upgrading its equipment. For instance, after practicing mountaineering and climbing skills in Alberta, it recommended the purchase of four-season, commercially made mountaineering tents. It also suggested switching from the rations that are standard in the Canadian Forces. While tasty, that food, contained in aluminum foil pouches, is heavy to carry. JTF2 operators suggested either using commercially available and much lighter freeze-dried food packages or similar such rations issued to NATO allies.

For intelligence-gathering JTF2 has access to digital cameras. Using this system, instant electronic images can be transmitted anywhere in a matter of seconds using a laptop computer hooked up to satellite communications. At the lower end of the technical scale, JTF2 has also purchased easy-load disposable cameras.

Since the unit is responsible for its own second-line maintenance and service support, additional demands are put on JTF2 staff. For maintenance work and for certain tasks, such as making targets, the Dwyer Hill compound has been outfitted with a full wood-working suite, complete with lathes and circular table saws. Since it also has to be self-sufficient on operations, the unit has welding equipment, automotive tools and portable motor vehicle lifts.

In 1997, JTF2 spent $1.9 million on equipment. In 1999-2000 that jumped to $3.6 million, reflecting the expansion of the unit as outlined in "The Way Ahead."

In the 1999-2000 period, JTF2 purchased a variety of equipment; $100,000 on cameras, $5,500 for targets, $100,000 for fitness equipment and $16,000 for climbing ropes.

UNIFORMS

JTF2 members adopt different dress according to their specific mission. At the Dwyer Hill Training Centre, the standard dress is a black turtleneck, black boots and black combat fatigues. In 1996 the unit briefly examined adapting

its own headwear, in the form of either a tan beret or a wedge-style hat. "It was decided that a wedgie was punishment for people who wanted a tan beret," wrote one cynical JTF2 officer in the unit's official history report. JTF2's Regimental Sergeant Major decided to look at grey color samples for a beret but the idea of distinctive headgear was eventually abandoned.

For JTF2 operations there are two basic categories of clothing, one for green operations, the other for black. The green operations uniform is identical to those worn by the rest of the Canadian Army. This is done so for good reason - to maintain a low profile so JTF2 operators can blend in with other troops. The JTF2 element deployed in support of the CCSFOR Battlegroup in Bosnia, for instance, wears the standard combat uniform complete with the unit identifiers and cap badge of the infantry battalion or armored regiment forming the basis of the battlegroup's F echelon. JTF2 is also in the process of adopting the new CADPAT camouflage uniform for its green operations. Eventually that uniform will be distributed to all Canadian Army units.

When performing bodyguard duties, some JTF2 operators wear civilian clothes with a tan safari-type cargo vest. Each soldier is equipped with a portable radio with the microphone within easy reach on his vest. A low-slung, black pistol holster is also worn.

For black operations there is a basic counter-terrorist close quarter battle ensemble (*see DND photo opposite page*). Included in that are:

1. Black Spectra-Shield helmet with a mount for night vision goggles. Included in the helmet is an ear protection system which, while allowing the JTF2 assaulter to hear transmitted orders over his radio, also restricts the level of high-pressure sound from grenades and gun fire.
2. Bolle Ballistic (poly-carbonate lens) Tactical Goggles.
3. Nomex (fire-retardant) balaclava.
4. On the right shoulder is an aluminum carabiner used to secure the shortened MP-5 sub-machinegun sling to body (rather than having the weapon slung across the body which could lead to tangling problems).
5. On the left shoulder is wiring for the Tactical Radio Earphone and Throat Microphone. The radio itself is worn in a pouch on the rear left shoulder of the load-bearing vest.
6. The chest is covered with Spectra-Shield Body Armor with trauma plates, front and rear, which are capable of defeating a bullet in a calibre up to

.308 Winchester / 7.62 mm NATO. That body armor is complemented by an olive drab ballistic nylon cover.

7. Also on the chest is a load-bearing vest constructed of ballistic (cordura) nylon pouches on a nylon mesh body. It has a zip-up front, and lace-adjustable sides. Pouches contain mission-essential equipment. A JTF2 assaulter usually carries at least three "flash-bangs" (stun grenades) in the grenade holders on lower right side of the vest. Also included is the standard MP-5 sub-machinegun. There are magazine pouches (tall) and pistol magazine pouches (short) on lower left side of the vest. On the bottom front left and right sides of the vest are flex-cuff restraints hanging from snap-release mounting points. The restraints are to secure the hands of any prisoners taken during a mission.

8. Protecting the assaulter's lower area is a Spectra-Shield Body Armor groin protector. That device zips on or off of the main body armor vest, depending on the mission and degree of required protection.

9. On the right thigh is a Kydex drop-leg holster which has a thumb-snap release for easy access to the pistol. The holster is designed to hold the SIG Sauer P-226 or P-229 handgun equipped with SureFire Light.

10. On the knees are pads secured with elasticized Velcro straps.

11. JTF2 assaulters tend to wear Rocky Magnum Law Enforcement/Duty boots.

12. On the hands are black U.S. Nomex Flight/Crewman (CVC) Gloves.

13. In the assaulter's right hand is the Heckler and Koch MP-5A3 sub-machinegun with a SureFire Light-equipped handguard.

14. The basic garment worn is a black, two-piece Nomex (flame retardant) SWAT-type suit with six-pocket pants and a four-pocket shirt. Assaulters are also issued black Gore-Tex outerwear for use in inclement weather.

Minor details of dress will vary from one assaulter to another, and from mission to mission. Possible variations, to give a few examples, would be the wearing of a gas mask instead of the ballistic goggles and balaclava or the attachment of night vision goggles to the helmet mount. The possible permutations for minor variations in dress are virtually limitless, and are dependant on a soldier's personal preference, the individual's assigned tasks and position within the mission, and any special mission-related requirements.

During missions in rural settings or on green operations, JTF2 snipers would use a ghillie suit to camouflage their appearance. When wearing such a suit, covered with material designed to replicate the foliage corresponding to a particular area, the sniper is almost invisible. The sniper's rifle is also wrapped in similar material to blend in with the terrain. Some ghillie suits are made of a material designed to reduce the heat being generated outward by the sniper's body. That feature is important to avoid detection since some surveillance systems are capable of detecting body heat.

VEHICLES

JTF2 uses a variety of heavy-duty commercially made trucks. The most common is the GMC Suburban, the vehicle of choice for many North American police tactical teams. Suburbans of varying colors can be seen going in and out of the Dwyer Hill compound. JTF2's assault ladder platform can also been installed on the roof of its Suburbans.

From 1997 to 1999, JTF2 received permission to purchase 24 vehicles of varying types but details of that procurement are unclear. It appears, however, that JTF2 has not been as fortunate as its foreign counterparts who have a variety of vehicles at their disposal for overseas operations. For such missions, the unit has had to make do with equipment already in the Canadian Forces inventory, such as the light support vehicle wheeled (LSVW). In 1994 and 1995, as many as five heavily modified LSVWs were spotted at Canadian Forces Base Uplands which was being used as a staging area for JTF2 operations and exercises. The LSVWs had been equipped with mounts, designed for heavy weapons, on the front and rear. The vehicles' cabs had been removed and there was no canvas on the rear of the light trucks. Wire cutters had been installed on the front of the vehicles. Two LSVWs had also been outfitted with Global Positioning Systems. The advantage of the light trucks is that they can be transported by CC-130 Hercules aircraft.

But the LSVWs are renowned in the Canadian Forces for their poor reliability and performance. The trucks have been plagued by engine fires and squealing metal-on-metal brakes, hardly a positive feature for a tactical vehicle. The LSVWs are also considered by operators to be under-powered. Between 1993 and 1997 the Canadian Forces purchased 2,879 of the vehicles as part of a politically motivated military procurement aimed at creating jobs at Western Star Trucks of Kelowna, British Columbia. Western Star has announced it will close down its production line but the Canadian Forces will continue to have the LSVWs for a long time to come.

JTF2's vehicle situation could somewhat improve in the coming years if the Canadian Army takes delivery of the Mercedes Benz 290 GDT, also known as the Gelaendewagen. The Gelaendewagen, while small, is fast and reliable and it is likely JTF2 would be among the first Canadian units to receive the vehicles. The Gelaendewagen is in service with German, French, Dutch, Danish, Norwegian, Austrian and Swiss armies as well as militaries in Africa, Asia and South America. The U.S. Marines have also purchased 100 of the vehicles. The Gelaendewagen is also being used for counter-terrorist work by Norwegian special forces.

AIR SUPPORT

CC-150 Polaris - JTF2 has access to the Polaris Airbus for either large-scale overseas transport or for use in counter-hijacking training. Over the years, the Polaris has been a stand-in for commercial aircraft, with military reservists playing the role of hostages. The scripted scenarios can last for hours or days and always end with a JTF2 assault on the plane. The CC-150 Polaris can carry 194 passengers or 32,000 kilograms of cargo. It has a range of 11,668 kilometres.

CC-130 Hercules -The workhorse of the Canadian Air Force is not only used by JTF2 for transport but as well for parachute training. The four-engine aircraft has a range of 3,960 to 9,790 kilometres depending on its load. It can carry up to 90 troops or 64 fully equipped paratroopers. The Hercules can be loaded and unloaded quickly and is especially useful in delivering supplies because it does not need a lot of room to land. JTF2 has prepackaged its equipment on well-marked pallets for easy transportation on the CC-130 or the CC-150.

CC-144 Challenger - JTF2 has used this twin-engine executive jet for some of its long-range transport needs, in particular to send close personal protection teams to Africa on several occasions. The CC-144 has a range of 4,630 kilometres and can carry 12 passengers. While most of the Canadian Forces Challengers have been sold off, the military still retains a small number for VIP use and it is likely that JTF2 will have access to those aircraft for future missions. The Challengers are based in Ottawa and operated by 412 Squadron.

Helicopters - The backbone of JTF's air operations is its helicopter fleet. In the beginning, the unit used three CH-135 Twin Hueys. A long-time veteran of military operations worldwide, the Twin Huey had a speed of 222 kilometres an hour and a range of 463 kilometres. It could carry 12 passengers. Flying operations were originally handled by the 450 Squadron at Canadian Forces Base Uplands. That squadron was disbanded in 1996-97 and JTF2 operations were taken over by 427 Tactical Helicopter Squadron.

The 427 Tactical Helicopter Squadron/B Flight was declared operationally ready on November 1, 1997, to use the Canadian Forces Utility Tactical Transport Helicopter (CFUTTH) CH-146 Griffon for JTF2 operations. The Griffon has a three-man crew - pilot, co-pilot and flight engineer - and can transport up to 12 troops depending on the equipment they carry. A combat load in the summer is around eight soldiers while in the winter, because of extra gear, the Griffon can carry six. The CH-146 has a maximum speed of 260 kilometres an hour. With normal fuel tanks its range is 630 kilometres but that can be increased with the use of two auxiliary fuel tanks, boosting the range to 1020 kilometres.

JTF2's Griffons were outfitted with a tubular A-frame device, also used in the Twin Hueys, for the attachment of a fast-rope used in infiltration or extraction. The frame juts out on the side of the helicopter. Rappel lines can also be anchored onto the floor of the aircraft. The Aerospace and Telecommunications Engineering Support Squadron at CFB Trenton, Ontario, was given the job of producing a fast-rope rappel/insertion/extraction system that will not only replace the existing system but also do away with the use of rappel ropes hooked up to the floor of the Griffon. It is not known whether that new system has been put in place yet.

Other modifications ordered for the Griffons include a new design in seating arrangements so snipers can sit on each side of the aircraft on the front of the skids. Armor-protection kits are also required for the JTF2 helicopters. The unit's Griffons have been outfitted for the installation of the Westcam Forward Looking Infrared camera, which has a range of up to two kilometres, as well as a specialized secure communications package. The unit works its helicopters hard. In 1998-99, for instance, JTF2 Griffons flew 625 hours, while in 1999-2000, they logged a little more than 850 hours.

JTF2's Griffons are scheduled to be among the first to be outfitted with the ERSTA system starting around 2003. This Electro-Optical Reconnaissance Surveillance and Target Acquisition system would give the unit increased intelligence-gathering capabilities. The ERSTA sensor package will consist of an infrared device with a range of about four kilometres, a camera for day use, a laser-range finder and a laser designator. ERSTA would also include a data link system to relay real-time information to ground commanders while the helicopter is airborne. The various missions will determine how that information is sent; it could be as simple as a text message or as advanced as a live video feed. A follow-on project would involve the purchase of ground stations to receive ERSTA information. Using the system, JTF2 commanders or senior military officers could watch an operation on a video screen as it actually takes place.

For JTF2 missions, the Griffon pilots are exceptionally trained. Standard flying tactics involve operating the helicopter low to the ground to avoid detection.

SKILLS AND EXERCISES

Parachuting - JTF2 practices two methods of parachuting - HAHO and HALO - which allow its operators to infiltrate undetected into a particular area. In HAHO, or high altitude, high opening, the commando exits the aircraft at a height of more than 9,000 metres and opens his parachute after free-falling several hundred metres. Once deployed, the parachute then acts as a glider and the soldier can fly along for tens of kilometres towards his target. The U.S. Navy's SEAL Team Six used HAHO to glide more than 15 kilometres onto an island off the coast of Puerto Rico. On a radar screen the soldier and parachute are barely visible. A Global Positioning System might also be used to help the JTF2 operator in directing his parachute to a specific area. The British SAS are reportedly the record-holders for the longest distance traveled using HAHO. In the early 1980s, an SAS team opened its parachutes off the coast of England and glided into France.

When British and American special forces were contemplating an attack in the 1980s against Libya's chemical weapons plants, one plan called for using operatives employing HAHO from a commercial jetliner. The airliner would be flying a regular route near Libya when the team would exit and glide to its target. Presumably the Libyans wouldn't suspect a commercial aircraft and the HAHO team wouldn't appear on a radar screen.

In HALO, or high altitude, low opening, the special forces soldier again exits the aircraft at around 9,000 metres but does not open his parachute until approximately 760 to 1,300 metres above the ground. Before the parachute has been opened, the commando freefalls most of the distance, using hand movements to stabilize himself. On an enemy radar screen, a JTF2 operator would be indistinguishable from a bird. HALO was used to insert SAS patrols into Iraq during the Persian Gulf War.

At the extreme exit heights of both HALO and HAHO, special forces soldiers have to be prepared to deal with ice buildup on their goggles and chest-mounted altimeters. As well, both HAHO and HALO require the use of an oxygen system for the soldier because of the high altitude from which they exit the aircraft. The Canadian Army plans to spend $520,000 for a new oxygen apparatus for its HAHO and HALO operations. JTF2 works closely with the Canadian Parachute Training Centre in Trenton, Ontario, both on equipment and practicing HAHO/HALO infiltration techniques.

Underwater operations -JTF2 places a great deal of emphasis on scuba diving, mainly for covert infiltration. Photos and video released by the unit show its operators using a breathing apparatus attached to a pack on a soldiers' chest. Although no further details have been made public, it can be assumed that like many special forces units, JTF2 would employ the German-made Drager system. The Drager is a closed-circuit breathing apparatus that allows an operator to remain underwater for up to four hours. It uses a soda lime cartridge, which not only purifies the air the soldier breathes through his mouthpiece, but prevents bubbles from forming on the surface of the water or underwater.

Close Personal Protection (CPP) - Bodyguard work, in two and four-man teams, for overseas missions accounts for much of JTF2's current operations. JTF2 has guarded Defence Minister Art Eggleton during his trips to Bosnia as well as various generals on visits to Canadian missions such as in Eritrea. CPP has been a double-edged sword for JTF2. Although it has given the unit a profile among senior leaders, it has also resulted in security breaches. Most of the readily identifiable public photos of JTF2 operatives, from Zaire to Eritrea, have come from this kind of bodyguard work.

The SAS and U.S. Army's Delta Force do close protection work but only if the threat level is extremely high and the likelihood of an attack on the person being protected is imminent. Otherwise they stay away from such duties because of the very security problems JTF2 has encountered. For instance, in the case of the Canadian VIP mission to Eritrea, where the threat level was low, neither the SAS nor Delta would have taken on such an operation. Such duties would have been left to military police or regular force soldiers.

JTF2 does close personal protection for military and political officials only when they are overseas or visiting a theatre of operations. For instance, when Defence Minister Art Eggleton and the Chief of the Defence Staff Raymond Henault visited CFB Esquimalt in Victoria in October, 2001, to bid farewell to sailors heading off to the war on terrorism, they were accompanied by two RCMP close personal protection officers.

Rappelling -Like all other special operations units, JTF2 uses rappelling as a quick-entry method for counter-terrorism missions. For example, operators slide down rappel ropes on the outside of an embassy to gain access to a balcony or window, or as a means to exit a hovering helicopter. A JTF2 team can rappel down to the ground from a helicopter hovering 20 metres in the air in less than seven seconds. Rappelling is also used to descend rough terrain and cliff faces.

The unit's rappelling equipment is all based on commercial rock climbing gear. An 11 mm diameter black polyester rope is used as the rappel line. That rope is run through a "figure-8 descender" which is attached to a climbing harness worn by the JTF2 soldier. The figure-8 allows the commando to control the speed of his descent down the rappel rope. Locking carabiners, oval-shaped aluminum devices through which the rope is threaded, are used to secure rappel lines to roofs and to the Griffon helicopter.

Another climbing technique that JTF2 uses is called jumaring. It involves having a JTF2 operator climb up a rope using mechanical ascender devices called jumars. The jumars are attached to the rope and are capable of sliding upwards while a locking system prevents them from sliding back down. An operator is either clipped into the jumars by a carabiner or has his feet in a sling attached to the jumars. Using two jumars at once, an operator can move up a fixed climbing rope until he reaches the intended target, perhaps a balcony or rooftop. JTF2 soldiers are also taught solo-climbing techniques which involve scaling a rock face or the outside of a building without the safety of a rope. For practicing climbing skills, JTF2 has an extensive indoor rock-climb-

ing wall at the Dwyer Hill Training Centre gymnasium. As well, JTF2 operators sometimes travel to the area of Canmore-Exshaw, Alberta to practice climbing on cliffs there.

Assault Techniques -Generally, during a hostage-taking at an embassy or in
a building, civilian police will establish inner and outer perimeters. The outer
perimeter is used to keep the public and news media safely away from the
site. In the inner perimeter, JTF2 would deploy its snipers on nearby rooftops
or other key positions. The initial job of the sniper/observer teams would be
to collect intelligence about what was happening in the building. They would
note the number of terrorists, how they were armed and, if possible, determine the number of hostages being held.

The JTF2 assault team would study the blueprints of the structure and determine where best to enter the building from several different locations. Then
explosives specialists would determine the best type of charges to use to blast
open entry points. Depending on the complexity of the mission, JTF2 might
build a full-scale replica of parts of the building to be attacked and practice on
that structure.

Previous hostage rescues by other elite units indicate that shortly before an
assault is to begin a diversion might first be created. One method, such as that
employed by Dutch special forces units in freeing hostages held in 1977 by
South Moluccan terrorists, might be to use low-flying fighter aircraft. The intense noise created by a fly-past of two Starfighters during that Dutch hostage-rescue mission was enough to temporarily distract the terrorists as the
assault team launched its raid. In any type of assault, JTF2 snipers would try
to kill as many terrorists as possible from the outset.

In a large embassy or residence, JTF2 might follow the model used by Peruvian and SAS special forces for their respective raids in Lima in 1997 and
London in 1980. One team might start on the upper floor of a building and
work downwards while the other would gain entry on the ground floor or
from underground such as from tunnels. All of those hostages rescued would
be handcuffed as a precaution. Such tactics are needed since past examples,
such as the SAS raid on the Iranian embassy in London, show that any surviv-
ing terrorists might try to hide among the hostages.

Similar tactics would be followed in a takedown of a plane or bus but in
those cases the assault team has an even more dangerous job since there are a

limited number of entry points on such a target. As well, once inside a bus or plane, there is less space to move around and fewer areas for the assault team to take cover from a terrorist who is shooting at them. For instance, during its ultimately successful December 26, 1994, raid on a hijacked Air France passenger jet in Marseilles, nine GIGN operatives were wounded.

Close Quarter Battle Training -Over the last two decades, firearms tactics for counter-terrorism work have evolved. Like many units, JTF2 operators still practice the "double tap" - a technique where two bullets are quickly fired off at the terrorist usually to the chest or head. In one drill, JTF2 commandos, with their backs to their targets, quickly turn around and fire two shots. In another drill, they quickly move away from the target, suddenly stop and turn, and then open fire, again with two shots.

But the SAS has realized that the double-tap may not always be enough to kill an attacker outright. An especially dangerous situation can develop if the terrorist, armed with a bomb, is not killed immediately. Even in his dying moments, a terrorist could detonate such a device. For that reason, the SAS has adopted a rapid-fire method. A whole pistol ammunition clip, some 15 to 20 rounds, is emptied at almost point-blank range into a terrorist over the course of a few seconds. Few ever survive such an onslaught. Although it not known for certain, it's expected that, like other special operations groups, JTF2 has followed the SAS-lead and has adopted this technique.

JTF2's ongoing emphasis on small arms training results in severe wear and tear on its firearms. In 1999 alone, JTF2 spent $245,000 on weapon parts, mainly for its MP-5 sub-machineguns and SIG-Sauer pistols.

EXERCISE SCENARIOS

Despite its move to green operations, JTF2 still spends a large amount of its time training for hostage-rescue and counter-terrorism missions. In 1999 and 2000, it held several such exercises to hone its skills:

In two, dubbed "Running Water" and "Poseidon's Eye 3," the emphasis was on practicing maritime counter-terrorism skills, an area that JTF2 decided it needed to develop further. "Running Water" involved a JTF2 raid on a ship that had been pirated by terrorists and sailed into a Canadian harbor. Once there, the terrorists planned to release a toxic substance. During the exercise, the unit, after receiving its initial orders from the Deputy Chief of the Defence

Staff, moved into position to launch its attack. Canadian Forces aircraft provided "real-time" intelligence by overflying and photographing the vessel. Once in place, JTF2 then received approval from the Chief of the Defence Staff to take out the "badgers" (Canadian military terminology for terrorists) who were on the ship.

"Exercise Poseidon's Eye 3" was designed to develop interoperability between JTF2 and the Canadian Navy so this scenario concentrated more on practicing beach-landings and using high-speed boats to board terrorist-held ships. A small JTF2 team practiced their shooting skills, firing at 45-gallon drums and using 2,200 rounds of small arms ammunition in the brief exercise. Also practiced were extraction maneuvers on the beachhead and linking up with small naval craft. "Poseidon's Eye 3," while a challenging scenario, had its problems. Boat motors continually broke down, radio communications were inadequate, and a planned live-fire exercise on targets towed behind ships had to be scrapped.

For "Exercise Bus Stronghold," a terrorist group staged a car accident as a pretext to stop, and then hijack, a busload of school kids. In all, 20 masked terrorists, played by Canadian Forces personnel, were involved in taking over the vehicle. In this scenario, the hostages included five teachers and 25 "students," again all played by military personnel. Initially, RCMP Emergency Response Teams surrounded the bus and negotiators began to deal with the terrorists, led by the "Commandante." Terrorist demands included the release of 172 political prisoners held in overseas prisons as well as an aircraft so the hijackers could safely leave Canada.

The negotiations continued until the terrorists killed one of the teachers. At that point, the RCMP handed over control of the situation to JTF2. The unit had a list of "doves," terminology to denote hostages, who were on board. As well, the few hostages who had been released earlier were questioned by JTF2 officers to gather any usable information about the terrorists and their weapons. The training exercise ended with a JTF2 raid, in which all the terrorists, except for the Commandante, were killed.

"Exercise Bold Staedtler" involved the JTF2 takedown of a commercial jetliner seized by terrorists. During that scenario, one passenger, who tried to escape, had already been shot. A few more, who had been released, were questioned by intelligence officials to gather any information about the terrorists.

JTF2 was flown into the airport at night on a CC-130 Hercules to take up its assault positions. Although the actual attack went off without a hitch, "Bold Staedtler" emphasized some of the problems that could result from such quick-reaction missions. There was an initial delay in the unit deploying JTF2 operators because some of them did not have their equipment ready to immediately put on board the Hercules transport aircraft. As well, "Bold Staedtler" was plagued by poor communications, resulting in additional delays in putting JTF2 members on alert.

The need for better communications was also highlighted in "Exercise Quadrant Brief," a JTF2 assault on a "hijacked" CC-150 Polaris aircraft. In the lead-up to the attack, there was poor communication between JTF2, not only among its soldiers, but with the Ontario Provincial Police which was taking part in the exercise. There were also problems in understanding battle procedures and which individual soldiers were responsible for which specific tasks. "Major education is required of how we should be doing business," the JTF2 after-action report determined. "A large number of shortfalls have been identified which must be addressed to ensure as a unit we are ready to fight in all respects."

WEAPON SAFETY

Safe weapons handling is a priority for any counter-terrorism team and at JTF2 proper procedures are strictly enforced. One JTF2 sniper received a $400 fine after he fired his rifle without proper authorization during a demonstration on October 21, 1999. Negligent discharges, where a gun is fired accidentally, result in fines ranging from $100 to $400 depending on the severity of the incident. Many negligent discharges happen during "transition drills" when a JTF2 operator finishes firing one weapon and quickly moves to using another. During the quick switch between firearms, a gun may go off accidentally. Persistent problems in weapons handling can mean immediate removal from JTF2 with the soldier being sent back to his home unit. Such punishment was handed out in 1998 to one commando who continued to have negligent discharges and safety violations during transition drills.

Other weapons accidents can be overlooked, depending on the particular circumstances. In November, 1999, a JTF2 soldier put two live rounds into an MP-5 sub-machinegun during exercises that required simulation ammunition.

The MP-5 had been outfitted with a simulation barrel device, an insert that fits into the machinegun. When the real bullet was fired it blew the simulation insert from the barrel and across the room. There were no injuries. A military police investigation determined the incident was an accident and that no range procedures had been broken. The JTF2 soldier involved was not punished.

TRAINING ACCIDENTS

JTF2's rigorous and realistic training scenarios, regularly involving live explosives and ammunition, can result in injuries. The most serious injury so far reported from JTF2 exercises took place in June, 1994, during "Exercise Praetorian" in Victoria when a non-commissioned officer lost his hand because of a malfunctioning stun grenade. There have also been some other close calls. In June, 1999, during close quarter battle training at Dwyer Hill, faulty ammunition blew apart a machinegun barrel but no injuries were reported.

In August, 1999, a JTF2 mobility operator received minor injuries when, during driver training, he tried to conduct a high-speed cornering maneuver. His vehicle went out of control and rolled over. During a November 9, 1999 practice assault on an aircraft, a reservist, playing the role of a terrorist, was injured when a stun grenade detonated too close to him. He was hospitalized for two days and later required plastic surgery. The reservist's injuries involved third-degree burns and a gash to his right thigh.

Rappelling can be another source of accidents. In April 2001, a JTF2 candidate was hospitalized with serious injuries when he fell eight metres during a rappelling exercise from the Method of Entry Building roof at Dwyer Hill. It was later determined that a piece of his clothing had gotten caught in the figure-8 rappel device.

RESEARCH AND DEVELOPMENT

Behind JTF2 is the research and development branch of the Department of National Defence. Defence scientists have conducted advanced studies for the counter-terrorism unit, in particular, in the area of scuba diving to enable JTF2 personnel to operate beneath the water's surface for longer periods. The scientists have developed an electric, closed-circuit hot-water heating system for underwater operations and, as well, are studying how to improve communications between divers.

Simulation is another increasingly important area for special forces. The U.S. Air Force Special Operations group uses the Combat 2 Talon Trainer to prepare its pilots for missions with as little as 48 hours notice. Sitting in the simulator, the aircrews can "fly" hostage-rescue missions or simulate inserting or extracting special forces teams. Canadian defence scientists are developing similar systems for pilots.

One of the more innovative devices developed by military researchers for special operations on land is a simulation program that can recreate, in 3-D, a highly detailed map of urban areas. Developed by Defence Research Establishment Valcartier and the Harris Corporation, the system allowed counter-terrorism planners at the April, 2001 Summit of the Americas in Quebec City to determine where best to place their snipers and react to threats against the international leaders at the event. The program recreated, in three-dimension on a computer screen, all of the buildings in downtown Quebec City where the summit was held. Using those images, sniper teams could determine their best vantage points. The computer program was also instantly able to determine the distance from a sniper team location to its target. Real-time images were also collected by the system, which gave security planners an immediate picture of what was happening on the ground and allowed them to monitor threats as they developed. JTF2 could use the system to create a three-dimensional model of any city landscape it has to operate in, at home or overseas.

"PERFORMANCE ENHANCEMENT"

Special operations by their very nature involve the need for incredible physical stamina. It's not unusual for troops to carry more than 45 kilograms of gear when on a mission. JTF2 operators may be required to be awake for days as they stake out a hijacked aircraft or conduct covert intelligence-gathering missions. A rapid burst of energy may be required for the crucial moments of a hostage rescue. While special operations troops spend long hours on physical fitness, being in the field on a mission can go far beyond what the human body is capable of enduring on its own. To deal with such situations, the special forces community has turned to various ways to "enhance" a soldier's performance. For Green Beret operations during the Persian Gulf War, particularly those requiring soldiers to carry large amounts of equipment in their backpacks, military doctors prescribed a weight-lifting regime with a high-carbohydrate diet shortly before the mission.

In the early 1990s, defence scientists from Canada, Australia, Britain, the U.S. and New Zealand undertook a research project to determine what kind of performance-enhancement drugs its special forces could safely use. The Canadian Forces has declined to release the results of that study and the recommendations it made for JTF2 for reasons of national and international security.

The Australians, however, have had no such qualms. In 1999, Australia issued guidelines, based on the international study, for its Special Air Service Regiment, 1 Commando Regiment and 4th Battalion Royal Australian Regiment, all of which handle special operations duties. Commanders and military doctors were given briefings on the dosage of specific drugs soldiers could take as well as the side effects to expect. Chris Forbes-Ewan, the senior nutritionist at Australia's Defence Science and Technology Organization, acknowledged that while many of the drugs studied are banned in international sports competitions, their use in wartime is a different matter. "All's fair in love and war," he explained to the Sydney Morning Herald newspaper. "What we are trying to gain is an advantage over any potential adversary. What we will have is a head-start."

More than 50 performance-enhancing drugs were rejected by the international group of defence scientists, which, in the end, approved six methods that special forces soldiers can use. They include:

Caffeine - Good old java was found to significantly boost endurance. For special operations, troops would take tablets containing the equivalent of six or seven cups of strong instant coffee.

Energy drinks -Commercially-made sports drinks such as Gatorade were deemed necessary to keep up performance in the field. Such drinks not only rehydrate a soldier but also replace electrolytes and carbohydrates lost during excessive exercise.

Modafinil - Modafinil, a medication prescribed for those with sleep problems, was found to be effective in keeping troops alert for long periods. Unlike amphetamines, Modafinil increases alertness without side effects such as anxiety. The drug was also determined to be more effective than caffeine. In testing, soldiers who took Modafinil were able to work for 60 hours straight without any problems and then sleep soundly.

Ephedrine - This substance, which stimulates the heart and nervous system, is banned in sports but for military purposes appears to be effective when combined with caffeine. Soldiers given caffeine and ephedrine were capable of doing short, intense amounts of physical exercise about seven per cent longer than troops who were given a placebo.

Blood-loading - This procedure involves having a soldier provide two units of whole blood, from which red blood cells are extracted, and then stored under cold conditions. Twenty-four hours before a battle or mission the small amount of red blood cells is infused back into the special forces operator. Some military scientists believe the process, which increases the body's capability to transport oxygen in the blood, results in an increased state of alertness and physical ability. In 1993, U.S. Special Forces commanders at Fort Bragg, North Carolina, started experimenting with blood-loading, also known as blood-doping.

Creatine - A typical diet will supply about one gram of creatine per day which is necessary for normal functioning of the muscles. Creatine is found in small quantities in foods such as meat and fish but for special forces' purposes the substance would have to be taken as a supplement, usually in the form of a power (a soldier would be required to eat 10 kilograms of meat a day to get the needed performance enhancement that creatine is believed to deliver). Creatine can boost an individual's anaerobic work capacity by up to nine per cent for a short period. It is also the one supplement the Canadian Forces will publicly discuss. After discovering that many of its soldiers, JTF2 as well as regular ranks, were using creatine, the Defence department issued recommended guidelines in 1999 for dosages. A daily intake of 10 to 20 grams of creatine for five days is considered effective. But the military has recommended that after that period, the daily dosage should be dropped to two to four grams since creatine levels can reach a saturation point in the body. The Defence department has also warned JTF2 and other soldiers about overuse of creatine as excessive levels of the substance are accumulated in the kidneys. Some users of creatine powder have reported nausea, diarrhea and abdominal cramps.

Another method being researched by Canadian military scientists to enhance JTF2 performance is the use of Respiratory Heat and Moisture Exchangers. Sports medicine doctors have examined this method over the years with varying results. Some believe it improves endurance in cold weather or dry climate conditions such as those found in the desert. The method involves using a device, inserted into the mouth, that will pre-moisten and heat air as it is drawn into the body. That reduces the amount of work, and thus calories, the body uses in heating and moistening incoming air. But other physicians don't believe that respiratory heat and moisture exchangers add anything to the body's performance and, in fact, may actually hinder it. Since the system requires using a special breathing device or mask, which can be heavy and cumbersome, a soldier may be burning up more calories than he saves.

ABOVE: U.S. military special forces member with an M-203 grenade launcher. JTF2 uses a Canadian-made version of the same launcher. (PHOTO COURTESY U.S. DEPARTMENT OF DEFENSE)

TOP: *JTF2 works closely with civilian police tactical teams who would be the first to respond to any terrorist attack. (PHOTO BY AUTHOR)*

ABOVE: *Israel's military has become expert over the years in battling terrorist groups. (PHOTOS BY AUTHOR)*

OPPOSITE PAGE: *A JTF2 assaulter takes aim with his MP-5 sub-machinegun during hostage-rescue training at Dwyer Hill. (COURTESY DND TRAINING VIDEO)*

TEN: FROM SELECTION TO SUPPORT

WHAT MAKES A JTF2 SOLDIER

Retired Colonel Michael Barr, a founding member of the Canadian Airborne Regiment and graduate of both Royal Marine Commandos and U.S. Special Forces courses, believes that a JTF2 operator must have a highly unique blend of qualities and skills. "Not unlike other special forces of the world, JTF2 soldiers are trained to operate in small teams," he explains. "Selection therefore is designed to find the individualist with a sense of self discipline, rather than the soldier who is primarily a good member of the team."

The self-disciplined individualist will always fit well into a group when teamwork is required, according to Barr, while at the same time retain the ability to work on his own when necessary. "Essentially the qualities needed are initiative, self discipline, independence of mind, ability to work unsupervised, stamina, patience and, believe it or not, a sense of humor," says Barr. "In their selection, instructors look for people they can live with during long periods of isolation, basically compatible souls who are not rigid loners, maniac teetotalers or fanatics of any kind."

Former SAS operator Alan Bell says that a special operations soldier is a "grey man. He doesn't have a fifty-inch chest and he doesn't have big pecs and he can't do 2,000 sit-ups," explains Bell. "He's Mr. Joe Blow on the street who blends in."

SELECTION OF JTF2 OFFICERS

A selection board comprised of senior National Defence Headquarters officers reviews the files of candidates nominated for Commanding Officer of JTF2. Criteria and personal attributes that are considered important include leadership, experience, maturity, vision, commitment and fitness. The board's recommendation is approved by the Deputy Chief of the Defence Staff on behalf of the Chief of the Defence Staff. For senior officer and NCO positions, a JTF2 board interviews candidates and passes its recommendations on to the commanding officer, who then makes the selection. The CO also personally interviews all officer candidates. Selection criteria for senior JTF2 leadership positions are similar to those used by the CO selection board.

SELECTION OF JTF2 SOLDIERS

Unlike the selection criteria for JTF2's commanding officer, the requirements for JTF2's operators have evolved considerably over the years. Here are examples of JTF2 selection messages sent out to Canadian Forces units in 1994 and 1999 (some of the wording has been slightly altered to fully spell out the military acronyms and abbreviations; the 1999 message has not changed significantly for year 2000-2001 selection):

CANFORGEN/94/ADM (PER)

SUBJECT: Joint Task Force Two Personnel Selection.

1) Joint Task Force Two is the CF unit responsible for counter-terrorism operations and armed assistance to civil power activities. Approximately 40 personnel in the rank of Master Corporal/Corporal, five Sergeants and two Captains are needed to top up the manning requirements of the unit and to offset the first rotation of personnel. These personnel will be drawn from regular force volunteers across the CF for a minimum tour of duty of four years (except for officers, two years).

2) Volunteers must be mentally and physically prepared to complete a very rigorous screening process. Successful candidates will possess exceptional leadership, instructional and weapon handling skills. Maturity and pro-

fessional ambition will also be important factors. Personnel who previously volunteered and participated in either phase two regional screening or a phase three selection course are asked to confirm their desire to proceed with training. Selection will be done in three phases and be followed by a basic course. It will be competitive both against a set standard and against other candidates. Only a percentage at each phase of the selection process will go on to the next phase. Those who complete the three phases will attend a basic course commencing 6 March, 1995 and if successful will continue team training until posted to the unit. The first three months at the unit are considered OJT (on the job training) and the candidate is still evaluated.

3) Selection phases are as follows:

 A. Phase 1. Unit Commanding officer screening and recommendation based on criteria listed at paragraph 4.

 B Phase 2. JTF2 selection team visits regional centres September 13 to October, 21, 1994.

 C. Phase 3. Series of six day selection sessions in Ottawa from November 5, 1994 to January, 13, 1995.

4) Phase 1 selection criteria as follows:

- Unit Commanding officer recommendation.
- Minimum of four years service with a minimum of three years left in current engagement.
- No known phobias such as fear of heights/confined areas/water etc.
- Minimum medical category 323325.
- Excellent physical condition. Minimum standard is as follows:
- One and a half mile run in maximum time of 11 minutes
- Forty consecutive non stop push-ups
- Five consecutive overhand grip, straight arm pull-ups
- Forty sit-ups in one minute
- Sixty five kilogram bench press (four inches from chest/full arm extension)
- Commanding officers are to have volunteers report to nearest location where above fitness standards will be verified. Member will be asked to carry out each fitness standard consecutively and to the best

level of ability (i.e. Best time, maximum number of repetitions and maximum weight for bench press)

1999 SELECTION

CANFORGEN 043/99 JOINT TASK FORCE (JTF 2) PERSONNEL SELECTION 1999. CANFORGEN 043/99 Adm (HR-Mil) 038 131012Z May 99

1. Intro: JTF 2 is the unit responsible for federal level counter-terrorist/hostage-rescue operations. This mandate demands personnel who possess very specific personal attributes and capabilities and who can be trained to perform a diverse range of unique tactics, techniques and skills.

2. The unit is comprised of three categories (cat) of employment: a. Cat A - Special Operation Assaulters (ASLTRS) who are directly employable in the tactical aspects of counter-terrorist/hostage rescue and other high value tasks. This cat is open to both genders of any MOC (Military Occupation) and rank from Private to Major. They must be volunteers and are selected based on successful completion of a selection process and the Special Operations Assaulter course (SOAC).

    b. Cat B - consists of personnel who are employable in combat support tasks during JTF2 ops. This cat is comprised of two groups as follows: 1) Mobility - this is a recently established group tasked with tactical mobility and other combat support tasks (eg. fire support). Members receive skills training in JTF 2 which will include high speed tactical driving in a variety of vehicles and watercraft plus extensive training with crew-served and personal weapons. This group is open to both genders of any MOC and rank from private to warrant officer. Cat B (mobility) members must be volunteers and are selected based on the completion of the selection process and successful completion of the skills training.

    Specialists - selected explosive technicians, radio operators and medics provide specialty skills that are directly related to their MOC. Cat B (specialists) should be volunteers and are selected based on their superior trade skills, the recommendations from their commanding officers and career manager, a review of their career and personnel file and finally a personal interview conducted by JTF 2.

    c. Cat C - consists of service support personnel who are selected from

Regular Force MOCs to fulfill JTF 2 support requirements. Members are selected from those who are volunteers, and those personnel identified and recommended by COs and career managers for service with JTF 2. A review of their career, personnel file and an interview by JTF 2 will be conducted.

3. Screening of CF volunteers for cat A and B (Mobility) will take place from May 10 to August 13, 1999. Pre-requisites are as follows:

a   Medical category - 32225;

b   Applicants must have a minimum of three years service and be eligible for a second basic engagement (BE) prior to commencement of Phase IV skills training.

c   Reservists must have a minimum of three years service and be prepared to commit to a three year period of service on completion of skills training.

ii)   Phase I - initial application at unit level:

d   Applicant volunteers through his/her chain of command;

e   Application for service with JTF 2 form to be completed by the applicant's unit;

f   Unit security officer is to have applicant sign a completed TBS 330-23 and to ensure it is included with member's application package.

g   Applicant undergoes PT test (Cooper's test) which must be administered at a CF gym. Min standard for the PT test is as follows:

i)   1 1/2 mile run - 11 minutes or less;

ii)   pushups (no rest stops) - minimum 40;

iii)   sit-ups (1 minute) - minimum 40;

iv)   overhand, straight arm chin-ups - minimum 5;

v)   bench press (4 inches from chest to full arm extension - 1 press minimum) minimum 65 kilograms Note: the overall test scoring is based on an aggregate point system. Historically, no one with a total score of less than 75 points has ever successfully completed the cat A and B selection process (i.e. achieving the bare minimum standard in each exercise as indicated above will not be sufficient to attain those 75 points).

vi) Unit to forward complete application package.

a) Application for service with JTF 2 form;

b) Cooper's test results;

c) Personnel file; and

d) Applicant's conduct sheet (if applicable);

e) No financial commitment to be made at this stage

c. Phase II screening:

1) Screening will be conducted at the respective locations and will include a diagnostic test to assess IQ/spatial recognition, and an interview;

2) Phase II documentation to commanding officer for onward transmission to Dwyer Hill Training Centre

d. Phase III selection process:

1) Cat A and Cat B (Mobility) - suitable applicants will be invited to attend one of the nine-day selection sessions. (This includes a six day selection process and three days administration) to be conducted at Dwyer Hill Training Centre in Ottawa between October 9 to November 27, 1999;

2) officer applicants will remain for two additional days for further evaluation;

3) the selection process is designed to assess if applicants are likely to succeed during the Special Operations Assaulters Course (SOAC) and mobility skills training and assess if they possess the personal attributes required for employment within the unit. These selection sessions are demanding and push applicants to their physical and mental limits;

4) applicants will undergo endurance runs of up to 10 km in PT kit interspersed with circuit training stands every 200 - 500 metres (eg. push-ups, sit-ups, squat thrusts, dips, fireman and deadman lifts, wind sprints, skipping). Applicants must complete runs with their peer group within a stringent fixed time margin;

5) applicants undergo phobia tests for water, heights and confined spaces;

6) individual and group tasks assess the applicants psychological profile, interpersonal and problem solving skills;

7) applicants must negotiate various obstacle courses dressed in PT kit or burdened with combat clothing, boots, helmet and other equipment. These assess physical dexterity/agility/strength/ coordination/speed and accuracy of reaction and power of recall;

8) tests are conducted in high stress tactical settings to assess the applicants ability to recall instructions, identify and react to threats, safely handle

weapons and make decisions in dynamic environments while under physical and mental duress and to assess his/her ability to assimilate new skills;

9) officer selection is in two parts - Part 1 - the officer will be required to successfully complete the six-day selection process. Part 2 - an additional two days - will assess the officer applicant's organization, analytical, communication and presentation skills under continued physical and mental duress;

10) the decision to progress an applicant onto skills training will be based on a review of overall performance up to that point;

11) successful applicants will be informed that they are loaded onto skills training by message and joining instructions;

12) unsuccessful applicants will be informed by message;

13) given the extensive resources expended during the screening and selection phases an applicant will only be granted a maximum of three attempts at phase III after which his/her application will not be considered again; e. Skills training: 1) Cat A and B (Mobility) - those members selected will be on restricted posting to JTF 2 and will attend training during the period April to August, 2000. Cat A and B (Mobility) members can expect a fixed four-year posting as an initial posting to JTF 2. Cat C members can expect a normal four to six year posting.

JTF 2 will commence screening CF members for Cat B (Specialists) and Cat C in January, 2000 to fill MOC specific position in 2000.

a. Volunteers for support positions and those personnel identified by COs and career managers will have their file reviewed by JTF 2 to verify their suitability based on job performance, skills, qualifications and personnel profile;

b. Selected members will be invited to Dwyer Hill for further screening which will consist of the Cooper's test, further evaluation of their trade/military skills and an interview;

c. Those members invited to Dwyer Hill will be informed of their selection status. Conclusion - the operational effectiveness of JTF 2 directly affects the interest of Canadian public safety, security and the fight against terrorism. The nature of its roles demands that intensive training be continually conducted to ensure precision skills are honed to the finest extent possible. Members must be operationally effective and ready to deploy at extremely short notice throughout their tour in JTF 2 - this environment results in a unique lifestyle and demands that the right people be selected for the job. JTF 2 provides an extremely challenging and rewarding career/life experience for its members. The wealth of skills, knowledge and experience gained by JTF 2 members serves to benefit not only the member but the CF as a whole.

With this in mind it is urged that any interest in volunteering for service with JTF 2 be supported to the fullest extent possible.

Questions regarding JTF 2 screening and selection should be directed to the Dwyer Hill Training Centre Recruiting Sergeant using the toll free number 1-800-959-9188.

COOPER'S TEST

The Cooper's Test referred to in the above message is a physical fitness regime developed in the early 1970s and used by Delta Force and the British SAS in its evaluation of potential operators. The Cooper's Test requirements, designed by former U.S. Air Force Dr. Kenneth H. Cooper, are outlined as JTF2's basic, minimum fitness quota for prospective recruits. As listed, the Cooper's Test consists of a one-and-a-half mile run in a maximum of 11 minutes, 40 consecutive push-ups, five consecutive overhand grip straight arm pull-ups, 40 sit-ups in one minute and the 65-kilogram bench press. JTF2 requires that a recruit have a total score of at least 75 of 100 points, but obviously those who score higher will be more readily acceptable for further training with the unit. To achieve 100 points (20 points per event) in the Cooper's test, a JTF2 candidate would have to accomplish the following: a one-and-a-half mile run in under eight minutes, 45 seconds, 58 continuous push-ups, 58 sit-ups in one minute, 14 overhand pull-ups with a full extension and a bench press of about 110 kilograms.

PAY

Complaints among JTF2 soldiers about their salaries were solved by the Canadian military leadership in May, 1998, when it instituted a special hazard allowance for the unit. Now JTF2 operators are among the highest paid in the Canadian Forces (outside of senior officers) if their hazard pay is factored in.

Details of what constitutes a particular hazard level are sketchy but it is assumed that it reflects the equivalent of a low-threat environment at its lowest level to wartime service at its highest. In 2000-2001, a JTF2 operator with less than five years service would receive $368 extra a month for level 1, $671 for level 2 and $1,067 for hazard level 3. Someone with five years or more would receive $428, $729 and $1,132 respectively.

COMMANDING OFFICERS

JTF2 has had a wide variety of commanders and deputy commanders over the years with varying backgrounds. Strong administrative and command skills, as opposed to a special operations background, were, and still are, key attributes for JTF2 commanders. As JTF2 captains and majors climb up the rank structure, it is possible that the unit could eventually see a commanding officer who has been totally immersed in special operations, almost from the beginning of his career. At the same time, the senior officers who commanded JTF2 may be eventually promoted to generals, giving those well informed about the unit's capabilities key roles in the senior rank structure. That presumably could mean an even more expanded role for JTF2.

Some JTF2 officers, such as Lieutenant Colonel David E. Barr, have had a strong special operations background. Barr served as deputy commanding officer of the unit in 1995 and was well respected for his unconventional warfare training and his operational experience. Barr entered the Royal Military College in 1976, graduating four years later with a Bachelor of Arts in Political Science, and a Commission in the Princess Patricia's Canadian Light Infantry. His early regimental duty with the PPCLI consisted of seven consecutive years of platoon commanding, beginning with two years as a Rifle Platoon Commander and two more as the Reconnaissance Platoon Commander with the Third Battalion PPCLI in Victoria, British Columbia. In 1984 he was posted to the Canadian Airborne Regiment, where he commanded a Rifle Platoon for one year in 2 Commando, and the Regimental Pathfinder Platoon in his final two years. During these years he completed the United States Army Ranger Course, and the Military Freefall Parachutist Course. Following that were postings back to 3PPCLI and a 1992-93 operational deployment to Croatia as part of the United Nations' Protection Force. In 1993-94 Barr attended the Canadian Forces Command and Staff College in Toronto, which was followed by a posting to National Defence Headquarters in Ottawa as the Coordinating

Staff Officer in the Directorate of Land Force Development.

In 1995, he was selected to be JTF2 Deputy Commanding Officer. A year later, he was posted back to NDHQ where he served in the office of the Director General of Strategic Planning for two years. In June 1998, Barr returned for his third tour of duty with 3 PPCLI - this time as commanding officer. On March 1, 2000, Barr and the 3 PPCLI Battle Group of approximately 900 all ranks, took over responsibility for the Canadian area of operations in North Western Bosnia-Herzegovina for six months, as part of the NATO Stabilization Force (SFOR).

Colonel Barry W. MacLeod, JTF2's commanding officer from 1997 to 2000, is an example of a well-respected officer with a more conventional military background. He enrolled in the Canadian Forces in 1975 and was commissioned as a lieutenant on completion of training in 1976. After serving with 3 Royal Canadian Horse Artillery (RCHA) in a variety of positions, he was posted to 1 RCHA in Lahr, Germany in 1979 for four years. In the 1980s, he served at CFB Gagetown, New Brunswick, and later graduated from the Army Staff College and the Canadian Forces Command and Staff College. On completion of his Canadian Forces Command and Staff College course in 1987, he took command of C Battery, 1 RCHA until July 1989.

MacLeod was promoted to Lieutenant-Colonel in January 1990 when he was appointed as a senior artillery staff officer. Two years later he assumed command of the Field Artillery School at CFB Gagetown and later went on to hold several key operations and training positions. In 1997 he was appointed JTF2 commanding officer. Later promoted to colonel, he became commander at CFB Gagetown.

AWARDS

Military honors for JTF2 personnel are, for obvious security reasons, not usually made public. However, several of the unit's soldiers, in rare instances, have received public commendations from Canada's Governor General.

On June 24, 1997, Chief Warrant Officer J.A.Y. Williamson received the Order of Military Merit at Government House in Ottawa. At the time, the tall and tanned JTF2 operator had 22 years of service in the Canadian Forces, mainly in the military engineering trade. Williamson, JTF2's Regimental Sergeant Major, received his award for the integrity he has displayed in his long military service, for his work as the unit's RSM, and for the example he has set for younger soldiers.

Chief Warrant Officer F.W. Grattan received the Order of Military Merit on May 29, 1998 for his role in standing up JTF2. CWO Grattan joined the Canadian Forces in 1966, serving with the 3rd Battalion, Royal Canadian Regiment and the Canadian Airborne Regiment. He also completed three tours in Cyprus. In 1992, he was instrumental in the standing-up of JTF2 and was the senior non-commissioned officer responsible for training in the unit, ensuring it maintained its high state of operational readiness. After service with JTF2, Grattan went on to serve as the Regimental Sergeant Major of the Royal Canadian Regiment Battle School in Meaford, Ontario.

In the late 1990s, JTF2 received another honor of sorts from one of the world's most successful thriller writers. Tom Clancy used JTF2 for the background of one his characters in his computer game, *Rainbow Six*, which follows the adventures of an elite group of freelance special operations soldiers. The background of the fictional character, Roger McAllen, combined both RCMP and military training. McAllen was a former member of the Canadian Army who later joined SERT. After SERT was disbanded, he re-enlisted with the Canadian Forces, being accepted into JTF2. There he served on a variety of operations, including missions in Bosnia to hunt down war criminals.

SECONDARY SUPPORT INSTALLATIONS

JTF2 also trains at the Connaught Range, located on the Ottawa River approximately 20 minutes west of Canada's capital. The Defence department site is remote and easy to secure so that training can be conducted in seclusion. Although covering 2,600 acres (1,058 hectares), Connaught's quarters, lecture rooms, and small-arms ranges are all within walking distance of each other. Connaught is home to the Area Training Centre Detachment Ottawa, made up of army and sea cadets and is also used by regular force units. But when JTF2 shows up for training and firearms practice, the range is locked down and other shooters are asked to leave.

Another location where JTF2 trains is at the RCMP's Technical and Protective Operations Facility in the Ottawa suburb of Orleans. The site is the former Canadian military Land Engineering Test Establishment which was turned over to the federal police force in 1996. The compound has an off-road test track where drivers can practice their skills on asphalt, sand, rock and gravel surfaces. JTF2's mobility operators use the site to train in evasive counter-terrorism driving techniques.

AFFILIATED UNITS

To maintain its high degree of readiness and skill levels, JTF2 needs a continual supply of quality recruits. While the unit selects individuals from the army, navy and air force, there are some groups within the Canadian Forces whose training mirrors that of JTF2 and as a result are natural "feeder" units for the commando team.

The army's combat divers, as well as their navy counterparts, are considered among the most skilled underwater operators in the world. For parachute skills, JTF2 has a source of recruits from the three Light Infantry Battalions located at CFB Petawawa, Edmonton and Valcartier. Their training includes fighting in built-up areas, desert operations and mountain and winter warfare. The LIBs have also conducted jungle-warfare training.

Perhaps the one specialized element that mirrors JTF2 training the most is the Canadian Army's Pathfinders. Pathfinders are trained to penetrate enemy lines, using a variety of methods such as high-altitude parachuting and offshore submarine insertion. The use of assault boats and helicopters is also emphasized in Pathfinder training. Other skills include mountain warfare, combat survival, escape and evasion, and intelligence-gathering.

The Patrol Pathfinder course, operated out of the Canadian Parachute Training Centre in Trenton, Ontario, runs for 48 days. It begins with an initial two-week training period in Trenton, after which soldiers deploy to the field for the rest of the course. It is not unusual for soldiers to be awakened well before sunrise to conduct a 13-kilometre march in full kit. During escape and evasion training, the Pathfinder candidates are required to move across country while avoiding teams sent to hunt them down. To help the soldiers, there are a series of designated safehouses where they can seek shelter. During the October, 2001 Pathfinder escape and evasion test, soldiers found themselves being hunted by 14 police officers from the Durham Regional Police Tactical Support Unit. The civilian law enforcement officials used a tracking dog and a helicopter equipped with a heat sensor to try to detect the soldiers over a three-day period. All Pathfinder candidates escaped the police dragnet and made it to designated safehouses.

A typical Pathfinder course may have around 25 candidates in the beginning with significantly fewer than half expected to make the grade. Sometimes the failure rate is even higher. Of the 34 candidates who began the Pathfinder Patrol course in August, 2001, only seven graduated.

Army snipers are also a natural fit to supply JTF2 with recruits. Observation and intelligence-gathering are part of the snipers' job, besides the more obvious elimination of enemy targets. "We would go in 72 hours or more ahead of time and pass back information to a battalion or a brigade on the enemy situation," one sniper explained in a Canadian Forces publication. "It's all covert. We want to get in there and not be seen."

Canadian Army snipers still use the C-3A1 Parker Hale rifle. It is considered a capable weapon within the limitations of the 7.62 mm calibre. Newly acquired McMillian stocks and pillar bedding have enhanced the accuracy of the weapon and snipers can engage targets up to 600 metres away with very little chance of collateral damage. However the C-3A1 is at the end of its operational life in the Canadian Army and Parker Hale no longer produces parts or replacement guns. It is likely that army snipers will move towards heavier calibres such as .300 Winchester Magnum and the .338 Lapua Magnum. The standard sniper scope on the C-3A1 is the Unertal 10 power scope. Some army sniper teams have also started to receive the M-82A1 Barrett .50 calibre rifle already in use with JTF2. They have also recently redirected much of their training to emphasize urban operations, reflecting the situation the Canadian military finds itself in on many overseas deployments. Studies have shown that in urban operations, the average sniper shot is around 70 metres.

As JTF2 expands its naval counter-terrorism expertise it will likely turn to recruits from the Canadian Navy's boarding teams. In the Canadian Forces these specialized teams take on the jobs that are handled in the U.S. by SEAL teams and the Marine Force Recon. They provide the capability to quickly seize vessels as well as provide security for jetties. After the attack on the USS *Cole* by suicide bombers, Canadian naval boarding parties also started being used as upper-deck sentries.

Each of Canada's major warships carries a 20-member naval boarding party. Typically, the team is organized into two "waves." Selection is based on previous naval skills, motivation and fitness levels, and knowledge of weapons handling and safety. When not taking part in boarding operations, the sailors continue their regular assigned duties on the ship.

In their training, boarding party members master a range of skills. After 12 days of basic individual training, the teams from each ship undergo a further four days of intensive training at the Fleet School facilities at CFB Halifax. Sailors become proficient in areas such as small arms safety and marksmanship, strength training, unarmed combat, small-boat handling and search and sweep tactics. They receive instruction from legal staff on topics such as the Law of the Sea. Practice boardings are carried out on decommissioned ships, in-service warships or Coast Guard vessels.

The teams use the same firearms as JTF2, namely the MP-5 sub-machinegun and the SIG-Sauer 9 mm semi-automatic pistol. Shotguns and C8 rifles are also used. Since 1991 the navy has boarded hundreds of ships while enforcing the oil embargo and other sanctions against Iraq in the Persian Gulf. The boarding parties can access a ship in various ways. One method involves the Canadian warship maneuvering to take up a position 200 to 300 metres off the target vessel. At that point, the boarding team launches from the warship using a rigid hull Zodiac boat. Once the squad reaches the target vessel, its members will climb up a "pilot" ladder on the side of the ship. The actual entry onto the vessel is done in less than two minutes. The team's second wave can usually be inserted within five minutes of the first.

Naval boarding parties can also be inserted onto a target vessel by helicopter. One of their most high-profile missions so far was the August, 2000, boarding of the GTS *Katie* transport ship off the east coast of Canada. The *Katie*, enroute from Bosnia, was carrying more than $250 million dollars of Canadian military equipment when it became the centre of a messy financial dispute between private companies. Worried that it would not get paid for its services, the firm owning the GTS *Katie* ordered it to remain at sea, effectively holding the Canadian military hardware for ransom. On August 20, a naval boarding team, using Sea King helicopters, seized the *Katie*'s bridge.

While not specifically a "feeder" unit, the Canadian Forces Nuclear Biological and Chemical Response Team (CFNBCRT) plays an important support role for JTF2. It is the unit that the counter-terrorism soldiers turn to for advice and information on how to deal with weapons of mass destruction. Formed in the 1970s, the team currently has 29 members but is expected to be expanded in the coming years as a result of the September 11, 2001, terrorist attacks.

Stationed at CFB Borden, Ontario, the team works closely with the RCMP's Explosive Disposal and Technology Branch. JTF2, civilian emergency preparedness planners, and the Canadian Security Intelligence Service all conduct joint training with the CFNBCRT, using various scenarios involving terrorists armed with weapons of mass destruction. Typical is Exercise Krypton Encounter 93, conducted over a two-day period in August, 1993, at CFB Trenton, Ontario. That scenario involved a highjacked aircraft flown from Europe to Canada by terrorists known to be armed with a chemical explosive device. JTF2 ended up storming the aircraft, "killing" the terrorists and capturing the weapon. The CFNBCRT then boarded the aircraft to defuse the device.

Such scenarios are valuable for the lessons learned. For instance, during Krypton Encounter 93, it was discovered that the CFNBCRT's specialized command post vehicle couldn't fit into the cargo compartment of the air force's CC-130 Hercules transport plane. Instead it had to be driven several hundred kilometres from Borden to Trenton, an unacceptable situation in the event of a real emergency.

In a September, 1994, training exercise, codenamed Klaxon Kounter, a terrorist slipped into a government building with a briefcase containing the nerve agent Tabun. The bomb accidentally detonated, "killing" the terrorist and contaminating the building. It was then up to the CFNBCRT to seal off the area and determine how best to decontaminate the site. As part of its training and to test its detection and decontamination equipment, the CFNBCRT has practiced with live chemical agents at CFB Suffield, Alberta.

LIFE AFTER JTF2

What do former JTF2 operators do after leaving the unit? Many, such as former Major Michael Rouleau, have found work in civilian police forces. JTF2 operators are particularly attractive to police tactical teams because of the wide variety of hostage-rescue skills they have. Another source of employment for former special forces operatives is in the growing field of private security work. Retired SAS soldier Alastair Morrison was among the first to tap into this lucrative market when he created Defence Systems Ltd. to provide security for business interests operating in high-risk areas. Others, such as former SAS soldier Alan Bell, who runs Globe Risk Holdings Inc. out of Toronto, provide security advice, personnel and protection for mining, oil and gas companies throughout the developing world. Some JTF2 officers have found work in this same field, particularly in Calgary where many of Canada's main resource exploration companies are based.

OPPOSITE PAGE: JTF2 soldiers practice with handguns at the Dwyer Hill Training Centre's 50-metre range. (COURTESY DND)

ELEVEN: FUTURE ROLES

EVEN BEFORE THE September 11, 2001 attacks on the United States, and the resulting war in Afghanistan, the Canadian Forces was considering a greater role for JTF2 in overseas operations.

One area that seems a natural fit involves using the unit in what the military refers to as Non-Combatant Evacuation Operations (NEO). NEO is essentially the rescue of Canadians trapped in foreign countries experiencing upheaval such as a military coup. As past experiences show, a NEO capability has been almost non-existent in the Canadian Forces. For example, in 1988, the army, navy and air force were put on alert for a potential mission to rescue Canadians caught up in political violence in Haiti. Although the tense situation on the Caribbean island eventually subsided, and Canadians were able to leave on commercial passenger jets, military planners realized the training and equipment they had for the job was totally inadequate. Not much has changed over the years. When several dozen Canadians had to be rescued because of increasing violence in Albania in 1997, British and Italian troops were called in to do the job.

Defence officials have considered using JTF2 in NEO missions since 1995. Then a military planning group examining the future of Canada's parachute capability suggested the commando unit could be a vanguard force for any such operation. Some leaders, such as Lieutenant Colonel David Pittfield, 3RCR's commanding officer in 1996, have also suggested using JTF2 as a covert reconnaissance force, similar to the role of Pathfinders, for overseas operations including NEO. A 1997 Canadian Forces College study on NEO operations also recommended employing JTF2 as a vanguard force. But it also noted that because of its limited size, the commando unit would have to rely on both helicopter airlift and manpower from allied nations. In return for such support, the study suggested that Canada offer JTF2's services to its allies for when they have to conduct NEO missions.

It was only recently, however, that military planners began moving ahead on using JTF2 in NEO operations. "Exercise Northern Brave," which took place March 19-21, 2001, in Vegreville, Alberta, is typical of how such a mission might unfold in the future. In that exercise scenario, an unnamed country had disintegrated into civil war, trapping 50 Canadians within its borders. A JTF2 reconnaissance element was the first to go into the country, not only to do detailed recce but also to develop a preliminary evacuation plan. In an actual mission, it is envisioned that JTF2 operators on the ground would be in direct contact with National Defence headquarters in Ottawa by secure satellite phone.

After the JTF2 evacuation plan was in place for "Exercise Northern Brave," the main body of troops from 3 PPCLI was used to secure the country's main airport and help Canadian citizens reach rescue aircraft. The lessons learned from "Exercise Northern Brave" outlined some of the problems associated with such an operation. It was acknowledged that Canada still has almost no capability to conduct NEO missions. As well, there were the usual equipment shortfalls. The aging jeep-like Iltis vehicle used by troops was deemed inadequate because it was slow moving and had no capability to mount machineguns or accept add-on armor. The planners involved in "Northern Brave" recommended that for future NEO missions, a fast-wheeled support vehicle should be acquired.

Another overseas role JTF2 has already reportedly conducted, and could further expand into, is in the hunt for war criminals. It could emulate its SAS counterparts who, in 2000 and 2001, conducted several "snatch" missions in Kosovo. In one operation, the SAS seized five Albanians suspected of bombing a bus that killed 11 Serb civilians.

A greater role in civilian law enforcement at home could also be in JTF2's future. A July, 2000, Defence department report suggested the Canadian Forces might have a greater presence in such domestic missions, particularly in the area of counter-smuggling. It noted that smuggling rings are now so sophisticated that they are akin to a small military organization, complete with intelligence-gathering capabilities and air support. JTF2, which conducted counter-smuggling operations against the Mohawk Warrior Society in the mid-1990s, has continued to prepare for such missions. In "Exercise Staedtler," the unit practiced a "law enforcement support scenario" involving an organized crime group smuggling weapons stolen from a government arsenal. The scenario later turned into a hostage situation and JTF2 was called in to raid the building occupied by criminals.

JTF2's mandate of handling missions that affect "national interests" could also be brought into play for border security operations. Other countries have used their special operations forces for such jobs. In August, 2001, the Australian SAS was deployed to seize a Norwegian freighter loaded with refugees. (The Australian government had denied the refugees permission to land and was worried the ship would ignore those orders). More than 30 camouflaged SAS troopers successfully seized the vessel.

WHAT JTF2 NEEDS FOR THE FUTURE
The desire to expand JTF2 into a full-fledged special forces unit similar to the U.S. Army's Delta Force or Navy SEALS will require new equipment and additional personnel.

The Canadian government's December 10, 2001 "security budget" approved $119 million for JTF2 over a five-year period but that's not much money, considering the unit has been ordered to double in size. Reportedly, JTF2 will expand from around 300 to 600 soldiers.

If JTF2 is to be effective overseas, it will have to improve in several areas. First, its firepower would have to be increased. Many special forces teams are now operating the Mk-19 automatic grenade launcher, a weapon particularly effective against ground forces. This belt-fed weapon fires a 40 mm explosive projectile up to a range of 1600 metres. Weighing in 34 kilograms, the Mk-19 is either used on a tripod or mounted on a special forces high-mobility vehicle.

JTF2 would also need some kind of reliable ground transportation for overseas use. The Mercedes Gelandenwagen that the Canadian Army wants to purchase as a replacement for the Iltis would handle some transportation needs but it is still considered too small for many of the unit's requirements. The existing light support vehicle wheeled fleet, plagued with various mechanical problems, is considered by many soldiers as too unreliable. There have also been problems with the Canadian Forces medium logistic vehicle wheeled (MLVW) fleet because of rust-out.

In contrast, Delta Force uses a variety of reliable vehicles ranging from the Humvee, commonly known as the Hummer, to the Steyr Pinzsgaur six-wheeled transport truck for its heavy-lifting requirements. Delta and other American special forces have also made extensive use of all-terrain Fast Attack Vehicles. The FAVs, capable of 130 kilometres per hour on flat terrain, were outfitted with AT4 anti-tank missile launchers and M-60 or .50 calibre machineguns. American units also used motorcycles, with heavily muffled engines, for work behind enemy lines during Operation Desert Storm.

The British SAS is in the process of receiving the Supacat all-terrain vehicle. That four-by-four vehicle will be outfitted with a Milan anti-tank guided missile, 40 mm grenade launchers and 7.62 mm machineguns. The SAS is also using the Shadow strike vehicle built by Alvis of Coventry, U.K. Designed for use in rugged terrain such as Afghanistan, the Shadow has been modified to reduce its profile on the battlefield. Alvis specifically designed the engine to be quiet and installed heat insulation to reduce the vehicle's infrared emissions. For their part, the Royal Marines have recently bought the BvS10 All Terrain Vehicle (Protected) from Hagglunds of Sweden. Similar in appearance to the Bv206, which is used in the Canadian Army, this tracked vehicle is armored and fully amphibious. It is small enough to be transported by Hercules aircraft or by the CH-47 Chinook helicopter.

Any of these specialized vehicles, but most particularly the U.S.-made Hummer would be suitable for JTF2's needs. The Hummer would provide JTF2 with the reliable transportation it needs to operate overseas. Using the Hummer would also give JTF2 the advantage of being able to obtain spare parts from the U.S. special forces units it operates with.

Larger, long-range air transportation, particularly in the area of helicopter support, would also have to be substantially improved. For insertion and extraction, the SAS uses the Chinook, capable of carrying 44 soldiers. With its lift capability of 12 tonnes, the Chinook was particularly effective during the Persian Gulf War not only for transporting SAS teams behind Iraqi lines but resupplying them once there. JTF2's counterparts in the U.S. also use larger and heavily modified helicopters such as the MH-53 Pave Low lll. The MH-53 with its rear ramp is ideal for fast-roping or allowing troops to exit via a flexible ladder being trailed from the ramp. The helicopter also has the capability for in-flight refueling for long-range work and is outfitted with mini-guns and other machineguns for protection. Heavily modified Black Hawk helicopters, also operated by U.S. special forces, are similarly armed and have in-flight refueling capabilities.

For maritime or long-range operations, JTF2 could use the Canadian Forces Sea King helicopter but there are obvious nagging questions about the reliability of the 35-year-old aircraft. In August, 2000, a Sea King was used to transport a naval boarding party to seize the GTS *Katie* cargo ship off the coast of Canada but that mission was hindered by mechanical problems. During the operation, one of the two helicopters that was to be used broke down, forcing the navy to rely on a single Sea King which then had to make two trips to the *Katie*. The actual lowering of the naval boarding team took longer than was deemed acceptable because of an ineffective and slow hoist system. "This resulted in an unacceptably long period for the helicopter to linger over the vessel," according to an after-action report produced by the air force. In total, the boarding took 45 minutes, three times as long as it would have if the Sea King had been outfitted with a modern hoist. In an actual combat special forces mission, such problems would have dire consequences.

The Canadian Air Force expects to take delivery of a replacement for the Sea Kings around 2006 but some officers estimate the older helicopters will still be flying until 2015. Until then it is likely that JTF2 will be without any kind of reliable larger long-range helicopter.

ABOVE: *Unlike the Canadian Forces, the militaries in other countries freely talk about many aspects of their elite units. Here, Norwegian special forces soldiers display some of their equipment.* (PHOTO COURTESY NORWEGIAN DEFENSE MINISTRY)

OPPOSITE PAGE: *JTF2 operators "take down" a bus during a hostage-rescue training exercise.* (COURTESY DND TRAINING VIDEO)

TWELVE: HOW MUCH SECRECY?

JTF2 IS ONE OF the most secretive units of its kind in the world and security is taken to the extreme. There is no better example than that of the JTF2 soldier who gently admonished his mother, also a member of the Canadian Forces, after she yelled out his name when she saw him at CFB Halifax. He told her that unit security is so tight she shouldn't have publicly acknowledged him.

"Quite honestly, I must admit that this is probably the only unit where operational security is constantly enforced," said another JTF2 officer.

In the past decade, the Canadian Forces has released six "official" JTF2 photographs, as well as the "Dare to Be Challenged" training video. At the beginning of the Afghan war, Defence Minister Art Eggleton and his generals insisted that almost no other details could be released about the unit since such a disclosure would put JTF2's operators at risk. Eggleton also claimed that other countries follow a similar strict policy and refuse to acknowledge any details about their elite counter-terrorism and special forces units.

Of course this isn't true. There are literally hundreds of highly detailed books, complete with officially released photos, about Delta Force, the SAS, GSG-9 and a host of other similar organizations. The Canadian military is glaringly absent from two major works on the subject, *The Illustrated Guide to the World's Top Counter-*

Terrorism Units and *The Illustrated Guide to the World's Top Naval Special Warfare Units*. Both books, by Samuel Katz, contain hundreds of color photographs of special forces operators in action as well as page after page of information on tactics and past missions. The photos, many clearly showing faces of individual soldiers as well as their weapons, were all released by the special forces units themselves.

But it is not only in the world of military literature that JTF2 is absent. More disturbing is that the unit received only a passing mention in the 1999 Senate Security and Intelligence report which dealt with Canada's preparedness to fight terrorism. For the most part, Canadian lawmakers, like the public, still remain in the dark about JTF2.

In the U.S., in particular, the American special forces community has realized the need for a controlled and limited amount of publicity, not only to send a message to the enemy about what they might face on the battlefield but also to build strong public support for such elite formations. U.S. Navy SEAL teams often stage public demonstrations, showing off their military skills to cheering American citizens who sit in bleachers watching the display of firepower and helicopter assaults. Tickets to such demonstrations are highly sought after.

Just weeks before the September 11 attacks on the U.S., the Australian government, concerned about illegal immigrants, used its Special Air Service to seize a ship full of refugees. Not only was the news media on hand to photograph the SAS soldiers heading off in Zodiac boats to storm the vessel, but journalists also identified mission commander, Lieutenant Colonel "Dirty Harry" Gilmore. Unlike JTF2, the name of Australia's SAS commanding officer and the size of the unit are public information. Both facts have not hindered the Australian SAS from conducting operations worldwide.

Even the previous Conservative government in Canada realized when it created the RCMP's SERT counter-terrorism unit that a certain amount of publicity was needed to let terrorists, as well as Canadians, know the country had such a team and was willing to use it. The RCMP toured reporters around Dwyer Hill on two occasions. Photos were taken and TV footage shot of masked SERT operators in training. No one's identity was revealed and the unit was never bothered by the news media again.

While a certain degree of secrecy is obviously needed, the total clamp-down on all information regarding JTF2 has arguably backfired on the Canadian Forces. The unit has not received any accolades, which it is due, and many Canadians, indoctrinated with the idea that their military is only used for peacekeeping, still remain blissfully unaware that JTF2 undertakes dangerous operations for the security of the country.

Some members of the current Liberal government have also questioned the wisdom of an almost total news blackout on JTF2. David Price, the one-time Conservative Member of Parliament who raised the issue of JTF2 in Kosovo, and now is a member of the Liberal Party, has questioned why Canadians couldn't be told at least some details about the unit. Price correctly noted that the British, Germans, French and Americans openly talk about their elite forces and the exceptional job they do, yet the Canadian Forces remains silent. "We have a great team," he said. "And most Canadians haven't a clue that we have these special forces out there, able to take care of us."

Even one of the country's top TV journalists couldn't convince Defence officials to budge on their JTF2 blackout. Shortly before the U.S. attacks, CBC anchor Peter Mansbridge flew to Ottawa to meet personally with Chief of the Defence Staff General Raymond Henault and try to persuade him to allow a television crew access to the Dwyer Hill Training Centre. The network was doing a series on the Canadian Forces and believed a segment on JTF2 would help inform viewers. The request was denied.

While Eggleton repeatedly talked about the need for security, the Defence department appears to have been violating JTF2's secrecy policy for years. Anyone going to the military's Web page could call up the biographies of JTF2 officers such as Colonel Barry MacLeod and deputy commander Lieutenant Colonel Dave Barr. In other cases, the department has mistakenly listed the names of current JTF2 operators in some of the documents it has released. If that weren't enough, shortly after the 1996 Zaire mission, the Canadian Forces inadvertently issued a photo of a JTF2 soldier guarding General Maurice Baril. Although the picture was supposed to illustrate Baril hard at work, two news editors picked up on the fact that the muscular armed man behind the general, his face clearly shown, was a member of the specialized unit. The photograph ran in *Esprit de Corps* magazine and the Ottawa Citizen newspaper to illustrate articles on JTF2. Soon after, a military public affairs official made a frantic phone call to *Esprit de Corps,* imploring the magazine's staff not to use the photo again. The Defence department then reissued the same picture, this time with the face of the JTF2 operator digitally blanked out. Of course, by that point the image had run in 6,000 copies of *Esprit de Corps* and almost 200,000 copies of the Ottawa Citizen.

Modern news-gathering techniques are also making it more difficult for special operations soldiers to work in the shadows. During the Persian Gulf War most journalists followed strict rules laid out by the Pentagon, which resulted in severely limiting what they saw and reported on. But other more intrepid journalists broke away from the official military-media pools and went off onto the battlefield on their own. Those that did were able to videotape and photograph U.S. special forces units in action in Kuwait City.

The Afghanistan war has taken this kind of independent reporting to a new level. Since the U.S. couldn't control access to the country, a number of journalists were on hand to record American and British special forces in action, something almost unheard of in previous years - for example, in missions in Panama and Somalia. A four-man American special operations patrol was photographed heading off into the Afghanistan countryside with Northern Alliance guides leading the way. CIA operatives arriving at a remote airstrip at Gulbahar in Northern Alliance territory were met by Western radio reporters as they got off the plane. The surprised spooks declined interviews as they were quickly hustled away by their Northern Alliance hosts.

Even more significant was the media coverage of the battle at the Mazar-e Sharif fortress in which Northern Alliance, CIA, Green Beret and SAS operators put down an uprising of Taliban fighters. A news crew videotaped the fighting and interviewed a CIA operative as the battle raged. Green Berets were shown calling in air strikes on the prison and there was footage of wounded American special forces officers being medically treated. Even the elusive SAS was captured on videotape. Video footage taken by an Afghan cameraman, and run on British television, showed SAS soldiers, their faces clearly in view, firing automatic weapons over the prison wall.

The Afghanistan war has also prompted the British to consider changing their long-standing policy about refusing to talk about SAS operations. Chief of the Defence Staff Admiral Sir Michael Boyce acknowledged that the military's official policy of not commenting on SAS missions had to be altered. Keeping SAS operations under wraps made little sense when, in the early days of the war, one of the main objectives was to put pressure on the Taliban regime to turn over al-Qaeda leader Osama bin Laden, he reasoned. After Boyce made his comments, the British military started leaking details about SAS missions, including a raid on an al-Qaeda cave network and the wounding of four SAS soldiers in that battle.

In Canada, the military leadership still embraces a confrontational attitude towards the news media and has yet to learn how to deal effectively with journalists. While U.S. Defense Secretary Donald Rumsfeld was showing off photographs of American special forces troops on horseback riding into battle against the Taliban, the Canadian military was refusing to even confirm whether JTF2 had left Dwyer Hill or not because of concerns for "operational security."

In fact, the Afghanistan campaign originally meant more secrecy than usual for JTF2. At first, Defence department officials refused to discuss the location of the commando team's base, saying such information is classified, even though Dwyer Hill is clearly identified in the Canadian Forces training videotape, "Dare To Be Challenged" issued to the news media two years ago. As well, the name of the female public affairs officer responsible for answering questions from the media about JTF2 - an easy job if ever there was one, for it usually means responding that the military can't comment on any aspect of the unit - is now considered secret. Defence planners are concerned she might be targeted by terrorists.

Officers were particularly incensed when, shortly after the government announced JTF2 would be involved in the Afghanistan campaign, National Post newspaper columnist Roy MacGregor drove out to Dwyer Hill looking for someone to talk to at the commando unit's headquarters. He chatted briefly with a gruff security guard at the gates before she sent him on his way. It never occurred to Defence department officials that journalists, when faced with a total lack of information about a subject, will rise to the occasion and start probing even further.

Such was the case with Ottawa Citizen journalist Gary Dimmock, who on October 24, 2001, reported in a front-page article the details of one of JTF2's secret counter-terrorism exercises. The night before, after receiving a tip from a source, Dimmock and a photographer drove out to the Ottawa airport where, on the south side, far from the main terminal, a Canadian Forces CC-150 Polaris Airbus had been parked. The two journalists watched 80 reservists climb on board the passenger jet to play the role of "hostages" for one of JTF2's assault exercises. After the reservists settled into the seats shortly after 6 p.m., an officer stood at the front of the plane and addressed the young, part-time soldiers. "O.K., you've heard the rumors so you can figure out who we are," said the JTF2 operator. "Just sit tight and enjoy the show."

Outside, Dimmock was looking for the best vantage point for him and his photographer to document the Polaris assault. At one point the veteran police journalist almost ran into a JTF2 operator sitting in a gold colored Suburban in a parking lot near the aircraft. The soldier briefly followed Dimmock's car but eventually decided he didn't pose a threat to security when the reporter drove and parked at a nearby golf course.

As Dimmock positioned himself, a caravan of JTF2 trucks arrived at the tarmac and the commandos began unloading their gear. In the plane, the action film Speed 2, ironically about the hijacking of an ocean liner, was being shown on the aircraft's video monitor. The reservists sat back and watched the movie, resigned to the fact that this assignment could drag on for a lengthy period. Similar JTF2 exercises at Pearson airport in Toronto and Mirabel in Quebec, had gone on for days, as "hijackers" and hostage negotiators acted out their roles.

At the front of the Polaris Airbus was one of eight "hijackers," being played by regular force soldiers. They played their parts by yelling out political slogans and warning they had pipe-bombs to blow up the plane. But unlike previous training exercises, this "hijacking" wouldn't last for days. Part way through a second video, this one the Tom Cruise spy drama, Mission Impossible 2, the hijacker, armed with a pipe bomb, started to act irrationally. "We're all going to fucking burn," he yelled out to the reservists, some of whom couldn't help but chuckle at the scripted drama.

Seconds later the lights went out in the aircraft and the JTF2 assaulters, armed with MP-5s and wearing balaclavas, began swarming through the front and rear doors. "Get your fucking heads down," one of the JTF2 operators yelled as he entered the Polaris. The first commando through the door grabbed the hijacker, stuck a gun in his face, and threw him onto the floor of the aisle. A second JTF2 soldier following closely behind tripped over the downed terrorist and landed flat on his face, while Mission Impossible: 2 played above his head on the screens. The attack was over in 10 minutes.

Outside, Dimmock and his colleague were watching and photographing the whole raid, along with members of the public who had gathered near a fence where the Polaris was located for a ringside seat of the attack. After JTF2 soldiers finished their mission, the crowd could see them unload their gear in a nearby well-lit hangar.

Military police are still searching for Dimmock's source. This was the second time the journalist sparked an investigation into the leak of JTF2 information. In February 2000 military police tried, unsuccessfully, to determine how Dimmock was able to obtain the names of commandos, their home phone numbers and JTF2 pager numbers for his series on the Darnell Bass case. A day after the journalist contacted the JTF2 members using their pagers, the phone numbers were disconnected.

As the Afghan war progressed, the lid on JTF2's secrecy was lifted somewhat. For the first time, the government announced that the unit would be used in an overseas mission, along with the number of troops it was sending and the general area where they would be operating. As well, in response to an Access to Information request, the Canadian Forces did indicate JTF2's budget in rough terms. Defence Minister Eggleton has suggested this type of "openness" could continue, but that remains to be seen.

Another serious implication of JTF2's secrecy is a total lack of oversight and accountability regarding the unit. The amount of money that will have been spent on JTF2 since its inception is expected to exceed $200 million by 2006. But a breakdown of unit's budget still remains "black" and parliamentarians and the public don't have a clue as to how the money is being spent. Any wrongdoing within the unit is also not made public because of the convenient and all-encompassing excuse of "operational security."

As well, for more than a decade the Defence department has been dispatching JTF2 on overseas operations with a total disregard for Parliamentary oversight. Through no fault of the JTF2 operators, the unit has engaged in missions, particularly in the area of training foreign security forces, that have the potential to seriously damage Canada's reputation abroad. What, for instance, would be the consequences of a human rights organization linking JTF2 training of foreign soldiers or police to abuses? The potential is already there.

Two years after JTF2 left Haiti, its protégés in the Haitian SWAT unit were being used not for the police work the unit originally trained them for, but to intimidate and threaten the government's political opponents and their families. One of the SWAT team's main targets in August 1998 was the International Republican Institute, a political organization with links to the U.S. Republican Party. The IRI had taken a lead role in Haiti in trying to re-establish a political party system but in the process had run afoul of the government as well as supporters of then former president Jean Bertrand Aristide who still dominated island politics and didn't take too kindly to any criticism.

Three days after the IRI publicly criticized how elections were being conducted, the Haitian police SWAT team raided the homes of IRI family members, and the political organization's top official, Stanley Lucas, was threatened. According to those in Arisitide's camp, the IRI was funding right-wing politicians who had supported the 1991 army coup which ousted the civilian government. The use of the JTF2-trained SWAT team was a pre-emptive strike to prevent the overthrow of the current Haitian regime, they claimed. But they never did explain why family members of IRI organizers were targeted.

Whatever the case, Canadian Members of Parliament never knew about the consequences of the JTF2 SWAT training program because they were never even told that the unit was operating in Haiti, or elsewhere in the world for that matter.

And what about the involvement of the military's CTSO branch in training the Nepalese army? It can be easily argued that the training was needed because the Maoist guerrillas threaten the stability of the Nepalese government. But atrocities by both the government and guerrillas have been growing. Caught in the middle, as usual, are the peasants of Nepal and since the war began more than 2,000 innocents have been killed. The guerrillas have launched a brutal campaign of retribution against villagers who refuse to take up their cause but government security forces are no better. The United Nations and Amnesty International have raised concerns that many of the 5,000 people who have been arrested over the last four years have disappeared or been tortured. So far, most of the abuses are linked to the Nepalese police but the country's army is now spearheading the offensive against the guerrillas. What responsibility does Canada have if it turns out that the military advice provided by the Canadian Forces somehow contributes to the deaths of innocent people?

JTF2's global reach and its use in clandestine operations make a strong case that some kind of oversight body be installed. Both the Canadian Security Intelligence Service and the Communications Security Establishment have civilian oversight agencies that, while generally seen as weak, would provide at least some kind of measure of accountability.

OPPOSITE PAGE: *Reputed to be fanatical fighters, the Afghan rebels were able to defeat the Soviet army using a collection of captured weapons such as this 12.7 mm machinegun.* (FRANK SPOONER PICTURES/GAMMA)

THIRTEEN: TERRORIST GROUPS – A ROGUE'S GALLERY

TO UNDERSTAND THE magnitude and complexity of the terrorist threat and the need for anti-terrorist and hostage-rescue units, one has only to consider the large number of terrorist groups that have come into existence during the last quarter century. The CIA lists close to 300 liberation movements, terrorist organizations, drug cartels and other para-state entities that it considers threats to national security. Though their political aims may vary widely, all share a basic philosophy that violence is an acceptable means to their ends. Here are just a few:

Abu Sayyaf Group (ASG): The ASG is the smallest but most radical of the Islamic separatist groups operating in the southern Philippines. Some ASG members have studied or worked in the Middle East and have fought and trained in Afghanistan. The group split from the Moro National Liberation Front in 1991 and since then has conducted a campaign of bombings and assassinations to promote an independent Islamic state in western Mindanao and the Sulu Archipelago areas. ASG has raided towns and kidnapped foreigners. The group is believed to have about 200 core fighters but have reportedly had an influx of about 2,000 volunteers motivated by the prospect of receiving ransom payments for foreign hostages. Throughout 2001, the ASG continued with its campaign of kidnapping foreigners, including a group of French tourists and two American missionaries.

Al-Gama'a al-Islamiyya (Islamic Group, IG): Egypt's largest militant group, active since the late 1970s, has vowed to overthrow the Egyptian government and replace it with an Islamic state. From 1993 to 1997, the IG launched attacks in Egypt, most notably a raid at Luxor that killed 58 foreign tourists. It also claimed responsibility for the attempt in June 1995 to assassinate Egyptian President Hosni Mubarak in Addis Ababa, Ethiopia. The group issued a cease-fire in March 1999, but its spiritual leader, Shaykh Umar Abd al-Rahman, incarcerated in the United States, rescinded his support less than a year later. Rifa'i Taha Musa, a hard-line former senior member of the group, signed Osama bin Laden's February, 1998 fatwa calling for attacks against U.S. civilians. Taha Musa has since sought to push the IG toward a return to armed operations, but the organization has yet to break the unilaterally declared cease-fire. In late 2000, Taha Musa appeared in an undated video with bin Laden threatening retaliation against the United States for Abd al-Rahman's continued imprisonment.

Al-Jihad (a.k.a. Egyptian Islamic Jihad, Jihad Group): This Egyptian extremist group has been active since the late 1970s and is closely allied with Osama bin Laden's al-Qaeda network. Its main goal is to overthrow the Egyptian government and replace it with an Islamic state. The original Jihad was responsible for the assassination in 1981 of Egyptian President Anwar Sadat. It is believed responsible for the Egyptian Embassy bombing in Islamabad, Pakistan in 1995. In 1998, it planned an attack against the U.S. Embassy in Albania but a series of arrests by security forces scuttled that proposed assault. Al-Jihad's exact size is not known but it is estimated to be around several thousand hard-core members and another several thousand sympathizers. Although it operates mainly in the Cairo area, it also appears to have members outside Egypt, mainly in Afghanistan, Pakistan, and the Sudan.

Armed Islamic Group (GIA): An Islamic extremist group, the GIA aims to overthrow the secular Algerian regime and replace it with an Islamic state. The GIA began its violent activities in 1992 after Algiers voided the victory of the Islamic Salvation Front, the largest Islamic opposition party, in the first round of legislative elections in December, 1991.Since then, the GIA has carried out frequent attacks against civilians and government workers. Between

1992 and 1998, it conducted a campaign of civilian massacres, sometimes wiping out entire villages. Since announcing its campaign against foreigners living in Algeria, the GIA has killed more than 100 expatriate men and women, mostly Europeans. The group uses assassinations and bombings, and is known to favor kidnapping victims and slitting their throats. The GIA hijacked an Air France flight in December 1994. That incident was ended by the successful raid by the counter-terrorist unit GIGN.

Al-Qaeda (The Base). Established by Osama bin Laden in the late 1980s, this group is believed to have operations in 60 countries and active cells in 20, including Canada and the United States. Supported by Pakistan's Intelligence Service (ISI), Chechen rebels and the KLA in Kosovo and Macedonia, al-Qaeda has been held responsible for the September 2001 attacks on the Pentagon and World Trade Center. Its goal is to establish a pan-Islamic Caliphate throughout the world by working with allied Islamic extremist groups to overthrow regimes it deems "non-Islamic" and expelling Westerners and non-Muslims from Muslim countries. It issued a statement under banner of "the World Islamic Front for Jihad Against the Jews and Crusaders" in February 1998, saying it was the duty of all Muslims to kill U.S. citizens—civilian or military—and their allies everywhere. Al-Qaeda was behind the August 1998 bombings of the U.S. embassies in Nairobi, Kenya, and Dar es Salaam, Tanzania, that killed at least 301 persons and injured more than 5,000 others. It also claims to have shot down U.S. helicopters and killed U.S. special forces soldiers in Somalia in 1993 and to have conducted three bombings that targeted U.S. troops in Yemen in December 1992. It is also linked to the following plans that were not carried out: the assassination of Pope John Paul II during his visit to Manila in late 1994, simultaneous bombings of the U.S. and Israeli embassies in Manila and other Asian capitals in late 1994, the midair bombing of a dozen U.S. trans-Pacific flights in 1995, and the assassination of President Bill Clinton during a visit to the Philippines in early 1995. Its exact strength is unknown but intelligence agencies estimate it ranges from several hundred to several thousand members.

Basque Fatherland and Liberty - Euzakadi Ta Askasuma - (ETA): This Basque separatist movement has carried out sabotage, car-bombings and kidnappings. Its operatives have also been responsible for numerous assassinations of Spanish politicians and judges. Most ETA operations have been carried out in Spain, although some have spilled over into France. Over 800 persons have been killed since the group began its attacks in the early 1960s. ETA's exact strength is unknown but it is estimated to have several hundred members. The ETA has established relations with the Irish Republican Army, and with the Algerian Islamic Group, for which it has provided training in the production of explosives, guerrilla warfare and urban terrorism. ETA has also obtained weapons, safe houses, and other logistics support from Islamic networks in Europe. Shortly after the September 11, 2001 attacks in the U.S. there was talk about the ETA entering into a peace agreement with the Spanish government. Those hopes, however, were dashed with the ETA assassination of a judge and the detonation of a car bomb in Madrid which injured 100 people.

Hamas (Islamic Resistance Movement): Hamas was formed in late 1987 as an outgrowth of the Palestinian branch of the Muslim Brotherhood. Various Hamas elements have used both political and violent means, including terrorism, to pursue the goal of establishing an Islamic Palestinian state in place of Israel. Hamas is loosely structured, with some elements working clandestinely and others working openly through mosques and social service institutions to recruit members, raise money, organize activities, and distribute propaganda. Hamas's strength is concentrated in the Gaza Strip and a few areas of the West Bank. Its activists, especially those in the Izz el-Din al-Qassam Brigades, have conducted many attacks—including large-scale suicide bombings—against Israeli civilian and military targets. One of the victims of a 1990 bomb detonated on a Tel Aviv beach was Canadian tourist, Marnie Kimelman. In the early 1990s, Hamas also targeted suspected Palestinian collaborators and Fatah rivals. In December, 2001, Hamas suicide bombers killed 25 Israelis in attacks in Jerusalem and Haifa.

Hezbollah/Hizballah (Party of God): This terrorist group is centred in southern Lebanon and dedicated to the destruction of the state of Israel. Funded and supported by Syria and Iran, it is responsible for attacks on Israeli settlers in the West Bank and suicide bombings in Jerusalem and Tel Aviv. Branches are also active in Bahrain, Kuwait, and Turkey. The Hizballah is an umbrella organization of various radical Shi'ite groups and organizations which adhere to a Khomeinistic ideology. Hizballah was established in 1982 during the Lebanon war when a group of Lebanese Shi'ite Muslims declared themselves to be the "Party of God" (Hizb Allah). Assisted by 1,500 Iranian Revolutionary

Guards operating in Lebanon, Hizballah cells began conducting attacks against Israel. Between the spring of 1983 to the summer of 1985 the Hizballah launched an unprecedented wave of suicide bombings. It is known or suspected to have been involved in numerous anti-U.S. terrorist attacks, including the suicide truck bombing of the U.S. Embassy and U.S. Marine barracks in Beirut in October 1983 and the U.S. Embassy Annex in Beirut in September 1984. The group also attacked the Israeli Embassy in Argentina in 1992. Hizballah continues to launch rockets at Israeli towns and settlements. It is estimated to have around 1,000 fighters.

IRA (Irish Republican Army): Long-standing Irish nationalist group fighting to unite Ireland and remove British forces from Northern Ireland. The military wing of the legitimate political party, Sinn Fein, it has been observing a cease-fire since July 1997. (It previously observed a cease-fire from September 1994 to February 1996). IRA membership is believed to be around 200 to 300 plus several thousand sympathizers. The cease-fire hasn't stopped IRA members from going overseas on various missions. In the summer of 2001, IRA terrorists were arrested in Columbia and accused of training members of the FARC guerrilla group. Some members of British intelligence believe the IRA operatives were in the country to test new types of bombs. Sinn Fein's decision to take part in elections and accept a peace agreement has led to creation of more radical IRA factions which have continued the terrorist war against British interests. These include the organization, the Real IRA, which in 2001 launched a series of bombings in England. In November, 2001 the Real IRA planted a car bomb on a street in Birmingham. While the detonator ignited, the main 27-kilogram explosive device did not and hundreds of pedestrians were spared serious injury.

Liberation Tigers of Tamil Eelam (LTTE): The LTTE is dedicated to establishing an independent Tamil state in Sri Lanka. It began armed conflict with the Sri Lankan government in 1983 and relies on a guerrilla strategy that includes the use of terrorist tactics. LTTE is most notorious for its cadre of suicide bombers, the Black Tigers, which carry out attacks against key targets. All Black Tigers have vowed not to be taken alive and are equipped with a cyanide capsule to kill themselves in the event they may be captured. The LTTE also has a naval group called the Sea Tigers as well its own intelligence service. Political assassinations and bombings are commonplace. LTTE is estimated to have 8,000 to 10,000 armed combatants in Sri Lanka, with a core of trained fighters of approximately 3,000 to 6,000. The organization also has a significant overseas support structure for fundraising, weapons procurement, and propaganda activities. The Tigers control most of the northern and eastern coastal areas of Sri Lanka but have conducted operations throughout the island. The LTTE exploits large Tamil communities in North America, Europe, and Asia to obtain funds and supplies for its fighters in Sri Lanka. In July, 2001, a Tamil Tiger suicide squad attacked Sri Lanka's only international airport. Thirteen Tigers were killed in that raid along with seven Sri Lankan soldiers.

People's War/Nepal Communist Party (Maoist): This guerrilla insurgency began in the northwest provinces of Nepal in February, 1996 in retaliation for a brutal police crackdown on Communists. It has now spread across the country. In its early days, the People's War guerrilla group armed itself with hunting rifles and home-made landmines made out of kitchen pots. Now it has access to more modern weapons and is capable of co-ordinating multiple attacks across Nepal. The Maoists want to abolish the monarchy and set up a socialist state. In November, 2001, Nepal's king declared a state of emergency after a series of attacks killed 76 soldiers and police. The People's War is believed to have about 1,000 guerrillas but many supporters.

Revolutionary Armed Forces of Colombia (FARC): Established in 1964 as the military wing of the Colombian Communist Party, the FARC is Colombia's oldest, largest, most capable, and best-equipped Marxist insurgency. The group has taken part in peace negotiations with the Colombian government but it still conducts guerrilla and conventional military action against political, military, and economic targets. Foreign citizens are often targets of FARC kidnapping for ransom. In March, 1999 the FARC kidnapped and later executed three U.S. native rights activists. The group also has well-documented ties to narcotics traffickers, principally through the provision of armed protection. FARC consists of approximately 9,000 to 12,000 fighters and an unknown number of supporters, mostly in rural areas.

Revolutionary People's Liberation Party/Front (DHKP/C): A Marxist organization commonly referred to by its former name Dev-Sol. This group opposes Turkey's pro-Western stance and its membership in NATO. Since the late 1980s it has concentrated attacks against current and retired Turkish security and military officials. Attacks against foreign interests began in 1990 with the assassination of two U.S. military contractors and the wounding of a U.S. air force officer. Turkish authorities thwarted a DHKP/C attempt in June 1999 to fire a light anti-tank rocket at the U.S. Consulate in Istanbul. A series of arrests over the last several years has weakened the group.

Sendero Luminoso (Shining Path): A Maoist Peruvian terrorist guerilla group responsible for numerous atrocities in the Andean highlands. The Shining Path was founded and led by Abimael Guzman until his capture in 1992. Approximately 30,000 persons have died since the guerrilla group took up arms in 1980. Its stated goal is to destroy existing Peruvian institutions and replace them with a Communist peasant revolutionary regime. The Shining Path suffered a major blow in 1999 when one of its top leaders was captured. Peruvian special forces and police continue to hunt for active guerrilla members and have conducted counter-terrorist operations, targeting pockets of activity in the Upper Huallaga River Valley and the Apurimac/Ene River Valley, where Shining Path cells continue to conduct periodic attacks. It is estimated the group has between 100 to 200 active members.

ABOVE: Elite Israeli troops begin their hunt for Palestinian terrorists in Gaza. (PHOTO BY AUTHOR)

FOURTEEN: SPECIAL FORCES OF THE WORLD

JTF2 IS A RELATIVELY new unit in the global lineup of special forces and counter-terrorism formations. Here are some of the world's top units:

THE BRITISH SAS

In the early evening hours of May 5, 1980, television viewers across Britain and around the world watched in fascination as explosive charges were detonated and eight black-clad and hooded figures, sub-machineguns slung over their backs, rappelled down from the roof of the Iranian embassy in London to a balcony below. Other hooded figures smashed through doors at the rear of the building. Seventeen minutes later, as flames licked through the shattered windows, six terrorists lay dead and hostages were led out of the embassy at Princess Gate. Then, as suddenly as they had appeared, the hooded figures hurried into hired vans and drove away. For millions around the world, this was their introduction to the British Special Air Service, the SAS.

The drama began six days earlier when Iranians opposed to the regime of the Ayatollah Khomeni had taken over the embassy, capturing 22 hostages in the process. Their demands included the freedom of political prisoners in Iran, something that British authorities had no control over. Yet, if their demands were not met, the Iranians threatened to execute the hostages and blow up building.

A constable on duty at the embassy had managed to radio an alert before he was taken hostage and the Metropolitan Police's D11 and C13 anti-terrorist squads had surrounded the embassy fairly quickly. The SAS received notice that their services might be needed by way of the old boy's net, when a former non-commissioned officer, now a dog-handler with the Metropolitan Police, telephoned the officers' mess at Hereford and tipped them off about the situation. When the call was passed on to the "Kremlin," the SAS operations centre, 6 Troop of B Squadron was in the "Killing House," a specially-designed facility for practicing standard hostage-rescue procedures. An hour later, they were on their way to London, where they set up a holding area inside Regent's Park Barracks.

As negotiations dragged on by telephone and television crews gathered in the surrounding streets, the terrorists became increasingly frustrated and the situation in the embassy began to deteriorate. For the men of the SAS's B Squadron planning the rescue raid, the Iranian embassy was unknown territory. Fortunately, two of the hostages who had been released on account of illness, a caretaker and a BBC journalist, proved to be a mine of information, allowing them to build a plywood model of the building. One thing they discovered was that the ground-floor and first-floor windows were armour plated and could not simply be smashed through with sledge-hammers; explosive charges would be needed.

On the morning of May 5, shots were heard, followed shortly by the body of the embassy press officer being thrown out the door. Police negotiators immediately began stalling for time to prevent more killings, telling the terrorists that their demands were about to be met and that they were working out details to fly them safely out of the country. In reality, they were waiting for the SAS to move into position.

"Operation Nimrod," the plan which was eventually put into effect, involved creating a diversion at the front of the building while entry was forced at the rear, with teams entering the ground floor by way of the embassy garden and rappelling down to the first-floor balcony. At 7:23 p.m. demolition charges went off at the front and CS gas was pumped into the building through the broken windows. As the ground-floor assault team rushed into position, they saw the inert form of one of their comrades above them who was caught up in his rappel harness and dangling too near the windows to safely allow them to use frame charges. Quickly adjusting to the situation, they cut him down and hacked and hammered through the hardened windows. Once those were smashed, they tossed in stun grenades and the raiding party then moved into the embassy, MP-5 sub-machine guns at the ready.

The team on the first floor rushed up the stairs to the second where the hostages were being held, while the ground-floor men systematically cleared the lower part of the building. There was total confusion: bursts of fire, men cursing, women screaming, smoke and tear gas billowing, and the roar of grenades. The two-man assault teams, weighed down with heavy body armour and their respirators misting up from perspiration, moved automatically, assessing and reacting. The leader of the terrorists was gunned down on a first-floor landing as his comrades started to shoot wildly, killing one hostage and wounding two others. Two of the terrorists were instantly killed along with a third who had tried to mingle with the hostages. Another, identified by the hostages, was cut down by an SAS soldier as he came down a staircase clutching a fragmentation grenade.

Then the order came crackling through the SAS men's headphones to abandon the building as it was on fire. After a quick look around for codebooks and other items of interest, they formed up on the stairs and bundled the hostages, none to gently, down to the back lawn where they were thrown to the ground and held at gunpoint until handed over to police. A few minutes later, they stripped off their assault gear, turned in their weapons for forensic examination, and were driven back to Regent's Park for a celebratory beer. Joining them, was a delighted Prime Minister Margaret Thatcher.

It was later alleged that on this occasion, the SAS was ordered to take no prisoners. The Thatcher government, it was said, had long since come to the conclusion that putting terrorists in prison would only lead to further hostage-takings by other members of the same group trying to force the release of their comrades. It is unlikely it will ever be known if such orders were actually given as few governments would admit to flouting the rule of law. But the allegation was taken seriously, as there had been several previous reports of SAS brutality in Northern Ireland.

As for the SAS, it wished no more than to slip back into obscurity and train for the next "incident." Despite its distaste for publicity, one can only assume that the unit was not exactly displeased, its success having demonstrated to other would-be hostage-takers that Britain was an unhealthy realm for such activities. It also enhanced the regiment's reputation with the public and increased overseas demand for SAS know-how.

The SAS was not really formed as an anti-terrorist unit, but as a commando and intelligence-gathering force. Founded by Major David Stirling, an eccentric and tough product of the Scots Guards, it was originally known as the "L" detachment of a non-existent Special Air Service Brigade. It first saw service in the Western Desert in 1941. Stirling chose the Sword of Damocles with wings and the motto, "Who Dares Wins," to symbolize what he determined would be the role of his unit - raids by small groups of men, often dropped by parachute behind enemy lines. By war's end, Stirling's force numbered in the thousands and had seen service in North Africa, Sicily, Italy, and Northwest Europe. Stirling was the military "Marks and Spencer," according to one of the unit's first recruits. "Like some vast organization of chain stores his force grew ... and grew ... nourished by success, fortified by prestige and an intriguing air of mystery."

In the post-war years, reconstituted as the 22nd Regiment Special Air Service, the SAS was primarily involved in fighting Communist insurgencies and providing training and support to Third World heads of state friendly to Britain. It saw service in Malaya, Oman, Aden, Kuwait, and many other parts of Asia and Africa. As the IRA stepped up its activities in Northern Ireland in the mid-1960s, however, it began to devote more of its men and resources to anti-terrorist duty, most notably to a hostage-rescue unit known as the House-Assault Group.

In time, 78 men would be assigned to a Counter Revolutionary Warfare Squadron (CWR) known within the regiment as the Special Projects Team. The squadron was broken into four operational troops of one officer and 15 other ranks, with each of these troops sub-divided into four-man operating groups. Each of the operational troops was divided into a containment group which included snipers and surveillance specialists and an assault group. So fearsome became its reputation that terrorists were known to give themselves up on learning of its presence. In 1975, for example, IRA gunmen ended a hostage-taking at a flat in Balcombe Street in London when the BBC broadcast that the SAS was about to move in.

Today, the SAS has its headquarters at the Duke of York Barracks in West London, where its Crisis Alert Unit is based. Its main training base and depot is at Bradbury Lines in Hereford. It is presently organized into five operational units: A, B, D, G (Guards), and R (Reserve) Squadron. The original C Squadron, recruited in Rhodesia, was disbanded when that country gained its independence from Britain. Each squadron has four operations squads of 16 men each, which are in turn divided into four four-man specialist units known as the Boat, Air, Mountain, and Mobility troops. Each squadron serves for a six-month period with CWR. It has its own communications support in the form of the 264th (SAS) Signals Squadron, which provides secure links for worldwide operations.

The 22nd SAS is further strengthened by the addition of two territorial units. The first is the 21st (Artists Rifles) Regiment. Established in 1946 as a reserve unit, this is the oldest SAS formation. It recruits highly-trained personnel in Southern England and specializes in intelligence gathering. The second is the 23rd SAS which recruits largely in the north of England and Scotland and keeps alive the skills developed by MI-9, the highly-secretive Second World War organization. Its specialties include combat rescue, interrogation and clandestine intelligence.

Both the 22nd SAS and the territorial units demand an extraordinary level of physical fitness, stamina, intelligence, and technical ability from their personnel. The regular regiment recruits from those already serving within the British Army, while the territorial regiments find their members from the civilian population. Although there is no typical SAS man, recruiters look for someone who is extremely fit, demonstrates strength of will and a balanced psychological profile. The average recruit is in his mid-twenties, has a good military record, and is already an NCO, although he will revert to the rank of trooper when he tries for the SAS. The process of selection involves a number of hikes of ever-increasing length over difficult terrain, advanced map-reading skills, referred to as "land navigation," and the carrying of heavier and heavier loads, to prove an individual's stamina and powers of endurance over a three-week period. Both officers and other ranks undergo the same ordeal. The failure rate is approximately 80 per cent.

On arrival at Hereford, each recruit must pass the standard British Army

Fitness for Battle test - which, surprisingly enough, means a 10 per cent reduction in numbers from the start. There is no shouting of orders and recruits are left to sort themselves out. In the first week, the men work as a group on a series of graduated hikes across the hills to build up their level of fitness. During the second week, loads and distances increase, as does the length of time each man must spend in the hills. By the beginning of the third week which is known as "test week," numbers have been reduced by half. The remaining men are now moved to Wales where they must swim the River Wye nude and climb a fearsome 3,000 foot (900 metre) mountain, the Pen-y-Fan three times in full combat gear. To finish the course within the set time, a man must jog wherever possible. The final endurance test, a fearsome ordeal for even the fittest of men, is known as the "Long Drag." It involves covering a distance of forty miles (64 kilometres) in twenty hours over some of the roughest terrain in the British Isles. Over the years, some men have died of exposure.

Continuation training lasts for four months and is designed to weed out anyone who was fit enough to get through basic selection period but is lacking in intelligence. Having successfully completed selection and continuation training, the handful of remaining candidates are called before the commanding officer and presented with the SAS's beige beret and badge. They are then assigned to a squadron and can choose their specialization. Those deciding on freefall parachuting, for example, will be taught both HALO (High Altitude Low Opening) and HAHO (High Altitude High Opening) techniques and must drop into a narrow Norwegian valley in full kit, and land ready to move off instantly. Mountain troop men will be taught the techniques of climbing on rock and ice anywhere in the world, while boat troop volunteers will train in the various specialties of amphibious warfare. Mobility troop members will be sent to the Gulf sheikdoms to learn the skills of navigating their Land Rovers in the desert with sun compasses. Training is so intense that the regimental motto has been corrupted to read, "Who Trains Wins."

THE AUSTRALIAN SAS

Closely modeled on the British Special Air Service, the Australian SAS earned its reputation in Borneo and in Vietnam where members of the regiment won four Victoria Crosses.

The Australian Special Air Service was formed in July 1957 as a squadron or company-sized unit and initially encountered many of the same difficulties experienced by special forces and hostage-rescue units in smaller and Third World countries. The competency level of such units varies greatly, and even some units which were at a reasonably high level of readiness when created and trained have declined through lack of use, misuse, or being split up and assigned to other units. One of the greatest difficulties in countries with limited budgets and limited pools of manpower is keeping a purpose-trained special force from being diluted or shifted to other duties. "Internal security" and VIP protection are the tasks most frequently assigned to such units and though both of these missions can validly fall under their mandates, concentration on these duties can adversely affect training for their primary purpose. Some have become little more than specialized police units like the London Metropolitan Police's D11 unit, the equivalent of a Canadian police SWAT team, and the FBI's national Hostage-Rescue Team. The Australian SAS seemed doomed to this fate until the war in Vietnam when two additional squadrons were raised, along with signals and headquarters units to form the new 1st SAS Regiment. Its solid combat record in Vietnam, in which it was credited with killing 500 enemy soldiers while suffering only one SAS combat death, ensured its continued existence.

Based at Swanbourne near Perth, the SAS uses its Tactical Assault Group as its primary counter-terrorist force. Later, an Offshore Installations Group, with combat swimmers trained to parachute into the sea, in addition to many other skills, was added, tasked with the protection of oil and gas platforms in the Bass Strait. This unit is similar to the Commachio Company of the Royal Marines charged with anti-terrorist responsibility for the North Sea oil rigs. Like the Commachio Company, this 300 to 400 man company has a large contingent of swimmer canoeists (SBS) assigned to it and has carried out numerous practice assaults on rigs from helicopters, small boats, and submarines. The extra responsibilities placed considerable strain on the limited manpower available to the parent unit. As the threat of terrorism grew more evident, however, the Australian government in 1996 significantly upgraded the unit's weapons, communications, and command systems to enhance its overall capabilities.

The selection process and training for the Australian SAS is quite similar to that of their British counterparts. The Australians, for example, have their own

"Killing House" with 360-degree shooting capability. One difference between it and the British 22nd SAS is that the Australians tend to leave a man on anti-terrorist/hostage-rescue duties longer - a year rather than six months - before rotating him to other assignments within the regiment.

Like the British SAS, the Australians carry out very rigorous training in close-quarter combat, using live "hostages" in some Killing House scenarios, reportedly including some political notables. Training is also carried out in abandoned buildings in Perth and on Quantas and other commercial jetliners. Parachuting and rappelling are standard skills for all members of the unit, while some are also scuba, small boat, mountain, HALO and HAHO trained. The unit is familiar with a wide range of weapons including M16A2 and lo-cally produced F88 (Steyr) 5.56mm assault rifles and Heckler and Koch MP-5K sub-machineguns.

The cooperation between the British SAS and its Australian counterpart is a real advantage for both and allows the Australians easy access to British intelligence, research, and equipment. Generally rated third in the world among anti-terrorist units, its reputation has led many Southeast Asian countries to send personnel to take part in joint training exercises in Australia.

GERMAN GSG-9

The German Army has long had a number of "Fernspah," Long Range Recon-naissance and Patrol (LRRP) units whose members are selected from airborne brigades and trained at the world famous NATO LRRP school in Weingarten. Although capable of special operations, they maintained a low profile through-out the postwar years and were not tasked with anti-terrorist duty. Indeed, the German Army had a well-known policy of disapproval of special opera-tions and of any type of military elite which might evoke memories of Nazi Germany and the Waffen SS. It took the death of 11 Israeli Olympic athletes at the 1972 Munich Games by Black September terrorists to graphically illustrate to the German authorities their lack of preparedness to deal with the growing terrorist threat. As a result, Hans-Dietrich Genscher, then Federal Minister of the Interior, was given permission to form a specialized unit.

Because the German Army again proved unwilling to create elite units, the para-military Border Police (Bundesgrenzchutz) was chosen to host the new unit. This has been an immense advantage as the unit has a much more flexible role under federal police control. Its highly-skilled personnel not only have the power of arrest, but they can also conduct long-term clandestine operations, infiltrate terrorist groups and carry out surveillance and counter-terrorist operations over a longer period of time and in a broader environment than a strictly military unit.

Designated Grenzchutzgruppe-9 (GSG-9), this new unit originally had an authorized strength of 188 men under the command of Ulrich Wegener, a 15-year veteran of the border police and an expert on terrorism. Before assuming his command, Wegener had trained with the FBI and the Israeli military. In 1976, he established even closer ties with the Israelis, participating in "Operation Thunderbolt," the raid on Entebbe, which was a watershed since it marked the first time that special forces had staged a long-distance strike to rescue hostages.

Wegener's unit was stationed at St. Augustin just outside Bonn so that it would be near the seat of government for the Federal Republic. Though primarily intended to act as a national hostage-rescue unit, GSG-9 was assigned other tasks such as guarding sensitive civilian installations such as nuclear power plants, providing security for VIPs in high-risk situations, and at German embassies in Beirut, Cairo and Tehran. Following the occupation of the U.S. embassy in Tehran in 1979, the GSG-9 found itself deeply involved in preventative protection as members of a highly-specialized unit advising on security measures at German embassies around the world. Later, personnel were regularly sent on assignments to embassies in Latin America, Africa and Asia, while GSG-9 developed a large, specialized VIP protection capability.

GSG-9 was originally organized into three strike units backed up by a headquarters, communications and intelligence unit, engineer and weapons units, a maintenance and supply section, and a training cadre. A fourth strike unit was added in 1983. Each of these strike units is made up of 30 men organized into a command section and five SETS (Specialein-satztrupp). Strength of the strike units has since been increased to 42 men. The five-man SET is GSG-9's basic operational unit and can be deployed in various combinations. SETS can function as assault or sniper sections as part of a large operation, or on special assignments such as VIP protection, a five-man SET might operate independently. GSG-9 has found, as have many other special forces units, that small units such as the SETs offer better command, control, and mobility, as well as greater flexibility. In a hostage situation, it is the SETs which actually go in, while a special sniper SET will take out a terrorist or terrorists at a distance should the opportunity arise.

Since intelligence is a critical part of anti-terrorist operations, GSG-9 is hooked directly into a computer system in Wiesbaden known as Komissar which keeps track of international terrorist groups, particularly those known to be active in Germany, and compiles information about their doctrine, organization, methods, membership, and movements. GSG-9 is also supported by the Bonn district BGS helicopter wing which is based next to its barracks. This unit works very closely with GSG-9 during training exercises and provides an integral airmobile arm.

GSG-9 recruits only volunteers from the Border Guards and ex-army personnel. To even apply, a candidate must have served at least three years with the BGS with a good record and be physically fit. If accepted, he must go through a three-day initial selection process consisting of a psychological and aptitude test, endurance and shooting tests, a physical-fitness test (including stress factors), an intelligence and general knowledge test, and a medical examination. Also included are extensive interviews with senior GSG-9 officers. This preliminary process weeds out about two-thirds of applicants.

For those who make it through the initial selection process, there is a five-month initial training phase, which about another 10 percent normally fail. During this phase, physical training, martial arts and shooting are stressed. The next, and final, phase of training lasts three months and emphasizes specialized skills, particularly assault tactics as part of a SET.

Firearms training in GSG-9 occupies four half-days a week on a state-of-the-art underground range at St. Augustin which features mockups of airplanes, trains, ships, and embassies. The unit takes advantage of German technological expertise and deploys some of the most sophisticated weapons and equipment available. The .357 magnum is the handgun of choice and an impressive armoury of sniper rifles is available with special-purpose optics. As with many of the world's counter-terrorist units, the MP-5 sub-machinegun is favoured. For VIP protection, a special briefcase is sometimes used with a concealed MP-5 which can be fired by squeezing a lever built into the handle.

GSG-9 troopers also learn to use foreign weapons, particularly the AK-47, which is popular with terrorists and guerrilla armies. Other shooting skills which are constantly practiced include weak-handed shooting, malfunction clearance drills, tactical reloads, use of cover, firing under assault conditions (including firing after the use of stun grenades or breaching charges), precise shot placement in hostage-taking scenarios, and firing from vehicles and helicopters or while rappelling.

Although this extensive firearms training makes a GSG-9 member an efficient killer if he has to be, the unit prefers to take prisoners, if possible. As a result, great emphasis is placed on the martial arts and using a rifle or submachine gun as a non-lethal weapon in hand-to-hand combat. GSG-9 members become very efficient at wielding the butts of their weapons.

Among other skills learned are HALO and other types of parachuting, scuba, demolition and explosive ordnance disposal (EOD), mountaineering, helicopter insertion, including rappelling, high-speed driving, police science, and law. A good deal of time is also spent studying airport operations and learning many related jobs to enable a GSG-9 commando to infiltrate a hijacked aircraft by passing as airline employees or crew members.

One of the hardest tasks GSG-9 faces is keeping the edge necessary to perform its task if called upon. Accordingly, 50 to 70 hours a week are spent training, and twice yearly each member of the unit must pass a qualification test to show that his skills are still up to standard. Members of the unit also engage in exchange training with the American Delta Force, British SAS, French GIGN and Israeli Sayeret Matkal.

During GSG-9's early years, there was considerable controversy about the unit's budget and questions were raised about its continued existence, especially since many of the German states had formed their own hostage-rescue units. This all changed on October 17, 1977 when GSG-9 went into action at Mogadishu Airport in Somalia to rescue 91 hostages aboard a hijacked Lufthansa airliner. The success at Mogadishu brought GSG-9 international fame and more than 40 countries have since requested assistance in forming their own anti-terrorist units along GSG-9 lines. Even the SAS asked Ulrich Wegener's advice prior to their classic operation at Princess Gate.

ISRAEL'S SAYERET MATKAL

Since Israel has traditionally termed any action against the PLO and many actions against neighbouring states "anti-terrorist," it is difficult to place Sayeret

Matkal within the framework of conventional counter-terrorism units. Although it has an anti-terrorist capacity, it is primarily a special operations unit similar to the British SAS.

Israeli anti-terrorist capability can be traced back to Unit 101 which was established in 1953 to carry out cross-border reprisal raids into Jordan and other states from which Palestinian fighters were infiltrating Israel. Largely due to criticism of its brutal methods, it was officially "disbanded," although in actuality it was merged with the Israeli Parachute Battalion which assumed responsibility for raiding and reprisals during the 1950s and 1960s. The Parachute Battalion has since worked closely with other Israeli special forces.

The most notable are the highly specialist Palsar, or long-range reconnaissance and patrol groups (LRRP) attached to each of the Israeli army's regular armoured and infantry brigades. These units carry out clandestine reconnaissance patrols deep behind enemy lines to ensure that the parent brigade has the best possible information at all times about any potential threat. The Field Intelligence and Military Intelligence Corps (AMAN), has a further range of specialized units such as Unit Yachman for intelligence and target acquisition, Unit T'zasam for special reconnaissance duties in the West Bank and Palestinian areas, and Unit-504 which handles undercover intelligence activities. In addition, there is a Sayeret Duvedevan, a secretive unit based on the Israeli-Egyptian border. Sometimes referred to as a "mistaravim," or "becoming an Arab" force, its role is deep-cover clandestine operations inside Egypt and its personnel are experts at merging with the local population.

With the increase in terrorist acts after the stunning Israeli victory in the Six Day War of 1967, a more specialized unit, the Sayeret Matkal (also known as the General Staff Recon Unit or Unit 269), was formed directly under the command of the Chief of Israeli Intelligence. The unit's strength is believed to number around 200 divided into 20-man operational sections. There is great competition to serve in the unit and it attracts top army recruits, paratroopers and naval commandos.

Training emphasizes infiltration, desert operations, close combat with firearms, knives and bare hands, languages (most members speak Hebrew, English, Arabic, and at least one other language), parachuting, small boat usage and scuba. Much training is of the on-the-job variety during raids across Israel's borders. Primary weapons used by Sayeret Matkal include the U.S. M16A1 automatic rifles and carbines, 9 mm Mini-Uzi sub-machine guns, Remington 870 combat shotguns, and Mauser SR82 sniper rifles.

Sayeret Matkal personnel have also been trained for service as sky marshals aboard El Al airliners. In 1972, it had the distinction of carrying out the first successful rescue raid on a hijacked airliner when four members disguised as mechanics assaulted a Sabena 707 with 100 passengers and crew aboard which had been diverted to Israel by Black September terrorists. All the hostages, except one, were freed without injury.

In September, 1972, Israel requested permission to send a Sayeret Matkal assault team to Munich to rescue the Israeli Olympic athletes taken hostage by Black September, but that request was denied. In retaliation for the subsequent murders, Israeli hit teams, including members of Sayeret Matkal, went after high-ranking Palestinian leaders in a series of raids into Lebanon. A deliberate policy of assassination has been continued against Hezbollah and Hamas leaders. They are targeted by deep-cover special operations personnel, then either shot by marksmen or ambushed by rocket-firing helicopters.

In 1985, a highly-secretive special forces base was established at Miktan Adam with a Special Training Installation, Maha-7208. Training is exceptionally tough, even by normal special forces standards, and includes demolition, sabotage, sniping, combat swimming, helicopter insertion and various parachuting techniques. Sayeret Matkal personnel are trained on standard assault weapons as well as a wide range of captured or specially-acquired small arms for under-cover operations. Shortly after the establishment of Maha-7208, internal hostage rescue operations were turned over to a special unit of the Israeli Border Police.

Sayeret Matkal is tasked with operations outside Israel, while its civilian counterpart, Unit Yamam, a GSG-9 style counter-terrorism unit is responsible for domestic duties. Both units are required to provide two action-ready teams at all times for counter-terrorist operations.

FRANCE'S GIGN

The French have a long tradition of specialist elite units, the most notable of which is the Foreign Legion. Today, France can still call upon the Legion, as well as a wide range of special forces provided by both the armed forces and national police.

The 1st Parachute Infantry and Marine Regiment, known as the Black Berets, is the French army's primary special operations unit. Similar to the British SAS, its main missions are intelligence-gathering, special operations and counter-terrorism. It owes many of its traditions to the Free French Special Air Service which served with such distinction during the Second World War. The 1st Parachute is supported by ALAT (Special Operations Aviation Unit) with two helicopter squadrons equipped with Puma and Cougar transports and Gazelle gunships. The Black Berets are now part of the Special Operations Command, formed in the aftermath of the Gulf War and designed to ensure full cooperation between the various special forces units and their parent services.

The Special Scout Team of the 2nd REP (Legion Parachute Regiment) is an experienced and particularly effective counter-terrorist unit. Its personnel are trained in long-range reconnaissance and patrol, deep penetration behind enemy lines, POW rescue, and clandestine operations. Based in Corsica, the regiment has been frequently engaged in Africa in recent years.

In 1972, France's Gendarmerie Nationale, a paramilitary police force under the control of the Ministry of Defence, was considering the formation of a special anti-terrorist unit. The Munich Massacre and the takeover of the Saudi Arabian embassy in Paris the following September acted as a catalyst, and in November, 1973, GIGN - Groupement d'Intervention de la Gendarmerie Nationale - was formed.

Based at Maisons-Alfort just outside Paris, GIGN has never numbered more than a hundred personnel. In addition to serving as France's national hostage-rescue unit, it is also charged with transporting extremely dangerous criminals, dealing with prison sieges, providing VIP protection and security for highly sensitive installations should a criminal or terrorist threat seem likely. Divided into five-man teams it is on constant standby for deployment anywhere in France or the world within 30 minutes.

GIGN candidates are all volunteers drawn from the Gendarmerie Nationale who have successfully made it through a preliminary screening and an interview with the unit CO. During this interview, the candidate's poise and dedication are evaluated, and he is made aware of the hardships involved in serving with GIGN. The candidate, once through the preliminaries, is then introduced to the physical fitness portion of the selection process. This involves an eight-kilometre run with full combat pack in under 40 minutes, a 50-metre swim in under 15 seconds, rope climbing and rappelling. Great emphasis is placed on marksmanship, with the candidate expected to already possess basic expertise.

Surprise tests - "sickener factors" as the SAS calls them - are thrown in at various points to evaluate the candidate's ability to think on his feet and to weed out those without the "heart" for GIGN. He might, for example, be subject to a sudden encounter with an attack dog or a GIGN martial arts expert. These various selection tests last about a week, at the end of which normally only one man will be selected. That man is then placed on eight-month probation while he is trained and assimilated into an operational team. The training is constant, diverse, and rigorous and will include karate and judo - most members are black belts - long-distance running, and ski and mountain warfare training at such schools as that of the 11th Parachute Division at Bareges.

Although all anti-terrorist units stress swimming ability, GIGN places even greater emphasis on it, and all members of the unit are qualified as "Nageurs de Combat." In addition to being able to swim 50 metres rapidly, the GIGN man is expected to be able to carry out a long-distance swim while pulling a 75-kilogram (165 pound) dummy behind him, the dummy representing someone being rescued. Up to four hours a week are spent on underwater swimming, both free diving and with scuba gear. One GIGN technique to develop confidence in a trainee's swimming skills and to help him cope with disorientation and panic, is to require him to dive to the bottom of the Seine and lie on the bottom as barge traffic passes overhead. Free-diving training includes a difficult exercise in which the swimmer must dive to the bottom of a pool, read a question on a tablet placed on the bottom, write it down with a waterproof pen, then return to the surface - all without breathing apparatus. GIGN men are also taught such sophisticated combat swimming techniques as locking in and out of a submerged submarine. The exercises are designed to allow a GIGN swimmer to infiltrate a hijacked yacht, ship, or beach-side hotel while remaining undetected.

All GIGN members are commando-trained and receive parachute training at the French jump school at Pau. To retain his jump status, each member must make five jumps a year including one "wet" jump in scuba gear. High-speed driving training takes place at Le Mans, which, of course, stands any GIGN man assigned as a VIP driver in good stead.

Although GIGN follows a police philosophy and prefers to avoid deadly force if possible, all members are highly-trained with firearms. Unlike some units which have specialized sharpshooters, each GIGN member is expected to be an expert with a rifle and is issued with a personal FR-F2 sniper rifle. He must be able to hit a target at 200 metres 93 times out of a 100. Most do much better: 98 times out of a 100 is the norm. Additional range time is spent with combat shotguns, sub-machineguns and various other weapons including a sophisticated slingshot which fires steel balls for a silent kill. Some range sessions include specialized exercises within mock-ups of aircraft cabins.

GIGN's operational record certainly justifies its existence. Since its formation it has rescued well over 500 hostages, most of these in barricade situations in France, since GIGN functions as the national SWAT team as well the nation's dedicated counter-terrorist unit. This has allowed it to keep skills sharp. It's best-known operation overseas, was the rescue of 30 French children aboard a hijacked school bus in Djibouti in February, 1976. GIGN has also been used to train Third World hostage-rescue units and many of France's former colonies have taken advantage of its expertise.

AMERICA'S DELTA FORCE

The United States lagged behind most of the other Western democracies in creating a specialized anti-terrorist formation, although it did have a robust special operations capability in units such as the Green Berets and Navy SEALs. But it was not until after the dramatic GSG-9 rescue at Mogadishu made world headlines, that the U.S. government was prompted to order the Joint Chiefs of Staff to enhance the country's anti-terrorist capability.

The result was the creation in 1977 of the U.S. Army's 1st Special Forces Operational Detachment - Delta, better known as Delta Force. The unit was the brainchild of a special forces officer named Charles Beckwith, a Vietnam veteran who also had close ties with the British SAS. At first, Delta recruited from the ranks of Green Berets and U.S. Army Rangers but that was later expanded to include the entire U.S. Army. Delta Force, nursed and guided by Beckwith, was originally organized and trained along SAS lines, but soon developed an ethos and character of its own.

Delta's first mission was the ambitious and ultimately unsuccessful 1980 attempt to free American hostages held at the U.S. embassy in Iran. The plan involved ferrying Delta Force operators by helicopter from a remote desert landing strip to Tehran. But the operation was hindered by poor support and internal bureaucratic bickering among the various U.S. military services.

On April 24, 1980 Delta landed in the Iranian desert but mechanical problems with several of its helicopters forced it to abort the rescue mission. As the strike force was preparing to return to a U.S. aircraft carrier, one of the helicopters slammed into a Hercules transport plane, killing eight U.S. servicemen. The problems encountered in the failed Iranian rescue mission led to a major shakeup of special operations forces in the U.S. and the creation of one command to oversee all elite units.

For its part, over the next two decades, Delta Force continued to expand in size and capabilities, conducting numerous operations around the world. It took part in Operation Urgent Fury, the U.S. invasion of Grenada in 1983, and Operation Just Cause, the U.S. invasion of Panama, where it successfully carried out the rescue of American citizen Kurt Muse who was being held hostage in the Carcel Modelo Prison. In the Persian Gulf War, Delta Force was covertly deployed within Iraq, tracing and destroying Scud missile launchers.

In October, 1993 the unit took part in a mission to grab key lieutenants of Somali warlord Mohamed Farrah Aidid from a hotel in downtown Mogadishu. The joint mission with U.S. Army Rangers and members of SEAL Team Six quickly turned into a major battle with Somalis, resulting in the deaths of 18 American soldiers. Six of the dead were Delta operators. The unit has also seen considerable service in the Balkan Wars where it was tasked with tracking down and capturing suspected war criminals in Bosnia, Croatia, and Kosovo.

In the 2001 war in Afghanistan, Delta Force operated with other American special forces units against the Taliban and Osama bin Laden. In late October of that year it linked up with U.S. Army Rangers to attack a compound near Kandahar used by Taliban ruler Mullah Mohammed Omar. Delta troops flew to their target area by Black Hawk helicopters from the aircraft carrier USS *Kitty Hawk*, located off the coast of Pakistan. The Rangers involved in the attack conducted a nighttime parachute jump on a Taliban airfield just southwest of Kandahar. Delta is also believed to have conducted hit and run raids on Taliban forces as well as searching for bin Laden and Taliban leaders in the

Tora Bora and Kandahar areas.

The U.S. Army does not acknowledge that Delta exists although the unit openly recruits in official American military publications. Delta Force has close ties with the British SAS, GSG-9, the Australian SAS, GIGN and JTF2. It is reportedly around 800 members in size, although some estimates of the number of personnel employed at its Fort Bragg, North Carolina base have been as high as 2,000.

Delta is probably the best equipped counter-terrorist/special forces unit in the world, having access to any of the vast resources of the U.S. military. It can call on helicopter support from the U.S. Air Force's Special Operations group as well as other regular force units. Since aircraft hijacking was foreseen as a primary threat to be countered by Delta, the Federal Aviation Administration, provided the unit with a Boeing 727 for training in assault tactics. Many training exercises are also conducted at Kennedy Airport in New York and other large U.S. airports. Members study all aspects of airport operations to plan assaults based on a variety of contingencies. All types of commercial airliners are studied in detail with special emphasis placed on identifying blind spots for an approach prior to an assault, location of hatches, and other features which might be critical during an operation.

Intelligence on terrorist groups is fed directly to Delta by the CIA and the FBI. Delta also has its own state-of-the-art communications equipment including a man-portable satellite link. Delta Force members have been allowed to visit foreign cities to familiarize themselves with potential terrorist targets and operating in unfamiliar environments.

Delta Force small arms include the M-4 5.56 mm carbine and the Heckler and Koch Offensive Handgun Weapon System. Delta snipers favor the Heckler and Koch PSG-1, and Remington M40A1.

SELECTED BIBLIOGRAPHY

Arostegui, Martin. *Twilight Warriors*, 22 Books, Kent, 1996.

Davis, Barry. *The Complete Encyclopedia of the SAS*, Virgin Publishing, London, 2001.

Directory of the World's Weapons, Blitz Editions, Leicester, 1996.

Geraghty, Tony. *Who Dares Wins*, Warner Books, London, 1993.

Griswold, Terry. *Delta: America's Elite Counterterrorist Force*, Motorbooks International, Osceola, WI, 1992.

Katz, Samuel. *The Illustrated Guide to the World's Top Counter-Terrorist Forces*, Concord Publications, Hong Kong, 1995.

Katz, Samuel. *The Illustrated Guide to the World's Top Naval Special Warfare Units*, Concord Publications, Hong Kong, 2000.

Macdonald, Peter. *The SAS In Action*, Sidgwick and Jackson, London, 1990.

Taylor, Scott, Nolan, Brian. *Tested Mettle: Canada's Peacekeepers at War*, Esprit de Corps Books, Ottawa, 1998.

Thompson, Leroy. *The Rescuers*, Dell, New York, 1986.

Tomajczk, S.F. *U.S. Elite Counter-Terrorist Forces*, Motorbooks International, Osceola, WI, 1997.

Waller, Douglas. *The Commandos: The Inside Story of America's Secret Soldiers*, Dell, New York, 1994.

Weale, Adrian. *Secret Warfare*, Coronet Books, London, 1997.

NOTES ON SELECTED SOURCES

CHAPTER ONE

Operation Apollo, Backgrounder, Department of National Defence (DND).

DND Budgets, 1992-2000.

Canada goes to war, Janice Tibbetts, Ottawa Citizen, October 9, 2001.

Ottawa's military boasting overblown, David Pugliese, Vancouver Sun, October 12, 2001.

Forces stretched too thin: analysts, David Pugliese and Joan Bryden, Ottawa Citizen, November 16, 2001.

War-bound Sea Kings lack defence, says report, David Pugliese, Victoria Times-Colonist, November 19, 2001.

CHAPTER TWO

Turkish Embassy Attack

Security Gap cited in terrorist raid, Barbara Yaffe, Globe and Mail, March 13, 1985.

Terror in the capital, Michael Clugston, Maclean's Magazine, March 25, 1985.

Attackers would have leveled embassy if grenade had gone off, court told, Abby Deveny, Ottawa Citizen, October 18, 1986.

Embassy guard likely alive when shot again, Abby Deveny, Ottawa Citizen, October 24, 1986.

SERT

New anti-terrorist team ready for action, David Scanlan, Ottawa Citizen, May 13, 1986.

A team against terror, Hilary MacKenzie, Maclean's Magazine, May 26, 1986.

RCMP killer squad issues warning to terrorists, Janet Steffenhagen, London Free Press, May 20, 1986.

RCMP's anti-terror team has yet to test its training, David Pugliese, Ottawa Citizen, November 21, 1991.

Elite RCMP anti-terrorist squad to be disbanded, Peter Moon, Globe and Mail, February 17, 1992.

Armed Forces team to replace RCMP anti-terrorist team, David Pugliese, Ottawa Citizen, March 6, 1992.

SERT Fact Sheet, RCMP.

Dwyer Hill Fact Sheet, RCMP.

SERT budget figures, RCMP.

Interviews by author with SERT officers.

CHAPTER THREE

Early Days

Author's tour of Dwyer Hill Training Centre (RCMP).

Personal Daytimer, 1992-1994, Robert Fowler.

DND Daily Executive Meeting notes 1992-1995.

Defence Management Committee Summary Record, March 26, 1993.

August 1994 Briefing Note on JTF2 to Deputy Minister.

Canadian Forces Organization Orders, Joint Task Force Two, November 15, 1993.

Colonel Michael O'Brien, various DND Performance evaluation reports, 1991-1993.

DCDS Warning Order, Aid of the Civil Power/Armed Assistance, February 2, 1994.

Operation Campus-Exercise Scorpion-Saxon, DND planning documents, message traffic, intelligence reports, February, 1994

JTF2 Annual Historical Reports, 1994-1999, DND.

JTF2 CANFORGEN, 1994.

Canada's secret soldiers: Tough, specialized and intensively trained, JTF2 is the elite unit of the Canadian Forces, David Pugliese, Ottawa Citizen, November 4, 1998.

Interviews by author with CF officers.

"Exercise Praetorian"

Speaking Notes for Jean Fournier, Deputy Solicitor General, May 27, 1994.

Military tightens up secrecy on injuries to crack soldiers, Gerald Young, Times-Colonist, June 11, 1994,

DND Summary Investigation - Bamberton (Victoria) Injuries, March 27, 1995.

Interviews by author with civilian officials involved in Exercise Praetorian.

CHAPTER FOUR

Freedom 55 and other missions

Army planned rescue raid; Secret unit was ready to free peacekeepers, David Pugliese, May 3, 1995, Ottawa Citizen. (Much of the information on Freedom 55 came from interviews the author conducted in Bosnia in April, 1995 with RCD and RCR soldiers, several months after the JTF2 rescue team left. CBC Radio reporter Michael McAuliffe also provided some excellent insight into the Visoko incident during an October, 1996 conversation with the author).

Tested Mettle by Scott Taylor and Brian Nolan also contains excellent descriptions of JTF2 missions in the former Yugoslavia, Rwanda as well as the Estai affair. Esprit de Corps editor Scott Taylor also talked with JTF2 Warrant Officer Gib Perrault in Croatia, and later Visoko, Bosnia in August, 1994.

The presence of JTF2 soldiers in Rwanda is also mentioned in a 1995 military police report into the death of a Canadian Airborne Regiment soldier in Kigali.

Airborne sends troops into Rwanda; Tragic mission in Somalia' put behind us', Jacquie Miller, Ottawa Citizen, August 4, 1994.

Troops waiting it out, talks continue to free 55 Canucks, Matthew Fisher, Toronto Sun, November 26, 1994.

NATO can't halt advance by Serbs, Associated Press, November 28, 1994.

Serbs fail to free Canadians but UN officials hopeful release may come today, Kitty McKinsey, Toronto Star, December 4, 1994.

Coping the Canadian way, David Pugliese, Ottawa Citizen, December 8, 1994.

Trawler Seized at Gunpoint, Doug Fischer, Dave Todd, Ottawa Citizen, March 10, 1995.

Security Breaches/Anjou Incident

Briefing Note for Minister of National Defence, David Collenette, May 10, 1995 by Commander J.C. MacQuarrie, Colonel Peter Maclaren.

Targeting of JTF2 Personnel (Suspected), SIU report, DND, 1995.

Joint Task Force Two Annual Training Plan March 1, 1994-March 31, 1995.

Army exercise a scare tactic, Parizeau says, Robert McKenzie, Toronto Star, August 10, 1995.

DND Media Response Line, "Counter-terrorism training exercise." August 10, 1995.

Gustafsen Lake

Much of JTF2's involvement at Gustafsen Lake was disclosed at the trials of native protesters. Of interest is Attorney General Ujjal Dosanjh's letter to Solicitor General Herb Gray requesting sniper rifles from JTF2. RCMP Assistant Commissioner Brown also kept extensive notes about JTF2; of interest are records from August 20 and September 13, 1995. Brigadier General Robert Meating's reactions about the use of JTF2 are also recorded in Brown's notes from September 13, 1995. Also released was an RCMP Fax from its 100 Mile Command Post on September 8, 1995 concerning JTF2.

RCMP tactics warlike, trial told, Ross Howard, Globe and Mail, October 8, 1996.

More militants surrender to police, soldier injured by stun grenade, Jeff Lee, Vancouver Sun, September 13, 1995.

Interviews by author of civilian police involved in Gustafsen Lake standoff.

CHAPTER FIVE

Haiti

The author received a full briefing (inadvertently as it later turned out) on JTF2 operations in Haiti during his August, 1996 visit to United Nations headquarters in Port-au-Prince.

Pressed by U.S. Haitian President begins purge of guards, Larry Rohter, New York Times, September 16, 1996.

Standing on guard for Haiti's president: Canadians keep President Rene Preval out of harm's way, David Pugliese, Ottawa Citizen, September 17, 1996.

Canada Facing Nightmare in Haiti, Linda Diebel, Toronto Star, February 22, 1997.

Soldiers transferred after criticizing mission, Linda Diebel, Toronto Star, March 12, 1997.

Constabulary of Thugs, Tammerlin Drummond, Time Magazine, February 17, 1997.

Human Rights Watch Americas Report, January, 1997.

Canada's secret soldiers: Tough, specialized and intensively trained, JTF2 is the elite unit of the Canadian Forces, David Pugliese, Ottawa Citizen, November 4, 1998.

JTF2 Annual Historical Reports, 1994-1999, DND.

Zaire

Canada proposes Zaire aid force, Barbara Crossette, New York Times, November 13, 1996.

Baril treks to rebel-held Zaire, Allan Thompson, Toronto Star, November 28, 1996.

Zaire rebel approves food drop but rejects western military role, New York Times, November 29, 1996.

Nobel Fever, David Pugliese, Saturday Night Magazine, May, 1997.

Author also relied on unpublished portions of his extensive 1997 interview with General Maurice Baril regarding Operation Assurance.

DND release, censored and uncensored photographs of JTF2 CPP personnel with General Maurice Baril.

Nepal

Message to Dwyer Hill Training Centre, Military Training Assistance Program - Nepal, August, 1996.

Report on Royal Nepalese Army Counter-Terrorist Posture, CTSO, DND, March 4, 1997.

Summary of 1996 annual report, Colonel John Bremner, CF Advisory Office, New Delhi.

Nepal struggles to cope with diehard Maoist violence, Jane's Intelligence Review, June 1999.

Nepal faces upsurge in violence, Jane's Intelligence Review, April, 2000.

Peru

DND Briefing Note - Hostage-Taking Incident in Lima, Peru, December, 18, 1996.

Reassessment of DND Role, Memo, December 23, 1996.

DND Briefing Note - JTF2 Actions, Lima, Peru, March 4, 1997.

See also the description of the JTF2 plan in Tested Mettle (Taylor and Nolan).

Memorandum for Minister of Foreign Affairs, Peruvian Hostage Crisis, February, 28, 1997.

Lima Hostage Situation, various updates, e-mails, message traffic, Department of Foreign Affairs.

Peruvian, Japanese leaders to meet in Toronto on hostage standoff, Juliet O'Neill, Ottawa Citizen, January 30, 1997.

Leaders want talks with rebels, Juliet O'Neill, Ottawa Citizen, February 2, 1997.

Hostages freed in bloody raid, Ian Lewis, April 23, 1997, Ottawa Citizen, April 23, 1997.

CHAPTER SIX

The Way Ahead and Expansion

Special Operation Allowance for JTF2, Briefing Note, November 16, 1995.

Problem Definition Paper, JTF2 Special Operations Assaulter Unique MO, DND.

The Way Ahead Report, JTF2.

Briefing to CDS, The Way Ahead, slide deck.

Briefing Note, JTF2 Capability Enhancement, 1996.

An Update on the Way Ahead for JTF2, Briefing package, May, 1997.

Master Infrastructure Development Plan, Dwyer Hill Training Centre, June, 1997.

Dare to Be Challenged, JTF2 recruiting video and brochure.

Canada's secret soldiers: Tough, specialized and intensively trained, JTF2 is the elite unit of the Canadian Forces, David Pugliese, Ottawa Citizen, November 4, 1998.

JTF2 Annual Historical Reports, 1994-1999, DND.

APEC/Medical Problems/Griffon Problems

A Study of the Treatment of Members Released from the CF on Medical Grounds, DND report, 1998.

Summary Investigation - Bamberton (Victoria) Injuries, March 27, 1995.

Issuing and Use of HI-6- APEC 97, Briefing Note, November, 1997. Also HI-6 and Diazepam Auto-Injector Information Brief and various DND documents related to the APEC 97 medical issue.

Vancouver Counter Terrorism Exercise, Memorandum for John Tait, Government of Canada, September 22, 1997.

CH146 Griffon Weapon System Support Plan 1998-2003 as well as other various Griffon maintenance reports.

Overseas Operations

JTF2 After Action Reports, 1996-2000.

Dallaire set for Rwanda tribunal, Allan Thompson, Toronto Star, February, 20, 1998.

Op Dubonnet, JTF2 Report.

Op Sphere, Post Operation Report.

Briefing Note for CDS, Security Support to BGen. Maisonneuve, April 6, 1999.

Briefing Note, BGen. Maisonneuve Security Advisors, April 9, 1999.

Briefing Note for Minister of National Defence, Tasking of JTF2, April 20, 1999.

Canadian commandos in Yugoslavia, MP says, Joan Bryden, Aileen McCabe and Hilary MacKenzie, Ottawa Citizen, April 20, 1999.

Transcript of DND Kosovo press conference, April 20, 1999.

MP cites covert Balkans unit, Graham Fraser, Globe and Mail, April 20, 1999.

MP retreats on commandos in Kosovo, Graham Fraser, Globe and Mail, April 21, 1999.

Transcript of DND Kosovo press conference, May 12, 1999.

CHAPTER SEVEN

Darnell Bass

DND Briefing Note, Darnell Bass Connectivity to JTF2.

DND Briefing Note, Sgt. Darnell Bass Incident, undated.

Heist suspect stockpiled weapons, David Pugliese, Ottawa Citizen, July 18, 1998.

Soldiers of Fortune, series by Gary Dimmock, Ottawa Citizen, April 22-23, 2000.

Briefing note on B. Countway, Deputy Chief of the Defence Staff, April 25, 2000.

Bank raider not a member of elite unit, letter, Major (retired) Mike Rouleau, Ottawa Citizen, April 26, 2000.

Interviews by author with Captain Bob Lanouette, NIS (Military Police).

COS J3 Briefing Note Executive Summary - JTF2 Connection - Calgary Robbery, May 10, 2000.

Briefing Note for CDS -JTF2 Connection to Calgary Robbery, May 12, 2000.

Somali questions disallowed, Kevin Martin, Sun Media, May 18, 2000.

Another soldier committed Brink's heist: defence, Ottawa Citizen, May 18, 2000.

Request from JTF2 Commanding Officer, Re-activation of CFNIS Investigation, May 30, 2000.

Ex-commando testifies on arms supply, Suzanne Wilton, Calgary Herald, May 24, 2000.

Brink's guard recalls shooting ordeal, Suzanne Wilton, Calgary Herald, June 16, 2000.

Ryan guilty of Brink's shooting spree, Suzanne Wilton, Calgary Herald, June 17, 2000.

Officers help robber win day parole: Former soldier convicted in botched Brink's heist, Suzanne Wilton, Calgary Herald, February 23, 2001.

Michael O'Brien

Colonel Michael O'Brien, various DND Performance evaluation reports, 1991-1993.

Military police investigation, Colonel Michael O'Brien.

Did Brass interfere with case? Dave Rider, Toronto Sun, March 28, 1997.

Colonel 'borrowed' anti-terrorist gear to flog real estate, David Pugliese, Ottawa Citizen, June 7, 1997.

Michel Rainville

Citizen special report: The Somalia story, David Pugliese, Ottawa Citizen, June 21, 1997.

DND letter, October 5, 1998, Response to request for records regarding Michel Rainville's service and training with JTF2.

Canada's Rambo, Marnie Ko, Western Report, November 20, 2000.

Former captain found guilty of raid torture: Subject of Somali inquiry: Corporal kidnapped and assaulted during La Citadelle exercise, James Cudmore, National Post, March 6, 2001.

Military Shocker, Peter Worthington, Toronto Sun, March 11, 2001.

Rainville escapes jail term for 'grave crime,' James Cudmore, National Post, August 11, 2001.

CHAPTER EIGHT

Secrecy surrounds role of Joint Task Force 2, David Pugliese, Vancouver Sun, October 10, 2001.

Committee wants elite JTF2 expanded, Tim Naumetz, Ottawa Citizen, November 8, 2001.

British troops played key role in advance, Michael Smith, Daily Telegraph, November 13, 2001.

Eggleton talks up special troops' skill, downplays hesitance to send in others, Robert Russo, Halifax Herald, November 21, 2001. Art Eggleton has compared JTF2 to Delta Force and the SAS on several occasions, including in response to a question from the author at a press briefing on October 29, 2001.

JTF2 not ready for Afghan duty: expert, David Pugliese, Ottawa Citizen, November 22, 2001.

Special forces get free rein, Rowan Scarborough, Washington Times, November 23, 2001.

Commandos hit supply lines, Catherine Philp, The Times of London, November 24, 2001.

Canadian forces told to stand down: Commandos never left country, Joan Bryden and Larry Johnsrude, Ottawa Citizen, November 27, 2001.

SAS forces the enemy back towards Kandahar, Michael Smith, Daily Telegraph, November 28, 2001.

Canada Special Forces in Middle East, The Associated Press, December 6, 2001.

Canadians join bin Laden hunt, Robert Fife, National Post, December 6, 2001.

Anti-terrorist unit to expand, Jim Bronskill and David Pugliese, Vancouver Sun, December 11, 2001.

Special Troops to Go After Al Qaeda, Steve Vogel and Vernon Loeb, Washington Post, December 14, 2001.

2 U.S. Soldiers Wounded at Tora Bora, Chris Tomlinson, Associated Press, December 14, 2001.

Chretien in dark, David Gamble, Ottawa Sun, December 14, 2001.

The Lost Regiment, by Peter Worthington, Toronto Sun, December 16, 2001.

Elite JTF2 goes into Kandahar war zone, Daniel Leblanc, Globe and Mail, December 20, 2001.

More JTF2 commandos in war zone, David Pugliese, Victoria Times-Colonist, December 20, 2001.

Canadian Airborne Forces Association Submission to the Somalia Inquiry.

DND Report - Exercise Defence Planner, CFC Toronto, June 1999.

CHAPTER NINE

Equipment

Information about JTF2's weapons can be determined from viewing the Dare to be Challenged video and brochure as well as the officially released photographs. Author also consulted CF members on equipment.

Details on CF firearms provided by DND and Diemaco.

For the full history of the Barrett see Guns Magazine, November, 2001 issue.

Briefing note to VCDS "Carrying of SIG-Sauer P225 with Chambered Round", November 5, 1998.

HK's MP-5, Bud Lang, Firepower Magazine, January, 1985.

JTF2 Equipment List. 1995.

Briefing Note on JTF2 to CDS, May 17 1995.

Details about Dwyer Hill accidents are contained in JTF2 Significant Incident Reports 1999/2000/2001.

Various problems with trucks are outlined in Fleet Wheel Problems Briefing Note for Minister of National Defence, January 5, 2001.

Performance Enhancement

U.S. special ops to study performance enhancing drugs, Debra Werner, Defense News, April 18, 1994.

Australia ponders doping for soldiers, Sydney Morning Herald, September 19, 1998.

Creatine overuse may be risky, Maple Leaf. Vol. 2, No. 14, 1999.

Letter from DND to author refusing Access to Information request on performance enhancement and blood-loading report, January 18, 2000.

Supplements banned for athletes are being considered for soldiers, Ira Dreyfuss, Associated Press, August 22, 2001.

DCIEM Report Number TR-1999-998 CA (Study on Heat and Moisture Exchangers for Dwyer Hill Training Centre/JTF2).

Exercises and Training

After-action reports for the following JTF2 exercises: Running Water, Poseidon's Eye 3, Bus Stronghold, Bold Staedtler and Quadrant Brief.

Threat Assessment: JTF2 Exercise, November 26-28, 1998, December 4-11, 1998, J2 Security Intelligence.

JTF2 charge sheets, 1998-1999.

JTF2 Court martials/summary trials, 1999-2000.

JTF2 recruiting campaign begins for 2000, Maple Leaf (DND newspaper), Vol. 3, No. 11, 2000.

Joint Task Force Two is recruiting, Maple Leaf (DND newspaper) Vol. 4, No. 25, 2001.

Simulation

Taming an Urban Maze; high-tech visualization system eliminates guesswork from operational planning, Armed Forces Journal International, September, 2001.

Affiliated Units

Exercise Klaxon Kounter After Action Reports, 1994, 1996.

Exercise Krypton Encounter 1993 After Action Report.

The Storming of the Katie, Zev Singer, Ottawa Citizen, August, 4, 2000.

The Next Wave of Naval Boarding Parties Trains, Sept. 17, 2001 The Lookout CFB Esquimalt. (see also Naval Boarding Operations, DGPA Backgrounder, Aug. 4, 2000).

Snipers compete at intentional competition, Maple Leaf (DND newspaper), October, 10, 2001.

Pathfinders strategize to survive, Maple Leaf (DND newspaper), November 28, 2001.

CHAPTER TEN

Resumes of JTF2 officers were found on DND Web site.

Both CANFORGENs released under Access to Information.

Briefing Note for Minister of National Defence, JTF2, April 20, 1999.

Details of JTF2 Honors were released by Government House.

Colonel Barr's comments are contained in a letter to the author.

JTF2 hazard pay details are contained in the CF Personnel Newsletter 8/98 and CF Personnel Newsletter Issue 12, 2000.

Peacekeeper turns talents to different kind of policing, Dave Rogers, Ottawa Citizen, December 18, 1999 (article on former JTF2 Major Mike Rouleau).

CHAPTER ELEVEN

Policy Issues Related to an Airborne Capability, DND report, February, 1995.

Canadian Army Reacts to Life after the Paras, Sharon Hobson, International Defence Review, December, 1996.

Ex New Horizons 1997-98 A Commitment to Canadians Abroad: a NEO Capability for the Canadian Forces by LCdr Richard H. Jean Paper written while attending the Canadian Forces College. DND Website.

Draft report, Potential Future Responsibilities and Roles of DND, July, 2000.

Responsibilities and Roles of DND, Asymmetric Threats and Weapons of Mass Destruction, July, 2000.

Sea King endangered Katie troops, Douglas Quan, Ottawa Citizen, October 31, 2000.

Refugee ship captain defies SAS takeover, Daniel McGrory, The Australian, August 30, 2001.

Northern Brave After Action Report, DND.

Interview by author of former SAS soldier Alan Bell.

CHAPTER TWELVE

Report of the Special Senate Committee on Security and Intelligence, DND Briefing Note for (ADM Pol) Ken Calder, January 20, 1999.

CFC identified source of comments JTF2, Major Rita LePage, e-mail sent to NDHQ, February 10, 2000.

.

Canada's very secret weapon, Roy MacGregor, National Post, October 10, 2001.

Price and Eggleton's comments on secrecy can be found in the October 18, 2001 minutes of the Standing Committee on National Defence and Veterans Affairs.

Elite unit quells 'threat' in seconds: Exercise so secret all participants sworn to silence, Gary Dimmock, Ottawa Citizen, October 26, 2001.

Mystery men on the first flight to new airstrip, Alan Philips, Daily Telegraph, November 5, 2001.

Five Americans hit by 'friendly fire' in battle to take prisoners in fortress, Associated Press, November, 27, 2001.

SAS are filmed firing in jail riot, Michael Evans, The Times, December 14, 2001.

Nepalese soldiers battle Maoist rebels, Associated Press, December 9, 2001.

People's War a one-sided battle, Nepalese Army fights Maoists, Claude Adams, National Post, December 29, 2001.

Republicans accused of plotting in Haiti, Michael Norton, Associated Press, August 14, 1998.

Haiti police raid opposition offices for guns, Trenton Daniel, Reuters News Service, August 22, 2001.

Various interviews by author of DND public affairs personnel.

CHAPTER THIRTEEN

For a complete listing of terrorist groups and their activities see the U.S. State Department's Web site or the Federation of Atomic Scientists' Web site report on "Liberation Movements and Terrorist Organizations."

CHAPTER FOURTEEN

See bibliography

GLOSSARY

Steeped in abbreviations, jargon, and slang terms, the military environment can often be difficult to comprehend for those unfamiliar with its terminology. The following is a brief selection of terms used in the world of Canadian counter-terrorism and special operations.

Adjutant: Officer, usually a captain, responsible for seeing that a senior officer's commands are carried out.

AK (47, 74, etc.): The most widely used family of assault rifles in the world. These Russian-designed weapons are found in the hands of terrorist and guerrilla forces around the globe as well as in the stockpiles of former nation clients of the defunct Soviet Union.

Assaulters: Used to describe those soldiers in JTF2 whose main job is to rescue hostages or to storm terrorist-held buildings, aircraft or vehicles.

Balaclava: Knitted hood worn by JTF2 soldiers for camouflage and to conceal their identities.

Badgers: Slang used during Canadian counter-terrorism exercises as a label for terrorists.

Black Budget: This term indicates that the budget for a certain unit or a particular equipment program is to remain secret. Specific details of JTF2's budget are considered black.

Black Operations: Counter-terrorism and hostage-rescue missions.

Body armor: Ballistic protection worn by assault units, commonly referred as a "bullet-proof vest." Body armor is often made of a material called Kevlar.

Breaching: Gaining entry to an area where hostages are held, usually with explosives.

Bungle in the Jungle: Slang used in the Canadian military to describe the 1996 mission to Zaire. Officially known as Operation Assurance.

CADPAT: Canadian Disruptive Pattern. A Canadian-designed camouflaged combat uniform.

Calibre: The term derives from the Latin *qua libre*, "what pound." It was first applied to the weight and later the diameter of a projectile (or the inside diameter of a gun barrel). Most armies use the measurement of the internal diameter of a barrel as a means of classifying weapons. Thus, a 20 mm or 76 mm weapon.

CAR: Canadian Airborne Regiment. This elite paratroop unit was disbanded by the Liberal government in 1995, two years after the regiment's mission to Somalia.

CDS: Chief of the Defence Staff. The senior Canadian Forces officer reporting directly to the Minister of National Defence.

CFB: Canadian Forces Base.

CPP: Close personal protection (bodyguard work). JTF2 engages in CPP for generals and politicians when they visit overseas operations.

CQB: Close Quarter Battle. A general term used to describe techniques of armed and unarmed close-order combat with knives, pistols, shotguns and sub-machineguns in physically restrictive surroundings such as in a building. Typically CQB engagements will happen at less than six metres.

CSIS: Canadian Security Intelligence Service. The main Canadian government spy agency collecting intelligence on internal and external threats. CSIS prepares intelligence briefs used by JTF2.

CSE: Communications Security Establishment. The CSE is the electronic eavesdropping organization which reports to the Minister of National Defence. CSE intercepts are also relayed to JTF2 for specific operations.

CTSO: Counter-Terrorism Special Operations, also known as Counter-Terrorist Specialist Operations. This is JTF2's liaison office at National Defence Headquarters. Many of its staff are former JTF2 officers.

Cyclic Rate: The number of rounds an automatic weapon fires per minute.

Dare to Be Challenged: JTF2 recruiting slogan used on its promotional pamphlet and video.

DCDS: Deputy Chief of the Defence Staff. The senior officer at National Defence Headquarters who has responsibility for JTF2. Any decision to deploy the unit, however, is made by the CDS, in consultation with the DCDS. Such a decision would obviously involve senior government ministers.

Delta Force: U.S. Army 1st Special Forces Operational Detachment-Delta. Delta is the army's elite counter-terrorism and special forces unit. The exact number of soldiers serving in Delta Force is unknown but is estimated to be around 800. The army does not officially acknowledge that the unit exists.

DND: Department of National Defence.

Doorkickers: Slang for JTF2 assault teams.

Double-tap: Two aimed shots, fired in rapid succession, at a terrorist at close range.

Doves: Term used in Canadian counter-terrorism training scenarios to denote hostages.

Dwyer Hill Training Centre: Main JTF2 base just outside Ottawa. The centre is also used on occasion by the RCMP and other civilian police tactical teams.

Emergency Response Teams: General term to denote specialized force that would respond to hostage-taking, criminal or terrorist attacks.

EOD: Explosive Ordnance Disposal unit.

Fast-Roping: Rapid insertion method akin to rappelling to allow special forces to quickly slide down a rope from a helicopter.

Frame Charge: A flat sheet of plastic explosives used by hostage-rescue units to shatter bullet-proof or reinforced glass.

Freedom 55: Name assigned to JTF2's 1994 plan to free 55 Canadian peacekeepers held by the Serbs in Bosnia.

GIGN: Groupement d'Intervention de la Gendarmerie Nationale. France's national hostage-rescue unit drawn from the ranks of the Gendarmerie but under the control of the Defence ministry.

Green Operations: JTF2's term for special forces missions such as intelligence-gathering behind enemy lines.

GSG-9: Grenzchutzgruppe 9. German federal border police hostage-rescue unit.

H&K: Heckler and Koch, a German firearms manufacturing firm that produces reliable and accurate handguns, sub-machineguns and sniper rifles favored by elite units.

HAHO: High altitude, high opening parachute jump from an aircraft. During HAHO the parachute is opened soon after the soldier exits the plane. This allows the parachute to be used as glider for covert insertion behind enemy lines or to access a terrorist target.

HALO: High altitude, low opening parachute jump from an aircraft. In this technique the soldier freefalls and then opens his parachute at a low altitude. This is also used for covert insertion behind enemy lines or to access a terrorist target.

Herc, Herk, Herky-Bird: Nicknames for the Canadian Forces CC-130 Hercules transport aircraft.

HRT: Hostage-Rescue Team. This is the FBI's hostage-rescue unit based out of Quantico, Virginia. "Hurt" is used for internal terrorist incidents.

HRU: Acronym for hostage-rescue unit, a widely used term to describe anti-terrorist or anti-hijacking units.

Killing House: Special room or group of rooms designed for practicing assault tactics and combat shooting. This term was coined by the British SAS.

MIBs: Men in Black. Nickname to describe JTF2. The name has its origins in the black uniforms that unit members wear.

Mobility Operators: JTF2 soldiers whose job is to get the assault group in and out of its target area. Mobility operators also provide fire support for the mission.

MP-5: German-made Heckler and Koch sub-machinegun. The standard firearm for many counter-terrorist units including JTF2.

NDHQ: National Defence Headquarters in Ottawa. Also known as Fort Fumble, the Puzzle Palace, the Glass Menagerie, and the Petrified Forest.

NVGs: Night-vision goggles. A device which allows a soldier to "see" in the dark by amplifying any available light thousands of times.

Operator: General term to describe a JTF2 soldier.

Ottawa Ski Mask Club: Another nickname for JTF2, coined because of the balaclavas that unit members wear when conducting counter-terrorism operations.

Polaris: Designation for the Airbus transport aircraft used by the Canadian Forces. JTF2 often uses the Polaris to practice hostage-rescue techniques.

PPCLI: Princess Patricia's Canadian Light Infantry.

R22eR: Royal 22nd Regiment. The Van Doos.

Rappelling: Method of rapidly lowering assault teams or snipers by rope from helicopters, rock faces, or from the top of buildings.

RCR: The Royal Canadian Regiment.

Recce: Pronounced "recky." The universal military abbreviation for reconnaissance.

RPG: Rocket-Propelled Grenade. RPGs, such as the RPG-7, are found in war zones around the world in plentiful numbers. The RPG-7 has an effective range of around 300 metres. It has been produced by China, Russia and numerous former Soviet client states.

RSM: Regimental Sergeant Major. Senior ranking non-commissioned officer in a unit, responsible for enforcing discipline and advising the commanding officer on matters of concern to the soldiers.

SAS: Special Air Service. The British elite military unit that routinely undertakes special operations and counter-insurgency missions. The SAS is viewed as the world's most effective special forces unit. Both Australia and New Zealand also have SAS units.

SEAL (Sea, Air, and Land): This is the acronym for the U.S. Navy's elite special operations unit. There are several SEAL units in existence, each having their own area of specialty (desert warfare, jungle warfare, counter-terrorism, etc.). The counter-terrorism unit used to be known as SEAL Team Six. It now goes by the name of Dev Group.

SERT: Special Emergency Response Team. SERT was created in 1986 by the RCMP as Canada's main counter-terrorism unit. It was officially replaced in 1993 by JTF2.

Sharp End: The operational end of the military as opposed to its headquarters or support elements.

Stun grenade: A non-lethal grenade which produces a bright flash and loud sound. Used to disorient terrorists or hostage-takers during an assault, while at the same time not permanently harming hostages. Another common term used to describe stun grenades is "flash-bangs."

Suppressed Weapon: A gun equipped with a noise-suppression device to muffle the sound of its firing. Commonly referred to as a "silencer."

SWAT: Special Weapons and Tactics. Normally, a police unit specially trained to deal with hostage situations and more fully equipped than normal police personnel. Also known as ERT or emergency response team.

Takedown: A general term meaning an assault on a target such as a hijacked aircraft, bus, or building.

Thermal Imager: Device used to track the location of an enemy by recording heat differentials between a body and the surrounding environment.

TOW (Tube-launched, Optically-tracked, Wire-guided): This U.S. designed anti-tank guided missile is capable of destroying armored vehicles up to a range of 3,750 metres.

TRU: Name for the Ontario Provincial Police's tactics and rescue unit, the main emergency response team in the province. JTF2 has conducted liaison and training with TRU as well as other similar civilian police units.

USSOCOM: United States Special Operations Command. A unified command established in 1987 and headquartered at MacDill Air Force Base in Tampa, Florida. It has overall operational command of the American military's special operations forces.

INDEX

ALSO AVAILABLE...

SHADOW WARS: SPECIAL FORCES IN THE NEW BATTLE AGAINST TERRORISM

Award-winning journalist and bestselling author **David Pugliese** provides a rare look into the clandestine world of special forces operations. In his detailed examination of SOF actions since 9/11, Pugliese looks at both what went right, and what went wrong. Although highly skilled and trained, SOF soldiers are not infallible and in the war against terror they have encountered a cunning and often elusive foe. (Book includes 16 pages of colour photos.)
ISBN 1-895896-24-X   *Retail price – $21.99*

AMONG THE 'OTHERS': ENCOUNTERS WITH THE FORGOTTEN TURKMEN OF IRAQ

Despite constituting approximately ten percent of Iraq's population, it is common to hear analysts make specific reference to Shiite Arabs, Sunni Arabs, and Kurds, while the remaining peoples of Iraq – the Turkmen, Yazidi, Sabia, Marsh Arabs, etc. – are often collectively referred to as the "others". In addition to presenting a history of the Turkmen people in Iraq, the book also includes several of author **Scott Taylor**'s personal observations of a people that has suffered through decades of political oppression and ethnic violence.
ISBN 1-895896-26-6   *Retail price – $21.99*

SPINNING ON THE AXIS OF EVIL: AMERICA'S WAR AGAINST IRAQ

This book, consisting primarily of **Scott Taylor**'s first-hand observations and interviews with the people who have become an integral part of this conflict, is a very personal account of America's war against Iraq. Put into historical context and with a rare inside view of Saddam's regime, *Spinning on the Axis of Evil* provides a unique perspective on President Bush's ill-conceived intervention in Iraq. (Book includes 16 pages of colour photos .)
ISBN 1-895896-22-3   *Retail price – $21.99*

MORE ABOUT CANADA'S MILITARY... EVERY MONTH!

Esprit de Corps, Canada's only independent military magazine, chronicles the current and historical exploits of the Canadian Forces. An award-winning combination of investigative journalism and informative history. Sign up today! Available on newsstands across Canada and by subscription.   *12-issue subscription – $34.95*

For more information on these and other titles visit our website at www.espritdecorps.ca